Flora Leipman was born in Glasgow in 1918, but moved to Russia when she was fourteen years old. After assistance from the foreign office, in particular Sir Geoffrey Howe, she returned to Britain in 1984. She now lives in London.

THE LONG JOURNEY HOME

The Memoirs of Flora Leipman

Foreword by Nicholas Bethell
Epilogue by Gwen Robyns

CORGI BOOKS

THE LONG JOURNEY HOME

A CORGI BOOK   0 552 12863 5

Originally published in Great Britain by Bantam Press, a division of Transworld Publishers Ltd.

PRINTING HISTORY

Bantam Press edition published 1987
Corgi edition published 1988

The translation of the poems of Sergei Esenin in Chapter 4 is by Peter Tempest (Moscow: Progress Publishers, 1982)

Copyright © Flora Leipman 1987

Foreword copyright © Lord Bethell 1987
Epilogue copyright © Gwen Robyns 1987

Corgi Books are published by Transworld Publishers Ltd., 61–63 Uxbridge Road, Ealing, London W5 5SA, in Australia by Transworld Publishers (Australia) Pty. Ltd., 15–23 Helles Avenue, Moorebank, NSW 2170, and in New Zealand by Transworld Publishers (N.Z.) Ltd., Cnr. Moselle and Waipareira Avenues, Henderson, Auckland.

Made and printed in Great Britain by
The Guernsey Press Co. Ltd., Guernsey, Channel Islands.

I dedicate this book to the memory of my dear mother, Marie Volpiansky Leipman.

To my sisters, Cecile and Mathilde, and my brother Samuel, who perished in labour camps.

To Dr Lass and other prisoners who helped me to survive.

Acknowledgements

I would like to thank from the bottom of my heart all those who worked so hard negotiating with the Russians for my return to Britain. In particular I would like to mention the Prime Minister, Mrs Margaret Thatcher; the Foreign Secretary, Sir Geoffrey Howe; the staff of the British Embassy in Moscow including the late Sir Iain Sutherland, then Ambassador, and the consuls, Simon Bonde and William Somerset; John and Brigid Edge; and 'Berthe'.

List of Illustrations

INTRODUCTION

It did not take long, when I met Flora for the first time in late 1984, to realise that there was a uniqueness about her. She had arrived in Britain just a few weeks earlier. She was homeless and living on social security. She spoke with an accent, but sounded not quite like a foreigner. She was a stranger to London, but somehow at home as well.

When she began her story, it all seemed even more bizarre. A women in late middle age, she had spent the past fifty years in the Soviet Union. Her entire family – mother, sisters, and brother – had been victims of Stalin's police. She had herself been tormented unbearably, imprisoned, starved, humiliated and then, after Stalin's death and the 'rehabilitation' of millions of his victims, left to fend for herself without so much as an apology.

It was an all-too-familiar story. Only one thing about it was strange. Flora was not Russian, nor did she belong to any of the Soviet Union's other nationalities. She was British born and British in the way she looked at the world. And throughout those fifty years of Stalin, Khrushchev, Brezhnev and Andropov it was to Britain that she longed to return.

It brings Flora's story so much closer to us. It makes the Stalin experience less foreign. Flora had her British birth certificate, her pictures of family holidays by Loch Lomond and her memories of a nice terraced house in London's Kensington. None of it, one would think, meant very much when she was weeding miles of sunflower in a Kazakh labour camp, sorting out the corpses in the camp 'hospital' or, aged only 18, standing in the prison's communal bath house under the watchful guard of armed NKVD thugs. It was these symbolic scraps, though, that helped her through. The link was maintained, in spite of the horrors of the fifty-year gap.

Only after years of poverty and frustration, as she

nursed the mother who had so innocently but recklessly taken them all to Russia, that she was able to think of reviving her Britishness. She kept herself alive by giving English lessons and sane by listening to such programmes as 'Round Britain Quiz' and 'Just a Minute' on the BBC World Service. She had her British passport and attended an embassy Christmas party, even though it meant a three-day train journey to Moscow from her 'home' at Batumi on the Black Sea.

The problem of Flora's exit visa became an international issue. Did her Soviet identity card cancel out her British birth certificate? It became a matter of some importance in Anglo-Soviet relations. Allegedly, when it appeared on the agenda of a meeting between Sir Geoffrey Howe and Andrey Gromyko, it caused one of the British foreign secretary's rare explosions of outrage.

Was it really true that they, foreign ministers of two important countries, were arguing over whether a sixty-year-old woman could travel from Moscow to London? Was this what summit meetings were reduced to? Was the world mad? The Soviet government, chastised at the highest level, was shamed into issuing the precious visa and Flora caught her train.

Her problems were, of course, not over. Where was she to live? How could she support herself? Could she make friends in a land from which, although it was her own, her roots had long since been pulled away? How would she fare emotionally, moving as she was into old age with no family whatever?

Then, in 1985, things began falling into place. The *Mail on Sunday* publicised her story. She appeared on radio and television. The much-maligned London Borough of Brent found her a council flat. She started writing her book. At last she had a home, a purpose in life, and friends.

Finally, most amazingly of all, it emerged that her brother Sammy had survived Stalin's camps and managed to reach the United States. At the end of 1986 sister and brother were reunited. Sammy was married with children. Flora had a family.

Her journey home was indeed long and painful. She has had to fight hard, but now, as she begins to enjoy a normal life, so much of which was stolen from her by tyrants, it all begins to look worth while.

Nicholas Bethell
January 1987

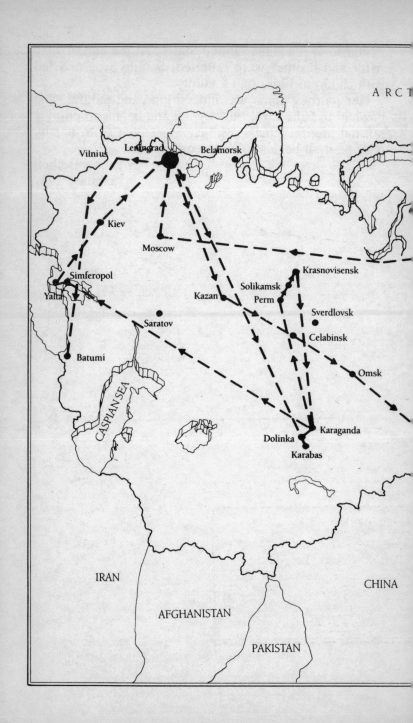

CEAN

Kresta

Pevek

Anadyr

ON OF SOVIET

ALIST REPUBLICS

Magadan

SEA OF OKHOPSK

rsk

Irkutsk   Cita   Chabarovsk

SEA OF
JAPAN

PACIFIC
OCEAN

DORA LEIPMAN'S RUSSIA

...ingrad 1932-1937	Yalta 1953-1954	Magadan
...abas	Kiev 1954-1960	Anadyr
...nka 1937-1941	Leningrad 1960-1963	Kresta 1963-1964
...aganda 1941-1948	Kazan	Pevek
...n	Celabinsk	Moscow
...kamsk	Omsk	Leningrad 1964-1965
...novisensk	Irkutsk	Vilnius 1965-1973
...ganda 1948-1953	Cita	Batumi 1973-1984
...eropol	Chabarovsk	

...osibursk	– KGB prison where Marie Leipman was interrogated
...morsk	– Marie Leipman's camp
...tov	– Samuel Leipman's camp
...dlovsk	– Cecile Leipman's camp

THE LONG
JOURNEY HOME

CHAPTER ONE

It was autumn in a prison in Leningrad in 1937, and I was nineteen years of age. I had woken at dawn from agonising pain and was stiff all over as the hard planks of the wooden bunk on which I lay pressed mercilessly into my right hip where I had a massive carbuncle, one of many boils spread over my body.

I was squashed in between bodies as foul-smelling as my own. In the sickly light I saw a block of people so packed together that they seemed to be a solid mass. They were quiet forms of humanity with their heads resting on one another's shoulders from the sheer exhaustion of standing all night. Now and then I heard whimpering sighs and moans and the repeating of names muttered over and over again. One cry distinct from all the others was 'Bozhe Moy' ('Oh my God').

Gently, so as not to disturb the sleeping forms on either side of me, I wriggled until I could lean on my elbow to get a better look at my surroundings. The people around me had pale frightened faces with a terrifying emptiness that comes from despair. Faces that had once loved and laughed now resembled statues carved from grey stone.

Where was I? Who were these people? I felt a smothering chillness as the full horror struck me that until last night I had been living in my own prison cell. For more than five months I had been in solitary confinement under investigation. In my twelve-foot-square cell there had been two iron beds, a lavatory, sink and tap. During the day I had not been allowed to lie on the bed as that was a regulation in all prisons, but sometimes when I did the guard on duty ignored it. It all depended who was on duty that day and what his mood was like. The only privacy I had was when I was using the lavatory, and then he could see only the back of my head through the peep-hole.

And then began the horrible interrogations. In those years of the thirties the investigations were always held late at night. The NKVD (now the KGB) worked only in the dark hours of the night as it confused the mind and the human spirit was then at its lowest.

The door clanged open and I was ordered by the guards to put my hands behind my back and marched through the prison. Everything was iron; through the iron-trellised floors you could see far below all the other landings with their iron-studded staircases and iron doors to the cells. The noise was shattering, with the sound of the tramping of the guards in their heavy high boots, the shouting and banging of the cell doors reverberating throughout the prison. It was like a gigantic iron maze.

I was pushed into the interrogation room. It was dominated by a massive desk and an old-fashioned high-backed sofa made of imitation leather – the fashion in those days. On one side of the wall was a portrait of Lenin and on the other one of Feliks Dzerzhinsky, founder of the Cheka (also now the KGB). His very name made people shudder.

Sitting behind his desk a young man looked at me with contempt and coldness in his bleak eyes. I was horrified and frightened of him. Drunk with authority, he dismissed the guards and commanded me: 'Sit down.' In the dimness I noticed another man sitting at a table taking notes. They were both dressed in drab uniform.

Suddenly a strong light glared into my face as my interrogator shouted: 'Flora Leipman, alias Kredji, alias Kaplan, what have you to say for yourself? We know who you are. We know all about you. You are the

2

daughter of an English spy. Your mother not only admitted to being an English spy, but confirmed to us that all her children had been collaborators.'

It was a sinister and unnerving feeling when I realized that within the files lying in front of him my life in Russia during the past four years lay exposed. Not only details of all my family, but also the fact that my first marriage had been to Karl Kredji, a young Austrian, and my second a marriage of convenience to Aaron Kaplan, a Russian Jewish boy.

My interrogator flashed some photographs of men's faces in front of me, asking: 'Have you seen them before?'

'No,' I answered.

He banged the table. 'You are a liar. These men were on the ship you came from England on.'

All this and more questions about my family were thrown chaotically into my face with the force of a tempest, bewildering me, stunning me and thrusting me into deep confusion. I began to cry hysterically. There was an ominous silence.

Suddenly I heard his voice saying to me: 'Sign these papers confessing that you are a spy or renounce your mother; then you will be allowed back to your cell.'

I picked up the papers and read them but I could not understand the legal formalities. Something held me back from signing them. It was as though I heard my mother's voice ringing in my ear, saying: 'Flora, be careful what you sign.' The whole injustice that had befallen my family filled me with such rage that I shouted: 'You bastards. I am not going to sign your bloody papers. Maybe I'll sign if you give me an English translation – and maybe not.'

'I'll give you an English translation,' he yelled back at me and, picking up a solid glass inkpot from the desk, he threw the contents straight into my face. Back in my cell I tried to wash the ink from my face and the blue and white polka-dot dress which was the only one I had. I

3

was surprised when I next received my food – a piece of sour black bread and dried fish – to see through the hatch a pair of amused eyes and a little piece of soap.

Sitting on my bed and reliving all that had happened to me during the last four years, I asked myself: Was my mother really a spy? Did she say anything at work that could have compromised the Soviet Union and that somebody might have overheard and so denounced her? This was the beginning of my doubts, and I began to wonder if I was being brainwashed.

Mamma was so gentle and naïve that she could not have possibly had anything to do with espionage; even so, subconsciously questions poured into my head. But my faith and belief in my mother conquered all suspicions. I was determined to live through this nightmare so that one day I would be able to restore my family's honest name.

On my next and final interrogation the younger officer was in charge. He had sleek black hair and despite his hard mouth he spoke quietly, almost confidentially to me: 'Citizen Kaplan, your case is now in my hands. You did not wish to sign, and as a result you remember what happened to you. You were lucky to get off the way you did. You behaved without respect to an official who was only doing his duty. You could have been sent to a punishment cell where you would not even be able to stand upright, let alone lie down. From now on this disorderly behaviour must stop. Don't forget where you are and don't make things worse for yourself. I am sorry for you because you are so young, and I want to make it easier for you. Do you realize that political prisoners like your mother get sentences of up to ten years? I advise you that if you officially denounce your mother, whom we *know* is an English spy, you will receive a milder sentence of about three years.'

To my complete surprise he calmly got up from behind his desk and approached my chair and, putting his arms around me, said: 'Well, now, don't get upset. Shush . . . come on and sit on the sofa and let's talk it over.'

4

It was only then that I realized that he was drunk as his breath reeked from the stale smell of vodka. Grabbing me by the arm he pushed me towards the sofa and, before I was aware of it, he was on top of me, kissing me clumsily and fumbling with my clothes. We began to struggle. I screamed in disgust and pain as the springs of the run-down sofa began pressing into the suppurating boils on my seat. In this ridiculously ugly situation I began shouting: 'You dirty dog . . . you dirty dog.' I exerted all the strength in my body and pushed him off me, which brought him to his senses.

Contorted with lust and rage he smacked me with the back of his pudgy hand right across the face, screaming: 'You fool . . . you stupid fool.'

I was returned to my cell. After a long period of solitary confinement Natasha came into my life. She was slim, with silky fair hair tied back and pale blue eyes. A serious girl who had come from a cultured background with a father in the Russian navy, she immediately reminded me of my sister Mathilde. Natasha's fate had been similar to mine as her parents had also been arrested.

She had come from a prison hospital where she had been under treatment for tuberculosis for more than six months from the day of her arrest.

To while away the time and distract ourselves from our misery, we used to mould one-inch dollies and animals from the bread we received with our lentil soup. By kneading the bread between our fingers we made it into soft dough. I made a funny little family of dolls, and Natasha was better at animals. We talked in whispers as speaking was strictly forbidden. It came as a break from the monotony of cell life when we were taken out for exercise, walking in circles round the high walled court-yard of the prison with our hands behind our backs, which was all right for me but exhausting for Natasha.

The nights were the worst for her. I used to lie in the dim light and watch her coughing as though her thin little

5

chest was being ripped apart. I did not know much about death as I had only seen one dead person in my life, and that was Papa when he lay in our flat in Glasgow and candles burned on the mantelpiece. But that was not only years away but also in another world.

Then came the night when her coughing was worse than ever and the hacking sound ricocheted into every corner of the cell until I became frightened. I banged on the door with all my force and began screaming until a guard came. By the time the white-coated doctor arrived Natasha had gurgled up blood and died. I sat on my bed crying. I cried not only for Natasha but also for myself and Mamma, Mathilde, Cecile and Sammy. I cried in protest against the whole rotten stinking injustice of the Soviet system.

Her young body had been covered with a grey sheet. The door banged open as two guards brought in a green wooden box with handles on each side. I remember thinking: Why green? Green is the colour of life – the sea, grass and forests of trees – but here in our prison world of washed-out khaki uniforms and drab clothes why suddenly a green coffin?

The guards did not even glance at me hunched on my bed as they lifted her from the bed and dropped her into the box, picked it up by the handles and left the cell clanging the door shut. I cried until there was nothing left inside me. Until I felt drained of life itself. Remembering my beautiful mother now in a concentration camp, Mathilde who had died so young in prison. Had the KGB reached my sister Cecile and her innocent baby? And where was Sammy, my brother, with his saucy smile, who had so loved to tease me? Had they suffocated the life out of him too?

The following night the door of my cell opened and the guard shouted: 'Sveshami!' ('Come with your belongings!') I collected up my comb and sliver of soap and looked for the last time at my bread family. Still dazed from sleep, with two guards on either side of me, I

6

was conducted down the corridor until they stopped outside a cell door and pushed me inside. The cell was lit by a naked light-bulb hanging from the centre of the ceiling. Hands appeared from nowhere, groping hands, guiding hands, until I found myself on a bunk against the wall where I squeezed between two shapeless forms.

As the morning light grew stronger I looked around and saw that I was in a huge cell that had once been whitewashed and was now smudgy grey. The walls were covered with the scribblings of former inmates, giving their names and the years they had passed through the cell: impersonal messages left with the hope that someone would recognize the writer and remember her with compassion. 'I was here in 1935 – T. Ivanova.' The ceiling was high, and near the top were cell windows sealed off with wooden boards, or 'muzzles' as the prisoners called them. The floor was cold cement, and the only door, made of iron, had one small peep-hole and a larger hatch where the food was handed in twice a day.

There was a movement as the mass began to disintegrate. Shuffling, pushing, cursing and shouting began as the prisoners surged in waves towards the one lavatory in the corner of the cell that must have contained about two hundred women. The noise that had begun as a murmur was now loud and strident like the tuning up of a symphony orchestra before the crescendo of the opening bars.

How could I perform the basic functions of nature in front of all these strangers? In my solitary cell, where I had lived for several months, this had not been a problem, but now I had to queue with the others waiting to use the stinking *parasha* (lavatory). I noticed that some of the elderly bodies never moved from the bunk, preferring to soil their clothes rather than lose their places.

I soon realized that I was much younger than the rest of the women and therefore a curiosity as they began

7

crowding round me. The fact that I spoke Russian badly and looked different made them all the more interested. They began plying me with a stream of questions. In Russian prisons the questions are always the same, only the name of the city changes.

'Are they still arresting in Leningrad? Are the people still waiting outside the Bolshoi Dom [the Big House]? What charge did they get you on? How many years did they give you?'

In the sharing of their fate prisoners felt comforted. They had been betrayed by their 'beloved Stalin' and were now part of a terrifying nightmare from which there was no awakening. The women looked bewildered when I told them I had been born in Glasgow, that I and my family were foreigners and that my only crime was that I had been 'accused' of being 'a daughter of an English spy'.

I asked them to tell me about themselves. The two neighbours on either side of me on the bunk had been charged with being members of a family of 'traitors', and most of those to whom I talked were in this category. This meant that somebody in that family had been found 'guilty of treason' or 'anti-Soviet activities' or even that there were members of their family abroad with whom they corresponded. Many prisoners did not even know the reason for their arrest, which was even more destroying.

Like me these women were totally confused because of what had happened to them. Although for the last few years they had seen queues of people standing outside the building of the NKVD at No.4 Liteinyi Prospekt in the centre of Leningrad, enquiring for the whereabouts of relatives, and they could not have failed to notice doors in apartment blocks with the Secret Police seals which meant that those families had been arrested, nobody thought that it could ever happen to them.

Humanity suffers from natural catastrophes – earth-quakes, floods, epidemics – and also from man-made revolutions, wars and religious conflicts, but why were these people suffering? The Soviet forced-labour system was harder for women as it destroyed family life. It tore children from mothers, brothers from sisters, husbands from wives, and mothers from the life they had created within their own bodies.

For what new Soviet ideological sin were these mothers and grandmothers, some as old as eighty, from respectable families, incarcerated in prison as the victims of Stalin's purges? That cell of about two hundred women was a tiny part of the ten thousand locked in the vast Kresty prison. They could not all have been spies and traitors.

Throughout history the Russian people have always cowered under tyrannical rule. People of independent thought and conscience have been persecuted without mercy – Pushkin, Dostoevsky, the Decembrists, right up to Andrei Sakharov. The forced-labour system of Soviet Russia, with its condemnation of innocent people, is pathological. It is impossible for Western minds to understand this phenomenon. The Soviet system deliberately and sadistically sets out to strip the prisoner of all human identity. No despair is so stultifying as being entombed in prison without knowing why. These women, some of whom became my friends, knew only that they were being herded like cattle towards some unknown Gulag hundreds of miles from home.

CHAPTER TWO

It was a crisp, cold day in Glasgow in 1929. The first snow of the year had fallen, and in Kelvingrove Park the children were rosy-cheeked and squealing with excitement as they tobogganed down the slopes on home-made sledges. We had badgered Papa to finish the sledge he had been making for several weeks, reproaching him that by the time he had finished there would be no more snow. Holding the rope of the sledge, as I was the front passenger, and nuzzling closely into my brother Sammy behind, I closed my eyes in sheer ecstasy as we slid down the hill with the wind whipping our faces. I felt that I was rushing into space. As the sledge came to an abrupt halt we tumbled over into the snow shrieking with laughter. Jenny Barrie, my classmate from the Garnetbank school, was throwing snowballs at us, and the scene of that winter day I remembered through all my life.

I felt somebody pulling me to my feet and looked up into the face of our French governess, who said: 'Come quickly, children. You are wanted at home.' We ran all the way home, a little disappointed that our first adventure in sledging was so short. I was eleven years of age and proud that I had made the decision to overcome fear for the first time in my life. Going into Father's room I saw my eldest sister, Cecile, who was already twenty-one, standing at the bedside and holding a mirror over Papa's mouth. 'Mamma,' she said, 'Papa is not breathing.'

Clasping both sides of her head, our mother cried out: 'Papa, Papa, what am I going to do? Why have you left me?'

10

We all stood hushed round the bed, my other sister, Mathilde, still a schoolgirl, crying in the corner, and as Sammy and I looked at the face of my father I whispered: 'Sammy, he is sleeping.'

Sammy, who was a year older than me, burst out crying and said: 'No, Flora, he is dead. We will never see him again.'

My father, who was only forty-nine, had been ill seven days before dying of a coronary, and our kind-faced family doctor had been visiting Papa every day. As Mother led him to the front door I overheard her saying quietly: 'Will you please wait for the money?'

Our neighbours opened their hearts. The Okrims from upstairs came with their two little boys, Sidney and Leonard, who were my schoolmates, to express their sympathy. Mrs Okrim took over the cooking and looking after the household. People came from everywhere until our flat was filled with quiet talk and the smell of fried fish from the kitchen. To comfort myself I crawled up on to the high coalbunker, the place where we all sat on bath night, when Papa would dry us with big warm towels.

I did not really understand what death was about. After Father's funeral Mother continually repeated: 'What are we going to do?' Our father had never spared us anything, but now that he had gone Mamma was faced with debt. Dear Papa, we never knew, as in his generosity he wanted to spare Mamma from worrying. 'Now we must sell the workshop,' Mamma resolved.

My grandparents had emigrated from Poland and Germany to Russia, but during the Jewish pogrom of the last century Mother's family had left Russia and gone to live in Switzerland and my father's family went to France. My parents, Alexander and Marie, had been married in Paris, and my eldest sister, Cecile, was born in Geneva. From there they moved to Dunkirk and, during the 1914–18 war, now with two little girls, they moved to Glasgow where they settled at No.435 Sauchiehall Street.

My father set up business as a furrier with a workshop

11

in our flat. During the war he was a special constable, and I remember the pride we children felt when he allowed us to play with his helmet. Father was an orthodox Jew, and we had a mezuza on the door. Every Saturday morning, dressed in our best, which in winter was fur coats with muffs to match, we would all walk up the hill to the Garnethill synagogue. A year after Papa's death, when Sammy was thirteen, he had his bar mitzvah and, sitting upstairs in the synagogue with my mother and my sisters, I looked down with pride at my brother in his white tallith. All four pairs of eyes filled with tears as we looked over to the place where Father always sat.

Father loved walking, and at weekends he would sometimes take the whole family for a picnic to Loch Lomond or take us to Sunday lunch at a restaurant. Every summer he rented rooms at the seaside in Ayrshire; on arrival one of the first things he did was to take us children and buy us red and blue tin pails with smart wooden spades. Every day we made long walks along the beach, Father with his trousers rolled up, and from my perch on his shoulders I clutched his braces like the reins of a horse. They were such joyous days, filled with the innocence of childhood, with Papa planning special treats every day. He used to take us to different tea-shops where we had a glass of milk, home-made scones with raspberry jam and sugar buns.

At Troon one year Father entered us children for a sandcastle competition. From two different-coloured sands, white and grey, I built a fairy castle complete with turrets and a moat festooned with green seaweed and coloured shells. I jumped with excitement and Papa shone with pride when it was announced that I had won first prize, and everyone looked bemused at the big fat tortoise Sammy had made. Sometimes we went to Edinburgh sightseeing and finished off the day with tea at Lyons, where we were allowed to eat as many sandwiches and cakes as we liked. Papa's patience with us children was endless. He loved us dearly.

12

We had four rooms in our flat, one of which was Papa's workroom. During the season, when the work was at its busiest, my mother used to make the patterned silk linings and Cecile was skilled at sewing fur. With the snippets of fur I used to make little animals and dolls.

We were considered to be well-dressed girls with Papa's fur coats, and Mamma made all our dresses, but I was the one who always grumbled because all my dresses had been remade from Cecile's and Mathilde's. It was not easy for a little girl to have two older sisters in those days.

All her life my mother had been fascinated by ballet and music, and ours was a very musical family. It was the early days of the gramophone, and Father brought home in triumph a new gramophone and a collection of His Master's Voice records. There was always music playing, and we girls spent our time dancing. It was natural for Mother to send us girls to the local ballet school. The talk was always about Pavlova, Karsavina, Nijinsky, figures who coloured my mother's fantasies.

With Father's death everything changed, and Mother had to take in lodgers. She gave up the main bedroom and moved in to sleep with us children. Our first paying guest was a consul from Buenos Aires who was jolly and often tipsy; a policeman was always bringing him home. On one occasion he was found lying on the tramcar rails stopping the tram. When confronted by the law he shouted: 'Don't touch me, I am a diplomat.' He brought in his Spanish friends and turned our kitchen into a restaurant. Life came back into the house again. He also used to bring girls back to his room. Mother made a big scene, saying: 'This is not a hotel. This is a private house and there are children here.' He left after that.

Our second lodger was Oscar Slater. Mother told us that there had been much written about him in all the newspapers as he had been wrongly accused of a serious crime and just released from prison after twenty-five years. Now he was well off as he had received a large sum in compensation from the Government.

13

He liked Mother to such an extent that one day he proposed to her, offering her security and independence on the condition that we children were sent to a private boarding-school that he would pay for. Oscar Slater was an intelligent man who took our education very seriously. He would sometimes take me on his knee and relate to me his experiences in prison, and this was my first encounter with a person innocently accused. If Mother could only have had a glimpse into the future she would never have refused this marriage, but destiny had prepared for her another fate.

Life in Glasgow with no financial security and the loss of Father became too much for her. The house that had once been filled with laughter now felt empty, and she wanted to escape and begin a whole new life. I remember before we left for London she ruthlessly sold all the furniture as well as the workroom and its stock. She sold everything down to the last tea-cup. She packed a suitcase of clothes for each of us and some linen and that was all. We arrived at King's Cross and, trailing our suitcases, searched the nearby streets for suitable accommodation.

Next day Mamma and Cecile put on their best clothes and went out to find work, but there was none and we were living on the money we had saved. Mamma, desperate and tired, returned to our room every night to cook our meal on the gas ring for which you put your pennies in the meter. We moved four times in six months, always hoping that the next district would prove better. Mamma looked at advertisements, notices in shops, and asked everyone she met, but it was hopeless.

One day my mother met in one of the boarding-houses an elderly Jewish businessman with a long grey beard and wearing a Jewish skullcap. He was short and fat, and we children made fun of him at the table. Mamma and he became friends, and like Oscar Slater he offered to move the whole family to Whitechapel if Mother would become his mistress. That was not for Mamma, although

14

clearly he could give us children support for our future. Mamma wanted to move west, not east, and she liked to live in posh places. Cecile and Mathilde were also against moving to the East End as they were both considered good-looking and had their dreams, too.

Through advertisements Mother found a two-roomed flat with a kitchen and bathroom on the first floor of Knaresborough Place in Earl's Court. It was a cream-painted Edwardian house with portals and a bow window, and we thought we were in paradise. Cecile got a job in a basement knitwear workshop, and Mathilde and Sammy went to work in the kitchens of the Regent Palace Hotel. One of Sammy's jobs was peeling vegetables, and I remember standing in the street and looking down into the basement to watch Sammy at work. He showed us how quickly he could peel an onion. He would squeeze it in his hands, and the inner part would shoot out. For me his dexterity was marvellous, like a magician.

Mother used to take me into the hotel where with the greatest delight she would give me a cup of water from the new automatic gadget. Mamma was now only forty-three years old and, although she was stoutly built and under average height, she looked very young for her age. She had a charming oval-shaped face with smooth ivory skin, sensuous lips and a slightly Roman nose. She had cut off her long brown hair and wore it in a bob with kiss curls on her cheeks. Mamma never went out unless she was well corseted, fastidiously dressed, and she always wore the chic little hats that were fashionable in those years and high-heeled court shoes and gloves. She was a strong and healthy woman, and the only time she took to her bed was to have her children. She was amusing and had a lot of humour, and in company lit up everyone with her strong personality. She brought us up very strictly, and as children our manners were impeccable. Yet in spite of all her frivolity she was sometimes terribly stubborn and egotistical.

15

She was always attractive to men, and now she had a new admirer, Camille. Although he was so strange with his beaky nose, hollow cheeks, black bushy eyebrows which reminded us of Niccolò Paganini,we all loved him. He was an intellectual and he was ten years younger than Mother. One day Mamma gathered us children round her and said: 'I have something important to tell you. You all like Camille. I am so lonely, and he wants to help us. He has asked me to marry him.' We saw no reason why she could not marry him as we realized she was still a young woman and he would provide for us.

Mother was married to Camille, and we lived as one big family. He got work as a travelling salesman and, although of course he did not replace our dear father, he was good to us and we had great fun with him. To our sitting-room in Knaresborough Place came many fascinating aristocrats from White Russia with whom Mother had made good friends. Our house was always filled with music, memories of the Russian ballet and the great dancers and of course of the New Russia. Many of the Russian émigrés were intrigued by Lady Astor's proposal to unemployed miners that if they were prepared to live under Bolshevik rule for two years she would pay their passage to Russia. A man called Morton from Liverpool took up her challenge and moved his family to Leningrad.

Bernard Shaw had recently accepted an invitation from Soviet Russia to visit the country because his plays, especially *The Apple Cart*, were popular there. He collected a party of the most unlikely assortment of friends, among them some of the richest capitalists in England, to take with him. It included Lord and Lady Astor, the Marquess of Lothian, the Hon David Astor and Charles Tennant, a kinsman of Lord Glenconner.

It was typical of Soviet Russia to splash propaganda about the industrialization of the USSR in English-language newspapers and journals. The Russian Motherland 'opened her arms' to her prodigal sons and daughters, and flocks of Russians and Jewish immigrants rushed to the call as well as the English and American unemployed.

Was it these circumstances that influenced Mother or was it the inherited genes of the Wandering Jew? Maybe a nostalgia for her native land or even some supernatural power forced her into the abyss of destruction. Certainly, she showed a recklessness that had no limit when she decided that the whole family should leave for the Soviet Union.

CHAPTER THREE

Mother's decision divided the family. Mathilde and Camille were on her side, and Cecile, Sammy and I were against. Sammy and I were sorry to leave because we were happy in our new school and I had two boyfriends, Nolly Bertram and 'Cuthbert Custard', and Cecile was working and now had a boyfriend. My knowledge of Russia was nil. I do not suppose that I even knew where it was on the map. I asked my teacher to tell me all about it and gained an impression of cobbled streets splattered with blood and Bolsheviks with long black beards. I do not think that my mother knew even that. I tried to tell her what I knew of Russia, and she would say: 'Stop talking such nonsense. Uncle Abraham lives there and your cousins live there and nothing has happened to them. Look at the nice letters he writes to us.'

The last golden days of that perfect English autumn were spent rushing about buying warm clothes, woollen underwear and presents for our relatives in Russia. Camille was still working as a travelling salesman and, because there had been complications with his visa, was not travelling with us but would join us later in Leningrad.

Standing on the deck and watching the coastline of England fading farther away I tried to cheer the others up. 'Adieu, adieu, my native land,' I shouted Byron's lines into the wind, and Sammy joined in with 'And if for ever fare thee well'.

Ironically, the ship was named *Feliks Dzerzhinsky*, after a Polish nationalist who hated the Russians and

18

was, it is said, responsible for the annihilation of thousands of the Russian intelligentsia. People called him 'The Iron Feliks'; he was the right hand of Lenin and head of the Cheka, now the KGB.

There were many children among the families on the ship, and we spent our days rushing round the decks and listening to the strange Russian talk of the sailors. They used to take us down to the hold to see the handsome Scots pedigree bulls which were also going to Russia.

All Russians are extremely kind to children, and these sailors were no exception. They took us to the engine room where we listened, fascinated, to the *tut-tut-tut* of the diesel engine, which was a novelty at that time. Then as we headed for the North Sea the weather changed and we were all sea-sick. The doctor was running from cabin to cabin with a tin of spiced sprats to cure our sea-sickness, but as we neared the port of Hamburg our spirits revived and all was fun and joy again.

At Hamburg some repairs to the ship had to be made, and the passengers were allowed to go sightseeing. Mother explained to us children that she had spent some years of her childhood there with her parents before moving to Switzerland and France. My memory of the Kiel Canal is that it was so narrow we could almost shake the hands of the passing farmers. By now the sun was shining and the trees were covered in bronze, and to my childish eyes the world looked a beautiful place.

During our seven-day journey the Russian émigrés had gravitated into little friendly groups within which they could exchange confidences and rely on one another for help. By now we had our own group of friends, and Mamma was enjoying herself, too. But the nearer we got to the Russian coastline the more apprehensive and quieter the elders became, and so did the children, catching the adults' mood.

It was a cold grey morning as the ship nosed into port on the Neva, in those days called Sovtorgflot for the Soviet merchant fleet. Looking down on the wharf from

19

the ship's deck all we saw was grey: grey sombre buildings, grey skies, grey people. The walls were hung with
flags, portraits of Lenin and Stalin, and red banners
covered with slogans: 'Long Live Our Great Motherland', 'Long Live the Communist Party'. As the ship
docked a band struck up the Russian National Anthem.
The impact was so emotional that Mamma, Cecile,
Mathilde, Sammy and I all burst into tears. So this was
Leningrad – and if this was Russia I did not like it.

The whole ship was hypnotized, and a feeling of
depression passed over us all.

'What are we doing here?' Mathilde cried. 'It is so cold,
and we can't even understand what they are saying.'

One by one we dissolved into tears again and putting
our arms around one another, had a very big cry. Feelings
of premonition and uncertainty crept into our bones, but
there was no way back. And all around there was much to
distract us children as they tied up the ship to the wharf
and a big crane swung into action unloading the holds.
The luggage was dumped in huge heaps, and as there
were no porters everyone scrambled to claim their own.
It was the confusion of Babylon, with lots of noise and
shouting and screaming.

After queueing at the Customs shed our turn came.
When the officer began to confiscate some of father's
clothes which we had brought as gifts, our fur coats,
lovely muffs, fur hats, new clothes and – most hurtful of
all – Mamma's jewellery, she became hysterical. Along
the long trestle table I could hear women screaming 'Give
that back to me' as Customs officers whipped out from
their luggage clothing and everything that was new or of
any quality. Family silver and cherished antiques that the
immigrants had brought for the new life ahead were
taken, too. It was like a bazaar in Whitechapel, but with
none of the good humour, only greed and a taste of the
official corruption that we were soon to discover
everywhere.

Customs formalities completed, we were taken outside

and whisked off in one of several shabby old buses waiting there. I noticed that there was nothing in the shop windows except a portrait of a man with a black tie. It was such a contrast to the London we had left behind, with its red buses, and shop displays packed with goods and dazzling with all the colours of the prism. The comparison was so incredible that everyone in the bus was too shocked to comment. I turned to Sammy sitting beside me and said: 'Oh, Sammy, isn't this awful?'

He looked at me and answered: 'Flora, I am going to run back to England and get away from this bloody place.' Could he have had a premonition of his own destiny?

After a long journey the bus passed a huge plant with tall smoking chimneys which in those years was called the Putilov Plant (now the Kirov Works) before arriving at the American colony. This was an area of two-storeyed wooden buildings which provided accommodation for the foreign workers. Standing in the inner courtyard of the hostels were some American men with their wives and children, and they smiled as they greeted us – the first smiles we had seen since we left the ship. We heard people saying all around us: 'It will be all right. Don't worry. It will work out. You must be tired. Come on, we will show you where you are going to live.'

A homely American woman patted Mother on the shoulder and led us up a wooden staircase where the masonry on the ceiling and walls was crumbling. The empty black gaps and cracks frightened me and did little to build our confidence. When she showed us into a room with two iron beds, a wooden wardrobe, two chairs and a table, the squalor of the place filled us with wretchedness.

She showed us the communal kitchen with its primuses for cooking on and explained: 'You go and get the kerosene yourself and you will have to stand a long time in the queue. Be careful how you use your kerosene as sometimes there is none for days. You will also receive bread and food ration-cards.' There was a school for foreign children not far away, she said.

In a couple of days, going by tramcar, we went to visit our Uncle Abraham. We had slept off some of our worries and were excited to see our new relatives. Uncle Abraham lived on 2nd Soviet Street, not far from Nevsky Prospekt. We knew that when Mother had gone to Paris to be married Uncle Abraham, who was two years older than her, had returned to Russia just as the Revolution began and that was why for many years there had been no contact between brother and sister. Uncle Abraham was then an electrical engineer working in one of the big plants. He was living with his second wife and two children, Zoya and Yura, from his first marriage.

It was a handsome house with, in the main entrance-hall, two female classical statues of great beauty. There was a lift, but it had not worked since the Revolution. Much of the marble had been chipped, and one statue had lost a toe, giving an impression of neglect and decadence. Walking up the marble staircase to the second floor we stood in front of a massive carved wooden double door. Houses of such grandeur, built in pre-Revolutionary Russia, can be seen in central Leningrad even today. It is a pity that tourists are not allowed to glimpse into their magnificent classical entrance-halls. I suppose the reason is that as they are in such a state of neglect, and as the elegant apartments in these houses have been converted into communal rooms and flats, the authorities prefer foreign eyes not to see them.

As we entered the apartment a stout man, very much resembling my mother, embraced her and greeted her in Russian. 'Marie, it has been a long time. Come in.' The two families of children – Uncle Abraham's two and Mother's four – from one root but two different worlds, stood staring at each other unable to communicate because of the language barrier.

We sat round a large table which was covered with a

Burgundy plush undercloth with a white lace cloth on top. In the centre was a large charcoal samovar. A pool of light fell from the orange silk-fringed lampshade hanging low from the ceiling.

My uncle was lucky as he had not been molested during the Revolution nor his apartment confiscated. Though he was not a communist, like many other Russian specialists of his time he managed to co-operate with the system and so survived the post-Revolutionary period.

Near the American colony there was a Russian school where we were enrolled. A few of the classes had been nominated for foreign children and they were isolated by a wooden partition. We were dressed in warm tweed coats and strong shoes and felt sorry for the Russian children, who were poorly dressed by comparison. They teased us by singing a made-up song that had no sense but was intended to be insulting: 'America and Europe, you are fried arses.' In my class were two girls and eight boys, and there I met Mary and Alan Morton whose parents had come to Russia four years before, their passage paid by Lady Astor. At school our behaviour was not very good. Ezra, an American boy, would tease the teacher who taught us English and, like a gangster, jump on to the desk threatening her with his toy revolver. 'I will shoot you, you bloody Bolshevik, if you don't give us good marks.'

Mamma began to pack again, telling us that she had arranged with relatives and my uncle that he would take my mother, Sammy and me while Mathilde and Cecile would stay with a distant relative called Aunt Sonya and her family in a communal flat, sharing a small kitchen and small bathrooom with other families. When I visited my sisters the whole place used to smell from the stink of primuses, fried potatoes, sunflower oil and lavatories.

Uncle Abraham was so 'kind' that we had to share one room with Zoya and Yura, while he lived in splendour in

23

the rest of the flat. Camille had joined us, and Mamma was happy to see her husband again, but now we were six in one room. Within days Camille had taken a job as a mechanic in a bus garage, Mathilde had got a job at the port as an English typist and Cecile was working in a dress factory. My mother, who spoke four languages, secured pleasant work in the kiosk of the Quissisana restaurant selling foreign newspapers, magazines, books from the House of Foreign Books, but even that small kiosk was under the control of the local Secret Police.

In their leisure Cecile and Mathilde were learning to ski and skate, or we would all go sightseeing, admiring Leningrad with its big squares, monumental buildings, elegant church spires, domes and romantic cupolas. We liked to go with Mamma to the Summer Park, which before the Revolution was only for the nobility. Mother told us that when she was a child she used to look through the eighteenth-century wrought-iron railings and watch the grand duchesses and fine ladies wrapped in sumptuous furs, velvet and brocade. But we saw only a park covered with a blanket of gleaming white snow as the classical statues had been encased in wooden boxes for the winter. To Mamma the park looked the same as she had seen it many years before, but she would say to us: 'Oh my God, how everything else has changed. There is no more of Old Russia.'

Despite the outward appearances of a seemingly normal life – if you can call a normal life living in a communal flat sharing one bathroom with fifteen or twenty people, or the claustrophobia of six people sharing one room – our hearts bled from the knowledge of what a mistake Mother had made in not realizing how backward the Soviet Union was, both in economy and in ordinary living conditions. But we concealed from one another our nostalgia for England so as not to upset her.

It was a warm day in April 1933 when Mother left

home to go to the Quissisana restaurant to collect her pay packet so that, although she was normally fastidious and vain about her appearance and would never leave the house without wearing her corset, on that day of all days she did not. And on that day she did not come home. I was then fifteen.

CHAPTER FOUR

Late that evening the family gathered together frustrated and anxious and with many different suggestions. We discussed endlessly what could have happened to Mother. Everybody had their own opinion. As there was no telephone in the house Camille had been to her workplace, and we knew definitely that she had not called at the office for her wages; while my sisters, with an older cousin, had been to several hospitals to make enquiries. The night passed and we all waited. That was the end of my childhood.

Days passed and no sign of Mother. I spent the time lying on my bed crying myself sick. There was no school for me. My relatives came to the conclusion that she must have been arrested. Uncle Abraham, trembling with fear, said, 'She should not have worked in that place,' and, looking at Camille and my sisters and brother, added: 'Your coming here will only bring trouble to my family. They will arrest me also because of Marie. The only thing left to do is to go to the NKVD and make enquiries as to whether she has been arrested or not. I have my family to think about and my work to consider and, oh my God, I wish you had never come here.'

'I suppose this is the place,' Cecile said next day outside the big grey building on Liteinyi Street. We were shocked to see hundreds of people standing in a queue. This was the time of the Stalinist purges sweeping the country with a huge wave of terror. Noticing some people standing with parcels, we approached an elderly lady and asked her how to make enquiries. 'Children, that is not easy,' she answered. 'You have to come in the late evening and stand overnight to get to the enquiry office the next day, only to be told whether your relatives have been arrested or not. Maybe you will be allowed to hand in a parcel.'

Standing in these queues overnight just to get an answer – 'Yes' or 'No'. People huddled together in their misery, exhausted and humiliated; it was beyond human imagination. After many attempts at enquiring we saw it was hopeless. We still did not know where Mother was. I constantly thought of poor Mamma without her corset. She had only her handbag with her and her powder-box, and our birth certificates that she always carried. Sammy and I wondered how we could get into that 'Big House' and help Mamma to escape. Sammy said that he could climb up the wall and get her out, and Camille would comfort us: 'Stop, children. Stop talking nonsense.'

Life went on. I still had to go to school, and Alan and Mary Morton, my schoolfriends, were kind to me as I spent much of my time crying. I was a frequent visitor to their beautiful house not far away from the Nevsky Prospekt. They had four spacious rooms that were filled with white Louis XVI-style furniture covered with flowered silk brocade. Mary and Alan both played the white grand piano. Everything was on the same affluent scale, and they had a maid called Paulina. I got to know that their father had met with a terrible accident in the Works – he was burned to death by red-hot lead – and now the Works had taken on supporting the family by giving them this luxury flat and Mrs Morton had received generous compensation for her husband's death. When I was sad Mrs Morton would cuddle me: 'Flora, you must be strong. You must study and be clever for Mamma's sake.'

The next sad event that came to me and Sammy was when one evening at supper Camille put his arms around us and said: 'Children, I am forced to leave Leningrad. "They" are sending me back to England.' With tears in

27

his eyes he added: 'I am so sorry that I could not do more to help you find your mother and I feel for you now that you are both left alone in this world. I advise you to contact the British consulate if you are in trouble.' He left us early in the morning, and that was the last we saw of Camille.

Through the factory Cecile was given a little room in a two-roomed flat where Mathilde joined her, but I was still living with my uncle. He paid little attention to me and gave instructions to the maid that I was to eat in the kitchen with his daughter, Zoya. Sammy had managed to find work with the River Transport and was living on board a boat, so, in my loneliness, it was natural that Zoya and I became close. She was also motherless as when she was ten years of age her mother, our Aunt Mary, had gone off with her lover, leaving her father to bring her up.

Zoya was about a year older than me. She was not tall and had narrow hips in contrast to her voluptuous bosom; her eyes had a squint, and she wore a fringe in the Charleston style. Zoya's way of living fascinated me. She used to dress up and go out in the evenings, coming home late at night. She was quick and bright and soon began to speak broken English, but she spoke German well; she had learned at a special school.

As it was summer, we would go out to the parks and dance together on the open dance-floors, and sometimes we promenaded up and down the Nevsky Prospekt to show ourselves off and look at everyone else. Going down from the Moscow Station to the General Staff Building the left side of Nevsky Prospekt was called Virginstreet, the opposite side Whorestrasse. We were dressed in the fashion of the day in dresses made from material decorated with patriotic motifs such as factories, engines, tractors, the sickle and hammer, and we wore white socks and canvas shoes.

One day she said to me: 'Come on, Flora. I'll show you a little bit of life, but don't tell anybody.' The restaurant she took me to was on the Fontanka Canal in a downstairs *podval* (cellar). It was filled with smoke like the Russian saying, 'You can hang an axe in the smoke.' I noticed that when we came in everybody greeted Zoya: this was not the first time she had been there. The men were dressed in baggy suits of cheap material. Some wore Russian overshirts with collars buttoned up at the side of the neck, a plain leather belt at the waist and baggy trousers thrust into high Russian boots. There they met and felt at ease drinking vodka, when they could get it, with pickled cucumbers and fried salami.

My life became full of continuous fun and sheer excitement – dancing, restaurants and going to parties to meet Zoya's friends. It was a time when some of the Russian young were aping the decadent Western world while other teenagers and students were inspired by the lyrics of Sergei Esenin. Esenin was the most popular poet of this century; he had been married for brief spells to both Isadora Duncan and Tolstoy's granddaughter.

We were fascinated by his vision of disruption as he saw the new industrialization destroying the beloved 'wooden Russia' of his peasant childhood. We admired his debauchery and 'skandalist' ballads, which we all sang and which had beautiful musical arrangements. These songs were from his 'hooligan period' and were about drunkenness, pub brawls, the treachery of love and the stench of human vomit.

> In the thick smoke
> In the turmoil of life swiftly spreading
> What tortured me was I did not know
> Where our step was heading.

In those years Esenin was banned by the State because it was believed that he corrupted the young, and his poems had to be circulated underground.

Typical of his romantic style was the song 'Letter to

29

My Mother', which still haunts me to this day as I was
unable to write letters to my own mother in prison camp.

> Still around, old dear? How are you keeping?
> I too am around. Hello to you!
> May that magic twilight ever be streaming
> Over your cottage as it used to do.

> That you often see in the blue shadows
> Ever one dream, giving you no rest.
> Someone in a drunken tavern scuffle
> Sticks a bandit knife into my chest.

Esenin died in 1925, hanging himself in a hotel room.
He left a suicide note written in his own blood:

> Au revoir, friend, no comment is due
> Your gaze let no sorrow obscure.
> In this life of ours dying's not new
> Nor is living, of course, any newer.

Cecile got me work in her factory, sewing on a
machine, and one day, remembering Camille's advice,
Sammy and I decided to contact the British consulate on
the Nevsky Prospekt. The officials were immensely kind
to us and gave us money to buy food in special shops
provided for foreign currencies, and sometimes we went
to the British Residence where we had tea. There was a
dentist there who put a filling in my tooth which I still
have to this day. Everybody was very considerate, and
when I became ill and was lying in the hospital, as I had to
undergo an operation because of some kind of abscess, a
lady officer from the Salvation Army used to visit me
every day bringing with her a pot of hot boiled carrots.
Looking back on these years I recall talks at the
British consulate about returning my brother and me to
England as orphans. But there were two reasons that
made this impossible. In the first place, I suppose, by

English law, it was necessary to get our mother's permission and she was 'missing'; and, in the second, even if the consulate were willing to act without permission, we could not have left the country not knowing whether Mother was alive or dead.

Cecile had been given a free voucher for a twenty-four-day trip to a sanatorium in the south. She wanted to take Mathilde, but she refused and said: 'Take Flora with you.' I was thrilled to go with Cecile, and we had an exciting time, the sunshine and the bathing bringing some colour back into my cheeks after my stay in hospital.

Returning home we were confronted with the appalling news that our dear sister was dead. Our relatives, friends from her work and the neighbours said only that she had been arrested and during the interrogation suffered a heart attack. She had been taken to the hospital, but it was too late. In our absence Aunt Mary, who was an extremely kind woman and very popular with us children, had been informed by the Militia of the tragedy and had taken over all the responsibility of the funeral arrangements; but she had been unable to write to us because we had not left an address.

Standing by her grave I remembered my dear sister, so delicate and fragile. She was a lovely ballerina in her white tutu. Mathilde was very sensitive and had many peculiarities. I suppose one might call them allergies today. She could not stand, for example, the smell of a burned-out match. It made her hysterical. What chance did this fairy-like, eighteen-year-old girl have confronting brutal coarse men from the NKVD, blowing smoke into her face and cross-examining her? They killed her! She would never have been able to survive the harshness of prison and labour camps. God spared her that, making her death a blessing in disguise.

CHAPTER FIVE

Unbelievable. Unexpected. After months of uncertainty we had news of Mother. She was alive. Breathless with happiness we rushed off to Uncle Abraham's apartment, where, with a few relatives, we read Mother's letter. The writing on the envelope was unfamiliar, and the post-mark was Novosibirsk. The letter, which was crumpled and soiled, had taken a month to get to Leningrad. It was absolutely amazing that it ever reached us.

She had been arrested on the Nevsky Prospekt, Mother wrote, not far from the Quissisana restaurant. Two men had grabbed her by the arms, she was thrust into a motorcar, standing nearby, taken to Moscow Station and there, under guard, placed in a compartment of a train. The abduction was done so quickly that she did not understand what was happening and, though she tried to speak to the guards, she received no answer. With the movement of the train, and the chugging noise of the wheels going round and round in her head as the engine gained in speed, she realized that she was being taken away from her children. She began to bang on the door, shouting: 'Open the door! Where are you taking me? The children are waiting for me. For God's sake have pity on me. They must know that I am here.'

The guards gave her food, but she would not eat and kept repeating that the children must be told where she was. She asked to be taken to the lavatory, and in a state of temporary insanity threw herself out of the open window. She was found unconscious at the side of the track and taken to a local sick-bay, and from there she

32

was finally transferred to Novosibirsk hospital where the interrogations took place. My mother was accused of spying for the English intelligence service and sentenced to ten years in a labour camp with an extra five years for attempting to escape.

Now, she wrote, she was feeling better, but her hearing was bad. She ended by saying that she was always thinking of us, crying for us, and implored us not to forget our poor Mamma. She had thrown the letter out of the hospital window with a message to anybody who found it to send it on to Uncle Abraham's address. Some unknown person, with a big soul and great compassion, responded to this desperate woman's appeal and forwarded the letter to us. It was sad horrifying news, but at least we now knew where she was.

Three months later we received an official paper from the authorities at the labour camp at the Belamor Canal, situated near the Swedish border, giving permission for any member of the family to make a special visit for three weeks as Mother was now considered a semi-invalid as a result of her accident. Only my mother with her persistence, strong will and obstinacy could have succeeded in getting such permission in that political situation of terror and of purges. It was fantastic.

Cecile and her fiancé, Innokenti, came to see me off with my small wooden-fibre suitcase bulging with clothes for Mother and as much food as possible – bread, sugar, hard-boiled eggs, cucumber and cold salted pork fat – because, although rationing was over, there was still a shortage of food. I was put on the train, and Cecile asked the attendant to look after me before she said goodbye. There were about forty people in the third-class – 'hard-class' – carriage, which had bare wooden berths.

There were a lot of roughly dressed men wearing the traditional canvas and pigskin high boots of the peasants and smoking 'goat's legs', a kind of pipe made from newspaper and filled with *makhorka* (cheap, strongly smelling tobacco made from the stalk of the tobacco

33

plant). The peasant women were dressed in long black skirts and flower-printed cotton blouses, their hair hidden under brightly coloured kerchiefs worn low over the brow like the Iranian women do today.

Because of the length of train journeys, Russian passengers take over from the moment they settle down in the long partitioned compartments. Within minutes my companions had arranged around them their belongings – cheap battered suitcases tied with string or rope, bundles tied up in cloth and cardboard boxes bulging with food for the journey. There was no past, no future, only this present journey.

Cecile had given me a little piece of blanket to sleep under, and next morning, after I had folded it away, I began eating breakfast from the food parcel she had prepared. While I was staring out of the window the man sitting opposite me began to ask me questions. 'What is your name?' 'Where do you come from?' 'Why do you speak broken Russian?' Remembering Cecile's advice, I merely told him that my name was Flora Leipman and nothing else.

The man was middle-aged and wearing a washed-out khaki military uniform that had seen better days, with the usual high Russian boots. He had a pleasant face and spoke to me slowly and distinctly so that I could understand what he said. When the train stopped he rushed out with the rest of the passengers to buy from the peasants and *babushkas* (grandmothers) hot boiled potatoes and pickled cucumbers, and to get a can of hot water to make tea which he shared with me.

As we neared my destination I told him that I was going to Medvezhaia Gora (The Bear Mountain), which was a small railway siding, and he answered that this was strange because he was going there, too. Sudenly he leaned across and said quietly: 'Your mother's name is Leipman?' When I nodded he added with a twinkle in his eye: 'Before meeting your mother wouldn't you like to buy her some flowers?' And then, very gently, he

34

inquired: 'Do you have any papers with you? Show them to me.'

I had been reluctant to mention that my mother was in a camp in case the other passengers heard, but he seemed to understand and immediately explained to me how to get there. 'When you get off the train turn left and walk about one kilometre. You'll see the camp ahead; you can't fail to notice the big gates, and if you turn left just before you get there you will see a little kiosk where you will find a woman selling flowers.'

When the train stopped I was surprised to see a commotion in the compartment as many people grabbed their belongings and got off the train, too. Clearly they were also going to the same place, though nobody mentioned it directly. With my suitcase in one hand and heavy parcels in the other I trudged along the dusty road until I saw in the woods a settlement of houses and not far away high wire walls and a huge iron gate.

Following the instructions, I turned left and there was the flower-kiosk. At first there seemed to be nobody there, and then I saw someone behind the kiosk watering pots of flowers. She was dressed in drab grey and black, her grey head bare, and she seemed to limp as she refilled her can from a nearby bucket. She looked old, and her movements were slow, as though everything was an effort. As I approached her she turned round and I saw that it was Mamma. We flew into each other's arms and, overcome with emotion, she shouted: 'Look, it is my daughter. My Flora has come.' Women came out from the nearby houses to see what was the matter and quickly came running to us. Mamma was hysterical with excitement as she cried out: 'Bozhe Moi, Bozhe Moi' ('Oh my God, oh my God'). Some of the women even smiled as they watched us hugging and kissing each other amid our laughter and tears. When Mamma asked about the family and Camille I bowed my head and said, 'He was deported,' and she replied: 'Thank God he is safe.' I then assured her that everyone was all right. There was nothing to worry about. I was horrified at what I was doing, but I wanted to spare Mother from the truth about Mathilde's death and was desperate that nothing should spoil our first day together. 'Come on, let's go home,' she said, cuddling me close to her, and this was how we made our way to the camp gates.

At the entrance the guard on duty admitted Mother, but I was refused. 'You have to get permission for your little girl to go in,' he explained. Mamma began shouting and screaming until finally the guard gave in. 'But you must go immediately and report to the administrative office,' he said. Once inside Mamma ignored his instructions and took me directly to her 'home'.

The whole camp was a series of wooden barracks with about one hundred people in each. Inside the prisoners slept in double-decker bunks, but because of her injuries Mother had a lower one. Some of the women had put up little curtains made from pieces of rag and the odd personal things they had in their handbags on the day they were arrested. It was horrible but, even so, one felt that here in this camp the human spirit had risen above barbaric Soviet injustice.

The other prisoners were also political and came from the professional world or were artists in their own right, singers, ballerinas, writers and wives of leading men from the intelligentsia. Through their capacity for survival, and resistance to being turned into human beasts of burden, they had been able to make life bearable even in prison camp. Besides, you cannot feel bad all the time when you can see trees around you and hear birds singing, as they could.

'My daughter is here . . . my Flora,' Mamma kept repeating. Women came from all over the barracks, old women and young women, crowding around me talking and laughing, rejoicing with Mamma in her happiness. They were all dressed like her except that they tied kerchiefs round their heads, which she was always reluctant to wear. Though her once ramrod-straight spine was now bent and in her fall Mamma had been concussed and suffered damage to her ear-drums, her skin was still alabaster white and she stood apart from all the rest. In some imperceptible way my mother had retained her own British character and personality and was to do this until the day she died.

After the rejoicing in the barracks Mamma took me with her to the small peasant cottage outside the camp where we were to stay together for the next three weeks. As no children were allowed in the camp the authorities had arranged that we stay in one room of this peasant woman's wooden hut. There were children running around without shoes, and the whole of the back garden was filled with potatoes, but to Mamma and me it was paradise.

Arms entwined we sat on the bed while she listened to my outpourings of news about the family. With Cecile's help I had made up my story in advance so that when it came to asking about Mathilde I play-acted, answering: 'Mamma, she is so happy. Mathilde met an Englishman and after their marriage he took her back to England.' I was such a good actress that my mother never doubted my story and rocked herself with happiness. At least one of her children had escaped from the Soviet Union and was now safely in England. The Secret Police could never touch Mathilde now.

Mamma had been given a day off, so we talked and talked the hours away. All the terror of the last fifteen months melted as we bathed in our love for each other. The peasant woman gave Mother some small potatoes, no bigger than marbles, which we cooked over the smoke fire and had a picnic in our little room. In the afternoon the woman left the house and went to the end of the garden. Some time later she returned with something squealing in her arms. I thought it was a pig, but looking closer we saw that it was a baby which she had given birth to amid the potato plants.

'Oh my God,' Mother shouted. 'Quickly, Flora, get

37

me some hot water' – and with that she led the young woman to her bed. Mother immediately became active and practical, and not only attended to the woman but also washed the baby. It was withered like a red apple and the first newborn baby that I had ever seen.

When Mother went back to work I stayed by her side at the kiosk, enjoying myself arranging the summer flowers – marigolds, marguerites and cornflowers – in their pots and carrying water from the nearby well. Our contentment was almost complete. It was a busy little town, and most of the people led near-normal lives and worked in the administrative offices of the prison camp. It was only in the early morning and evening, when I saw the long line of men prisoners, five abreast, shovels over shoulders, walking to and from their long day's work digging the canal that I realized the infinite sadness of their lives. They looked tired, dirty and dispirited, shadows of their former selves. Other prisoners, including women, were put to work clearing the forests and cutting wood, all of which was done by hand.

I was perturbed by such scenes, but to my mother they had become just part of the daily scenario of camp life. This was 1934, one of the worst years of the Stalinist purges, but life at this camp was tolerable as it was far away from the Kremlin and close to the ever watching eyes of Finland. There was also still an element of humanity between the guards and the prisoners as the KGB was not so sophisticated and psychologically orientated as it was to become a few years later.

A few days after my arrival I was resting outside the peasant's hut as Mamma had gone to the camp. Suddenly someone came running to me and said: 'Your mother is ill. Come quickly.' The woman caught my hand and we ran the short distance to the gate, where the guards let me through without any fuss. I found my mother lying on the floor surrounded by other women prisoners. She was writhing and screaming as she clutched something in her hand. On seeing me she got to her feet and, her eyes flashing with anger, lunged towards me. Her fury rose like that of a wounded animal and, unable to control herself, she hit me across the face, shouting: 'You liar. My own daughter is a liar. Have I not suffered enough that you do this? Why did you lie to me about Mathilde? She is dead . . . dead . . . dead!'

Mamma thrust into my face a letter that she had received from Aunt Mary telling her of Mathilde's death under interrogation in prison. By now she was so hysterical that someone called the camp doctor, who gave her an injection to calm her down. Once again, like a terrifying octopus, the tentacles of the Soviet system had stretched out and squeezed the last drop of happiness left to mother and daughter. I stood hanging my head in shame. It was not the stinging of my face, nor my humiliation in front of the other camp women, but the sight of my beautiful mother completely beyond my reach that shocked me. From my downcast eyes I saw a pair of official boots and slowly looked up into the face of the 'man on the train'. There was no recognition in his eyes. Mamma had by now sunk to the ground wailing and weeping. 'Stop screaming. Be quiet. You have another daughter to think of,' he ordered. 'Get up off the ground.'

Numb with emotion Mamma obeyed him. I was only sixteen and not mature enough to handle such a complex situation. I knew only one thing: that I had lost a part of my mother for ever. Our relationship would never be the same again. The sharp intolerable pain was like an incurable ache which would remain with me until this day. When Mamma's rage had spent itself we embraced and wept together.

Though Mamma had begged the authorities that I should remain with her, this was not possible. There was no school, and I would have been one teenager among thousands of convicted women prisoners. When the day came for me to leave, my mother gave me letters for Sammy and Cecile, and her camp friends asked me to take mail for their families, too. As they gathered to see me off I felt part of my heart was left behind the barbed wire as I took the dusty road back to the railway to pick up my train. I turned to look at Mamma, a speck in the distance as she stood waving bravely. Fourteen years and much suffering would pass before we met again.

CHAPTER SIX

As I returned to Leningrad in great sadness at my separation from my mother, my only comfort was that she was not alone in her plight. I also pondered on her last warning to me: 'Flora, be careful what you say about what you have seen.'

I had a premonition that this was not the end of all my troubles. I was living with Cecile and Innokenti, who were now married, and we were surprised when Sammy came to us, frightened, and told us that he had been given twenty-four hours to get out of Leningrad. His passport was remanded. During that last twenty-four hours we tried as much as possible to comfort him and prepared warm clothes to take on his journey.

We went to the Moscow Station, where his train was leaving, and, standing by the carriage, I looked at Sammy, tall and handsome with his broad shoulders in his brown suede English jacket. His pale face was expressionless except for his eyes, which were filled with misery and reproach. He looked so like Mother, every muscle of his body protesting against the humiliation and injustice done to him. 'Goodbye, Flora. Don't worry. I will take you back to Scotland one day.' That was the last I ever saw of Sammy.

I remembered with sadness and a feeling of amusement how Sammy and I had plotted to escape from this terrible country, and one warm summer night had gone to the port where the overseas ships berthed. Taking off our clothes we bundled them up in black cloth and fastened them on to our heads. We were both strong swimmers and set out towards a ship riding at anchor. When we reached it we clutched the anchor chain hanging from the prow. We shouted, but no one answered. Cold and trembling, I said: 'Come on, let's go back, Sammy. It's no use.'

My brother was furious with me, calling me a cry baby, and replied: 'I should never have taken you with me.' How we were never caught I cannot understand to this day. As there were no tramcars running so late at night we had to walk in our damp clothes all the way back to 2nd Soviet Street.

That was Sammy's first attempt at escape. After Mathilde died I did not see him for a long time, and when he finally came back to Uncle Abraham's home his face was covered with sores and he looked thin and worn out. He confessed to me that he had been arrested and caught in his second attempt to escape by ship, but for reasons that we did not understand the port authorities had let him off.

Three months after seeing Sammy off at the station, we received a letter from him explaining that the deportation had been a bluff; he had been arrested on the train. When they arrived at Saratov he was immediately taken to prison and sentenced to ten years under 'article 58/6 espionage'. That was the only letter we ever received from Sammy, and to this day his fate is still a mystery.

Everything was going wrong. It was terribly embarrassing for me to live with Cecile and her husband in one room despite the screen that was put up at night, and I felt that I was spoiling her happiness. I lied to her that Aunt Mary had invited me to live with her, but instead went to live with Zoya in the tiny room which her father was paying for so that he and his second wife could occupy the whole flat. I was still working in the factory and able to see Cecile every day. She was very pleased, and as it was summer I did not take all my belongings but left some with her.

After work I used to go with Zoya to the public beach

on the River Neva in front of the Peter-Paul Fortress. Sometimes Zoya and I would not go home but would sleep on the beach or crawl into the recesses between the rocks, and early in the morning after a quick swim rush off to work. I was young and reckless. After our late nights dancing we often wandered into some sophisticated building and made our bed on one of the wide window-sills, lying there looking at the beautiful rococo cornices and sculptures. The mantelpieces were particularly beautiful, and we would fantasize ourselves into grand duchesses coming home from the Winter Palace after the ball. But this did not last long as the Soviet Educational and Militia had better thoughts for our welfare. One night we were wakened by a torch in our faces and hurriedly pushed into a prison van with other 'ladies'. We were shut up in a cell for the night and in the morning I was told to get out of Leningrad within twenty-four hours and given a ticket to Izhorsk, a hundred kilometres away, courtesy of the Soviet Union, where I was to report. Zoya was accused of contact with foreigners and sentenced to three years' imprisonment. We lost touch until many years later.

I returned to Cecile to get my things. She was upset and annoyed at my deception, but when we parted she promised to help me and send money if I was in need. At Izhorsk the Militia sent me to a hostel for the accommodation of wild teenagers, and there I began my Soviet upbringing, building communism by sweeping the streets with a makeshift broom. They forced on me a Soviet identity card which meant that I was now a full Soviet citizen. My Britishness was slipping away from me.

After serving my 'time' as a street-sweeper I was allowed back to Leningrad as a fully fledged Soviet citizen. Cecile, thank God, was happy in her marriage and now had a baby daughter called Marina. I knew that I could never return to live with her. Husband, wife, baby and me in one small roon was just too much! But where could I go?

In a state of deep depression I went down the wide concrete steps on the Neva embankment opposite the Peter-Paul Fortress. My heart was heavy, and the scar from my recent appendix operation pained me. I was only seventeen. An overwhelming thought came into my mind. I wanted to die. Why shouldn't I drown myself? What was there to live for? Staring into the gentle lapping of the water I became lulled into a temporary insanity until youthful logic took over. How can I drown myself, I thought, when I am a good swimmer? That fleeting glimmer of light and humour saved me. In preparation for my watery grave I had taken off my coat and beret – my last reminders of Glasgow – but now, reason restored, I quickly put them on again. Life was for living – and there was no easy way out.

Suddenly in my reverie I heard the pattering of little paws, and two fat puppies with their leads trailing behind them came sniffing up to me. As I patted them I heard a strident woman's voice calling in English: 'Fuzzle and Puzzle . . . come back here *immediately* . . . heel, heel.' As the figure approached I recognized Mrs Morton, the mother of my schoolfriends Alan and Mary. 'Flora, what on earth are you doing here?' she inquired in her unmistakable voice. 'What's the matter with you?' I burst out crying with all my woes, and the outcome was that Mrs Morton invited me to come and live in their lovely flat, where I quickly settled in and became part of the family.

On our free days we used to go together to the Foreign Workers' Club, which was situated on the Square of Labour not far from the Astoria Hotel. There all different nationalities met and enjoyed various entertainments and lectures as well as playing chess and other games. Poor Sammy had loved to go there with Alan and would spend hours reading English books in the library and talking with the other young people.

Sitting in the lounge we remembered our school romps, how we decorated Lenin's portrait with flowers and ribbons and what fun it was going to camp with the Pioneers, the equivalent of Girl Guides and Boy Scouts except that their activities had a political background. We laughed at how I edited the English wall newspaper and how Alan was chairman of our English and American Pioneer organization. Alan was my first cherished secret love, though unrequited because he was infatuated with an American girl.

As the great October Socialist Revolution holiday approached I was worried that I had nothing to wear, and Mrs Morton told Mary to give me one of her dresses. It was all frills, and the colour was candy-floss pink, but there were no shoes to match because the pink shoes that went with the dress had a hole in one sole. But what is a hole in a shoe to a seventeen-year-old? I stuffed the inside with cardboard and, looking like a fairy on a Christmas-tree, went off to the party with Mary and Alan. When we arrived everybody was already dancing in the ballroom. Someone spoke to me in English, inviting me to dance, and looking up I saw a tall handsome young man a couple of years older than myself with piercing blue eyes, shiny black hair sleeked back, and a lively smile. We danced together several times, and I was enjoying myself until I looked down and saw that the cardboard had slipped through the hole. I was so embarrassed that I tripped and fell between his legs. Taking the easy way out I pretended to faint and was carried to a couch where someone produced some smelling salts. When I 'woke up' after a convenient time the kindness and consideration in Karl's concerned face banished my shame and confusion, and that was the beginning of our love-story. I was his Juliet and he my Romeo – it was as simple as that. It was so nice to feel myself lying in his warm protective arms as he supported me and accepted my explanation that I was weak from my recent operation.

In a week's time Mrs Morton, beaming with pride, seated me on the sofa beside her and read out Karl Kredji's letter asking for my hand in marriage.

My joy was momentary. 'How can I marry him, Mrs Morton, when two members of my family are in prison? How can I tell him that they have been accused of spying? There is too much loaded against me and I must wait for Mamma and Sammy.' All the fun had fizzed out of me when stark reality hit me in the face. I had already accepted the fact that my family carried a curse.

Karl was a Schutzbundler, an Austrian Social Democrat, so the situation was rather comical; he with his communist ideas and the daughter of a 'spy' with my hidden hatred of the socialist system, but he was persistent and I was young and I loved him. He was the first human being that I had all to myself. His parents in Vienna sent a big photograph of the whole family – my new family – and the broken pieces of my life fell into place when we married in one of the registry offices in the district. I was grateful when Mrs Morton got me a simple little brown wedding dress, though I thought it sad that she could not have bought better material. There were no bells ringing, no Mamma fussing over me in a billowing white wedding dress, no big family party surrounding me with happy faces – only a strange feeling that I was dreaming. I was seventeen and he was eighteen. It was child's love, but I was Mrs Karl Kredji.

The Putilov Plant where Karl worked had given us a little room for our honeymoon night, and some of his friends in the Austrian colony had prepared a modest festive supper of small things to eat and drink. It was in a daze of make-believe that we consummated our marriage and promised to be true to each other – for ever.

Now that I was married it was easier for me to get a job as a telephonist in the plant where Karl worked. I was part of a team of sixteen girls who giggled our way through the obscene telephone calls that we had to accept from time to time. In addition to my bad Russian I was always making mistakes with the numbers, but was clever enough to cover up, and it was great fun.

The Putilov heavy industrial plant was one of the most

46

important in the whole of the Soviet Union, and I used to dissolve into laughter when I realized my absurd position in being employed there at all. There I was, the daughter of an English 'spy' and the sister of two English 'spies'. It was a crass example of the illogic of the Russian mind. I could have done any amount of sabotage within the plant or, even worse, been used as a tool by some superior brain. How could I respect a country who threw into prison millions of people who were not spies and yet allowed people from all over Europe to do high-priority jobs in their factories without any security check?

Mixing in the evenings with the Austrian workers and their families, though my German was almost non-existent, I could not help catching a glimpse into their minds. They, too, felt that the great Russian adventure was in reality a myth with no substance, and their only thought was how to get back to Austria. They were disillusioned, disappointed, their only hope to escape from the irrationality of the Soviet system. Though unemployment was rife in Austria, anything would be better than this Russian imprisonment of the soul.

Like many of the other Austrians, Karl had been a member of the Schutzbund, a political party formed in 1923 as a spin-off from the collapse of the Habsburg Empire. These 'worker guards' became an official arm of the Social Democrats and took part in the civil war of 1934. They were defeated partly because their leaders let them down, and many fled the country to make a new life in a communist paradise.

In the evenings Karl and his friends gathered and talked in whispers long into the night. They were forming a plan to escape to Czechoslovakia. They would go ahead and then, in some miraculous and naïve way, get their wives out later. Karl explained it all to me, saying: 'Flora, we will get you out. Remember you are my wife and my family is waiting for you. Just be patient.'

There never seemed time for long discussions, but I

47

knew that I could not leave with Mamma in prison and Sammy missing. Just imagine my mother coming out of prison and no one there to meet her. No, I was not going, and no one could persuade me. There were nights when I became angry and argued: 'You can't leave me like that. They will put me in prison if you do that. Don't you understand, I will be implicated if you go ahead with your plans to escape?' But Karl was adamant, and our love of five months was not binding enough to deny him this chance to escape. It is ironic that, had I gone, I might, as a Jewish woman, have become a speck of humanity in Hitler's holocaust. I do not know whether it would have been worse or maybe better, only that the dilemma I faced at the time was almost overwhelming.

CHAPTER SEVEN

On the last night we lay in bed together hugging each other and crying. In the warmth of our embrace I whispered to Karl: 'You are the only person who believes in me. You are all I have to protect me.' At 1 a.m. we met up with the other conspirators. The whole room was filled with Austrians whispering their farewells. Wives were crying and I cried, too. Though our love was immature, innocent of the marital intrigues that come with age, I was losing the only person outside my family who had shown real compassion for me.

As the young Austrians strapped on their rucksacks 'scouts' went out into the streets to see that they were clear. The end was quick as they slipped out into the night – away to freedom.

Once their absence was noticed at work, within hours I was kicked out of my room. Men from the plant confiscated the furniture, and I was homeless again. Though I had made friends among the Austrian wives, I could not stay with them; they were only a part of five months of happiness that had now passed. There was no way that I would ever go back to Uncle Abraham's uncaring hospitality or burden myself on Cecile and her little family. Only one person had never failed me, and that was Aunt Mary. She listened quietly as my tears flowed, as I poured out all my fears that because of Karl's defection the NKVD would be after me now.

'There is only one thing we can do,' Aunt Mary told me in her straightforward logical manner. 'We must get you married again and change your name.' In those days divorce was not a problem. Church weddings were forbidden and consequently marriages in registry offices had lost their sanctity. Within weeks I had been divorced and Aunt Mary had found a nice young Jewish man called Aaron Kaplan who was willing to marry me for a sum of money. I arrived with Aunt Mary at the appointed time and saw my 'husband' for the first time. Within five minutes the papers were signed; I had lost my Austrian identity and become Flora Kaplan. We left the marriage office and went down to the park where I shook hands with Aaron Kaplan and Aunt Mary slipped an envelope into his hands. Then he walked out of my life.

How odd that of all Russian names Aunt Mary should have picked Kaplan. It was the notorious anarchist Fanya Kaplan who had attempted to shoot Lenin in 1918. She was arrested and executed, and the incident marked the beginning of the 'Red Terror'. In Russian history her name was hated and reviled. Whenever I had to give my new name I was always subjected to the most serious scrutiny and schoolchildren would shout after me: 'She killed Lenin.'

When Karl had disappeared I felt that the only person who could advise me was Aunt Mary. She was a handsome woman of perception and strength of character, and she helped me a great deal over the years. She understood when I told her that I felt that I could no longer go on working at the Putilov Plant. At that time Aunt Mary was in charge of the box office at a theatre, and she suggested that I might like to work in a cinema on Nevsky Prospekt. It was just the thing for me; I became an usherette.

The pictures were mostly revolutionary propaganda feature films and horribly boring. I saw Lenin seven times a week and Stalin about twenty. There were films about the foundation of the Pioneers, the foundation of the Communist Party, the foundation of the Komsomols (Young Communist League), industrialization, nationalism, civilization. On good days I saw Charlie Chaplin,

Ramon Navarro and the spy serial *Miss Mend*. There were Russian films, too, featuring the top star Zoya Fyodorova, who was later to be taken prisoner when she shared her life with an American naval officer, Captain Jack Tate. At the time I was supposed to look like Zoya and was happy when people commented on this as she was considered a great beauty.

Cecile and Aunt Mary rented a room for me with an old lady in a communal flat. It was dirty and poky next to the kitchen and clearly had once been the room occupied by a maid in pre-Revolution days. There was no bathroom, so once a week I had to go to the *banya* (bath-house) which looked like a Finnish sauna. All the fat women scrubbing away reminded me of when Mamma used to bathe me in the camp at Belomorsk.

One day at the cinema I met a young boy called Boris Kozlovsky. He was a year or two younger than me, and told me that his father was a captain of one of the big ships in the Soviet navy. On the walls of his parents' flat hung diplomas of appreciation from Stalin, who had travelled in Captain Kozlovsky's ship, of which the family was very proud. It was a solid bourgeois apartment with a long corridor leading to two steps that went down into the kitchen, and a little turning led to a small room which Mr Kozlovsky used as a study. It was in this little room that Boris and I used to sit and recite the poetry of Esenin when I visited the family. I was always welcome, and they were exceptionally kind to me.

One night about midnight I was lying in bed in my little room which overlooked the courtyard when I heard an urgent knocking on the window and a boy's voice saying: 'Flora, let me in . . . let me in.' I jumped up to see Boris's white face and opened the window to let him in. He was crying and desperate. 'Oh, Flora, they have arrested my father and my mother. They've taken them away and ransacked the whole house. What can I do?'

We sat on my bed as he explained the whole story: how the NKVD had knocked on the door and, realizing that it could only be the Secret Police at that time of night, his mother had rushed Boris to his father's study and hid him in an alcove in the wall in front of which stood a massive old-fashioned wardrobe. She handed him a glass of water and cautioned him that whatever happened he was to keep quiet, if necessary for hours. Boris had heard the NKVD talking as they went through the flat, ripping out drawers and throwing the contents on the ground, searching cupboards, combing the bookshelves and shaking every book for hidden evidence. Eventually he was exhausted with fear, and nature took over. Boris fell asleep, waking some hours later. All was silent. Cautiously he squeezed himself from behind the wardrobe and listened. The moonlight spilling on to the floor revealed that the men had even come into the study when Boris was sleeping, searching his father's desk with expert hands. It was the same all over the apartment. Every room was in chaos.

Officially, when an apartment or house was ransacked by the Secret Police an inventory of the contents was supposed to be taken and presented to the owner in prison for his or her signature. But in the Thirties this was a complete farce; the NKVD took their pick of the valuables for their own use. The homes of the officials were often filled with beautiful objects such as porcelain and silver, paintings and furniture which they could not possibly have owned otherwise. Stealing, plain ordinary stealing, comes in many guises in the Soviet Union.

Boris's one thought was to escape, but on opening the front door he broke the seal left by the NKVD, which left no doubt in his mind as to what had happened to his parents. All night we talked, and I tried to comfort him saying that I would get in touch with Aunt Mary, who would tell us what to do. Early in the morning we stole out of my room and went to see her before she left for work. 'There is only one thing to do and that is to get in touch with your relatives, Boris,' she told him. She allowed him to stay with her until his aunt came.

Together they wept, clinging to each other for comfort. This fear for the unknown was something that I understood so well.

During these two years of my life I received only two letters from my mother. There was no self-pity, no self-recrimination. Mother had accepted her fate knowing that to survive in the camps it was necessary to bend to the system and live only from day to day. She wrote that now her health had improved a little in the summer she was sent to work in the forests gathering branches off trees that had been felled. It was her job to gather them up and stack them into piles that would be used for fuel in the winter. She had been issued with warm clothing consisting of cotton wadded trousers and jacket, canvas boots. In Mamma's humorous way she described herself: 'I look a sight with a red kerchief on my head.'

After Karl had disappeared from my life I grew further and further away from the Morton family. My shyness over the breakdown of my marriage left a scar of hurt and perhaps resentment, and I felt that I could not impose myself on them again. Alan and Mary were the children of esteemed 'English communists'. I was nothing. They had nothing to fear. Nothing to hide. There was a barrier between us. I was an outsider, an outcast. I was dishonoured as my whole family had been branded as 'spies'. It made me feel unclean. At seventeen I was mentally unprepared for such a burden. My hurt was devastating.

A single arrest in any family made the other members nervous, waiting for the knock at the door which meant the NKVD. Some families even prepared a bundle of belongings which they kept ready in case, and I had gathered together a comb, brush, piece of soap, two pairs of knickers and some home-made flannel sanitary towels.

I was in my room one evening, tired and reading English books that I had got from the library. It was a tiny room: a bed, a chair, a little table, and nails stuck out from the wall on which hung my meagre wardrobe.

53

Reflecting on my relations with Cecile, I wondered why she no longer wanted to see me or let me play with my funny little niece, Marina. I supposed that it was Innokenti who was keeping us apart, but what right had I to complain? She was a happy wife and mother, and my marriage was a failure. I wondered where Karl was. Was he unhappy and lonely, too?

Suddenly I heard the sound of the doorbell and my landlady screaming my name. There was noise and confusion, and loud voices shouting: 'Kaplan, Kaplan.'

The landlady knocked on my door. 'There are two men to see you,' she told me in a scared voice.

They rudely pushed her aside and walked straight up to me. 'Come on, you are under arrest.' There was no warrant, no explanation. They were dressed in plain clothes and rather young. They just gave me time to take my handbag and the bundle I had prepared, then they took me by the arms and led me out to a black car standing outside.

I tried to struggle and gasped out: 'Where are you taking me? What have I done?' Desperate thoughts flashed through my brain, terrified that Mamma and especially Cecile would not know where I was.

Sitting there between these two men with their expressionless faces, seeing through the window laughing faces passing by – free people – sobbing hysterically as we reached the prison gate. The iron doors opened and we passed on as they clanged behind, robbing me of my freedom.

Held tightly under the arms through endless corridors I vaguely remember in some kind of office an official asking me a few questions and that I signed a paper. Two guards in military uniforms led me to my prison cell. The door opened and suddenly I felt Mother close to me and heard her voice: 'Flora . . . I have been through this . . . you must be strong . . . I am always beside you.' The door closed behind me and I distinctly heard it locking. *I am a prisoner*.

CHAPTER EIGHT

Thank God, no more interrogation. It was over. Finished. Here I was with those other wretched victims of Stalin's purges, waiting for our destiny – the great Etap (transportation of convicts under guard). Etap, the very word in Russia terrifies. In pre-Revolution days, under Tsarism, wretched convicts were chained together and forced to march thousands of kilometres through wild Russia to Siberia, but now prisoners were transported by train in cattle-trucks.

During my short 'rendezvous' with my prison mates we talked politics as now there was nothing to fear in being overheard, nothing to lose. We discussed the latest events that had been in the newspapers, in the cinema newsreels and public meetings over the last year in connection with the execution and imprisonment of historic personalities such as Trotsky, Zinoviev, Bukharin and Rykov, and of the old Bolshevik 'traitors' Marshal Tukhachevsky and many other famous generals of the Soviet Army. Many of the women had been present at meetings condemning these people, putting up their hands and shouting: 'No mercy for class enemies. Kirov's murderers will be punished.' Stalin's reaction to the murder of Kirov was to arrest thousands of innocent men all over the Soviet Union, some of whom had never even heard of the name of Kirov. And these women beside me were their wives, widows, mothers and sisters who had been caught up in this terrifying political whirlpool.

There was also the frightening talk that we would be

sent to concentration camps. In the afternoon I was called out with other women and sent to the *kapterka* (clothing depot). I was still wearing my blue polka-dot dress, which by then had lost all its buttons and one sleeve had been torn in the struggle with the drunk interrogator. I had fastened the top together with my torn stockings, used as a belt, and my legs were bare. Two grades of clothes were issued to prisoners – new, and old ones that had been fumigated. I clearly fell into the second category; only by bribery was it possible to get new clothes.

The woman behind the window of the depot pushed towards me an old worn-out black wadded coat, a cotton skirt and coarse petticoat, heavy rubber *chunies* (clogs) that had been made from motorcar tyres, and a cap with ear-flaps. On receiving the clothing we signed our names in a big book. I pleaded to the guard standing beside me: 'Please, could I have some medical attention because of my boils?' He was kind and, as by chance the sick-bay was near at hand, he stopped the column and I went in. It was full of women, lying on the floors, occupying every seat and even standing, and the nurses had their hands full trying to cope as best they could. When it came to my turn I asked for dressings and some ointment for boils. The nurse was very helpful and quickly handed me some gauze and black ointment wrapped in oiled paper. Returning to the cell I dressed up in all my new 'finery' and clowned in my rubber clogs and scarecrow wadded coat. Cocking the hat so that an ear-flap fell in front of my nose, I twirled and posed like a model demonstrating the new convict fashions.

Late in the afternoon the cell door opened and the officer on duty, a list in his hand, shouted for attention. 'Silence. Names called, collect belongings and out of the cell with no questions.' Name after name was called, and one after another, taking their belongings, the women left the cell. Words passed: 'God bless you', 'Goodbye', and 'Please don't forget my name; I'll never forget

56

yours'. This was the way prisoners were able to pass on messages to other prisoners. When I heard my name I shuddered. I was so frightened. I kissed and hugged all my cell friends. 'God bless you, Flora,' they said. 'You are young and you will survive.' With tears streaming down my face I left the cell.

From the corridor we were marched quickly down the steps into the courtyard where a large bus was standing. Butting us with rifles and bayonets the guards shoved us into the bus like cattle being herded to the slaughterhouse. Everyone had eyes like cows, so wide with fright. All the windows of the bus were heavily curtained, and into this dim interior we were packed, some sitting, some standing. The bus moved on with a lot of commands from the guards who stood at the two entrances. Somebody shouted, 'We are on Nevsky,' and then a woman's scream as she was hit on the head. 'Anybody who moves or opens the curtains,' a guard threatened, 'will be shot.'

The bus came to a stop and we were ordered out. We saw a long train standing at a siding far away from the station. Huddled together, we stood holding on to each other, humbled, mortified, degraded. Lost people. Hovering in the background a sea of people were prevented by a wall of soldiers from getting too near the prisoners. It was no secret to those who had somebody in prison that these 'evacuations' took place regularly, and the courageous people, desperate to know the where-abouts of loved ones who were missing, defied danger and the fear of persecution.

We were marched up to the trucks, but the height between the stony ground and the wagon made it difficult for many of the older women to climb into them. They were pushed from behind and pulled up by the help of stronger prisoners. Inside the wagon at both ends were roughly constructed wooden bunks made of planks, and in the centre, because it was early spring and still cold, was a small iron stove. The lavatory was a hole in the floor covered with a wooden lid. There were thirty of us, of all ages, but mostly elderly, and everybody rushed to get a place on the bunks as the side of the truck was closed and locked with a clang. We were all exhausted and upset, hopeless in the thought that outside these wooden walls was freedom and relatives suffering for us. We lay motionless, each with her own thoughts.

Day followed night, night followed day as we journeyed farther and farther away from Leningrad. At the stops the truck sides were slightly opened and the guards handed up a pail of water and another of lukewarm *skilly*, a thin slimy gruel with tiny stinking fish. We were hungry and we took our tin bowls and spoons and shared the food. Sometimes we would receive fuel to keep us a little bit warm. The blast of cold air from the opening was refreshing, and we all turned our faces to recharge our lungs. It was like a breath of life to us in comparison with our inescapable hell.

The motion of the train made us sleepy, and thank the Lord for that. We snuggled together for warmth and comfort, only interrupted by the continual use of the latrine because of upset stomachs and to urinate. Whenever we stopped at a station I would get up on the back of my prison friend and, stretching up to the bars high up on the walls, pull myself up and try to get a glimpse of our situation. Through the bars I would also throw out pieces of paper that women had given me, hoping that someone would send them on. Those who did not have paper wrote messages on bits of their petticoats and tore them off; if the train stayed for an hour or two the whole platform would be covered with these messages.

We had lost all sense of time when the train stopped with a terrific jerk, the wagons banging into one another. We were alarmed by shouts of 'Get out, get out, get out' and the marching of heavy boots on gravel. Our truck side was forced open and we could see soldiers. As far as the eye could see was bare steppe which seemed to stretch towards the horizon and meet the sky. We grabbed our belongings and with great difficulty, helping each other, scrambled down. Some of us were so weak that we could not stand, and just sat down on the ground. We had been without exercise for twenty-five days.

It was a cold early-spring morning, but the fresh air was delicious and the brightness of the day so intense that it hurt our eyes. When we had grown used to the light we looked at one another. We were very dirty as for the whole of the jouney we had not washed. Our faces had a bluish pallor; our eyes were sunken and lustreless. We looked like ghosts. After a short rest we were ordered to get into a column, five abreast. Rumours passed from one prisoner to another that we were in Kazakhstan, one of the largest republics of the Soviet Union, which borders with Afghanistan and China. The soldiers looked funny under their pointed caps called *budyonevka*, named after a famous cavalry officer of the Civil War. Their dark faces, with shining black pupils peering through slit eyes, seemed ferocious.

Under a convoy of about six guards we began our long weary march. Soldiers armed with rifles guarded a miserable bunch of elderly women who were dumb with grief. The Soviet consideration for the convenience of political prisoners who were travelling had presented us with a cart and a scrawny horse to carry our meagre belongings, and by human instinct everybody more or less strong took under her protection the feeble and elderly. About twenty kilometres a day we marched along a frosty rutted road sprinkled with the last of the winter snow, stopping only when it became dark at special transit halts where we lay on the mud floor of the dugouts unconscious of any feeling. From a camp kitchen, early in the morning, we were given our prison rations of soup and bread.

On the third day I was feeling very ill. I could not walk as something had happened to my legs and the rubber clogs had blistered my feet. Stumbling along I fell. On the first part of our journey we had tried to help one another, but by the third day people were weak and exhausted. Even so, when I fell a little old woman dressed in black with a large brooch on her lace-frilled neck tried to help me up, saying: 'Poor little girl . . . Lean on me.' I fainted. When I recovered consciousness I was lying on top of the bundles on the cart and my bare legs were covered with an old-fashioned Russian shawl. Beside me on the cart and holding my head was the kind old woman. That day, late in the evening, we saw the black silhouettes of the wooden watchtowers of the camp far away in the distance. That evening we finished our journey. We had reached the Dolinka camps.

At the camp we were put into barracks, the older women separated from us younger ones. I embraced my old lady and we looked at each other with tears in our eyes as we parted. I lay down on the mud floor, with others. There was no food that night, but exhaustion replaced hunger.

When I woke in the morning I saw at eye level a pair of laced up American boots. I looked up to see a man dressed in breeches and a sheepskin-lined jacket. Something about him – perhaps it was the way he was dressed – gave me the feeling that I could speak to him in English and impulsively I did so. Under the cover of the shrieking *blatnaya* (a term for criminals with special privileges) who was yelling 'Out you get, you snivelling bastards' at the top of her voice, he signed to me to follow him, pushing me into the corner of the dim hut.

We spoke in hurried hushed voices and, in a few words, I managed to tell my story. He then told me that his name was Smith and that he was from Moscow. He had received ten years for espionage and counter-revolutionary activities and had already served eight years. 'I have some friends in authority here,' he whispered. 'Be brave, don't rebel.'

We went out to where columns were gathering, all going to different destinations. He gave me a rough push. 'Brigadier,' he said, 'she'll do for you,' and, under his breath, 'Goodbye, Flora . . . luck'.

Getting into line, I threw him one last look and went out of his life for ever. Many years later, in Karaganda, I met his wife and two children. From a letter he had managed to smuggle out to her she had learned of our meeting and remembered my name. Quite accidentally she heard someone call me Flora and so we met, but she never saw her husband again.

After a day's march we reached a group of *zemlyankas* (earthen dugouts) and as we went down the steps cut out of mud I felt the musty dampness of my new home. On either side of the long hut were wooden bunks where we were told to put our belongings. There was a stove in the middle with a tin pail of tepid water. A prisoner with a hunched back was on duty by the stove. The brigadier shouted at us: 'Get some sleep, *countras*' – *countra* was a slang expression for counter-revolutionaries. 'No talking. Tomorrow at five a.m. you will go to work.'

CHAPTER NINE

Our new 'house' was in reality a hole in the ground. Wooden poles supported the walls, which were covered with dry clay and manure. The ceiling was so low that you could almost touch it, and there was more smoke than heat from the little iron stove which stood in the middle of the barracks. We lived on the level of the Kazakh nomad but without his *bish-barmak* (Kirgis stew) and *khoumiss* (horse's milk).

During our tedious journey we had taken every opportunity to try to get rid of the lice. They would accumulate under the armpits and in the seams of our underwear. The only technique was to squeeze the lice and eggs between our nails. It was indecent and repulsive, but there was no other way to get rid of them.

Early in the morning a warmly dressed woman would rush into the barracks, swearing horribly, screaming at the top of her hoarse voice and smoking a 'goat's leg' pipe. 'Out you go,' she shouted, and grabbed anybody within reach and pulled them off their bunks. She filled us with disgust and hatred. These *bytoviks* (brigadiers) were drawn from the criminal prisoners and came from backgrounds of thieving, petty crime and prostitution. They hated the political prisoners with a ferocious intensity and took every opportunity to insult them.

At sunrise, still dazed with sleep, we were marshalled in the crisp cold air, carrying our *kotelok* (tin can), we convicts had the honour of conquering the steppes. In those early years of the Thirties there were no days of rest, no Sundays. The Kazakhstan steppe was a flat

62

yellowish brown, arid land which stretched as far as the eye could see. There is nothing more desolate as it has no trees or friendly vegetation, just barren earth and small scrubby plants such as the camel thorn. When I was there a huge programme had begun to cultivate the steppes with sunflowers, for valuable oil can be extracted from the seeds. Thousands of acres were furrowed by primitive machines and then kept free of weeds by women prisoners from the labour camps.

The vast fields near our camp were trellised with long rows of small sunflower seedlings that were smothered in weeds. Taking me to the end of the one row, the brigadier showed me how to weed the three rows allocated to me. We all knew that if we did not complete the work we would be given only half the 400 grams of black indigestible bread which was our daily quota. That is why everybody was desperate – hunger made them work.

I noticed that some of the prisoners worked quicker than I did because I was not used to manual work. As a city child in Glasgow I had never weeded in my life. By midday I was behind the rest, and the burning sun, which could be as hot as 26°C, beat down on our heads. I took off my worn prison jacket and worked until sunset, when we returned from the weeding to collect our bread and soup. This monotonous routine continued for a week or more, rising at dawn and returning at sunset. But when the brigadier came to check my work she was horrified and stared at me and then down at the ground. 'You bloody whore,' she shouted, 'what have you been doing?' Then she suddenly hit me across the face. 'You dirty saboteur! You've pulled out all the sunflowers with the weeds, you fool.'

She called for some guards, who took me by the collar and pushed me away from the field. I was crying bitterly. The other women were far away and there was nobody to protect me as with the brigadier at my back and the two guards with bayonets they led me to a punishment cellar. I was shoved in and, stumbling down the steps, fell on my face on the hard ground. The door was closed, and I was in utter darkness. How long I was there I do not know and I was shivering with the damp cold. Maybe they had forgotten about me? Maybe they were going to shoot me? I was called out next morning and, half-dead with fright, came out into the glaring sunlight and was taken to the barracks to collect my pitiful belongings. My 'carriage' was waiting – two oxen harnessed to a cart that was carrying a large barrel for water. I was ordered to sit beside the driver, and my papers were handed to him.

'Tsop tsibi,' the driver shouted, hitting the oxen with his whip, and we began our journey.

'Where are you taking me?' I asked, but I do not think he understood, because as a Kazakh he did not speak Russian. He was about my age with slit eyes in a Mongoloid face and he sang to himself as we continued our journey. I took out of my belongings a piece of bread which I offered to share with him, but he refused. Far away in the distance I saw *kurjans* (burial-mounds) in the deserted landscape.

This vast region of Kazakhstan has an area of about 2,700,000 square metres and an extreme continental climate. The land cools rapidly and it gets cold in September and October, bringing frost which remains as late as April. In winter the temperature in Karaganda could drop to $-40°C$ and sometimes the snowstorms and blizzards continued for weeks with the snow lying thick and in high drifts which blocked the roads even in the camps. I was to find that we often had to dig our way out of the barracks. There is virtually no spring or autumn, the weather changing from heat to intense cold within a few weeks.

After five hours' rolling along on the hard wooden wheels we came to another camp. On either side of the street where the camp officials lived there were low whitewashed huts. We stopped at one of the houses with a board outside, where my driver grabbed me and passed

64

me on to a sentry standing outside. He gave the man my papers, and I was taken to a prison cell.

Later the sentry took me to an office where a stout elderly uniformed man was sitting at a big desk. I knew that I was again in the special headquarters of the Secret Police for the surveillance of camps. The man looked at me and then at the papers, and then again looked at me with a glint in his eyes and a slight smile on his lips. That man was to change my prison life. Suddenly he said, 'Take her away,' and as a young guard took me by the arm I began to scream. I felt I had misunderstood his expression and was deeply disappointed in him.

'Don't shoot me,' I shouted. 'I have done nothing wrong.'

He got up from his chair, said something quietly in Russian to the guard. Then he said to me: 'Don't be afraid. We are not going to shoot you. Go with him.'

I walked some distance with the guard before we came to a little hut with smoke coming out of the chimney. It was a *banya* (bath-house). The guard left me beside an old man with a long white beard like Santa Claus. He poured some kerosene on my head and wrapped it up in a clean rag to get rid of the lice. I told him that I was hungry and there sitting on the bench I ate a piece of bread with some *shzpik*, cold salted pork fat, which he produced. He seemed kindly disposed, and sitting there, dangling my feet on the high bench with the kerosene working on my head, eating my food with the gentle watching face beside me, speaking some kind of language I did not understand, I felt absurdly happy. Taking the bandage off my head he placed a piece of newspaper on my lap and started to comb out the lice from my hair; they fell in little thuds on to the paper.

After this procedure I so trusted the old man that I undressed in front of him and while he took away all my clothes I went into the *banya*. He returned bringing me buckets of cold and hot water, coarse brown soap and a rough towel, and left me to wash myself. The sensuous pleasure of the hot water and soap was unbelievable, but wonders were still to come when he produced a pair of clean knickers, a skirt, blouse, stockings and boots, and gave me another plain wadded coat and a white kerchief for my head. It was like a birthday for me. He then brought me a bowl of macaroni with a little milk and, sitting there in the sunshine drying my hair, devouring my macaroni, I thought that perhaps life was still worth living after all.

Delighted with my new clothes, my bath and my clean hair, I was escorted back to the headquarters of the NKVD, back to the same man whom I supposed the chief official there. He told me to sit down, and there was something sympathetic and fatherly about him when he said to me: 'That's much better. . . . You've had some food and now we can talk.'

He looked at the papers on the desk, reading them with a puzzled frown. 'Who put you up to sabotage, pulling out all the sunflower plants? Tell me what really happened at the weeding.' I explained that I had never seen a sunflower plant in my life and that the brigadier told me to pick out all the green ones, which I did. He insisted, raising his voice: 'But you plucked out all the little sunflowers.'

'As I don't know Russian well, maybe I did not understand. Please don't shoot me . . . have pity on me.' And I began to cry again. 'I didn't understand that I was doing anything wrong.'

'Why don't you speak Russian well? Where do you come from?' he asked.

I do not know why, but before I realized what I was doing I blurted out between my sobs the whole sad story, and stopped as impulsively as I had begun. There was a silence.

Looking down at my papers he wrote something and then said to me: 'For the meantime you are going to work in the camp hospital, where we can keep an eye on you until I make some more investigations on your case.'

66

He called out to the guard, who was given some orders, and we parted.

The hospital was a long barrack, and along the corridor on the left I saw windows and on the right the open doors of the wards. The chief of the medical unit looked at my papers and told the guard to take me to the living-quarters, saying: 'Tomorrow at eight o'clock you will begin work as a charwoman.'

The staff hostel was an ordinary barrack except that the wooden plank beds had thin straw mattresses and a single sheet and blanket; one electric bulb for the whole place was operated from a generator until 11 p.m. I was delighted with my new 'home'. The small staff at the hospital consisted of a lady doctor, a chemist, a midwife, two nurses and two chars, kitchen staff and an old man called Ospan who took care of the stoves and other odd jobs.

The majority of the patients were *katorzhniks* (convicts) from the nearby Rudnyi labour camps, which were under a special strict regime, and their bodies were covered with vermin. They were brought in half-starved and seriously ill; most of them suffered from dysentery, and brucellosis and tuberculosis were common. These were the lucky ones. The others died from the appalling conditions in their camps. My task was to wash these men, shave them and rid them of lice, but despite all my efforts the lice were always crawling into the hairy parts of their bodies and laid their eggs there which were difficult to destroy. It was a hopeless job because with the arrival of new patients it would begin all over again, and there was not always hot water in our hospital because there was not enough fuel to keep the stoves going. There was a general shortage of medical supplies, and drugs to ease the pain were almost nonexistent and only given to the very desperate cases.

My regular work was to wash the floors and keep the wards clean, but my other 'special' work was to help the old man bury the bodies. Two or three men died every day. Gradually I became accustomed to the faces around me and I grew to respect them, especially Dr Lass, head of the hospital, and Dr Arnov the pharmacist, who were both political prisoners.

My duties also included cleaning the dispensary, and when I noticed that the bottles on the shelves had soiled labels I decided to make fresh ones in my spare time. I did this purely for my own amusement and so that I would not forget the Roman script, as the labels were written in Latin. One day Dr Arnov caught me doing this and was very angry.

'Who gave you permission to change the labels on my bottles?' he asked, and, 'How do you know Latin? You could have made a mistake and caused a serious accident.'

'I have done it very carefully,' I replied, 'and the letters are the same as in English. Please don't punish me.' And here again I explained my story to this nice man.

'Don't do it again without my being here,' he cautioned. 'But if you really are interested I'll teach you about the medicines and their uses.'

The incident was over, and a few days later Dr Lass invited me into her little office. We exchanged our sad histories in low voices, and she asked me if I would like to study medicine. She was a small woman of about fifty years with a smooth round face and high red cheeks, and she spoke a little English.

By now all the medical staff and the patients knew me, and even the guards were familiar faces, but I still spoke Russian with a terrible accent and was called 'the English *devochka* [girl]'. In the evenings in the barracks after work I used to sit on my bed and sing to myself to take away the tension. It came naturally to me to think in English, and my prison companions would ask me to sing to them. I began to regain confidence in myself and secretly would arrange little home-made concerts. My English repertoire was 'It's a Long Way to Tipperary',

'Pack Up Your Troubles in Your Old Kit Bag' and 'Keep the Home Fires Burning', with translations into bad Russian. After the interval, when we checked that there were no guards around I would continue with my Scots programme, in national costume. I pulled my skirt above the knees to look like a kilt and turned down my stockings to make them knee high. In Scots fashion my blanket was thrown over my shoulder, and I hung my hat in front of me like a sporran. My voice soared with pride singing 'Annie Laurie', 'Ye Banks and Braes o' Bonnie Doon', always finishing up with 'God Save the King' – without translation! I was determined that the Soviet machine would not, could not, destroy me. I might be physically living in bondage, but mentally, emotionally and even spiritually I remained a free woman.

After I had finished my performance I would fall down on my straw bed and shriek with hysterical laughter that would lead to tears and memories of my family, my schoolfriend Jenny Barrie from Glasgow and our cosy home in Sauchiehall Street. Returning to my senses, the reality of terror, humiliation and all that Stalin's men were throwing into my face would reduce me to black despair. It was not enough that the system had robbed me of freedom, but that I should be subjected to live my life in this human cesspool was almost too much to bear.

CHAPTER TEN

To my surprise I saw my stout NKVD saviour again when he came to have some treatment in the hospital. Dr Lass examined him and found that he had a slight attack of lumbago. She told me to apply cupping-glasses to his back, the only remedy that we used in Russia in those days. Cupping was employed in cases of deep-seated congestion to draw blood to the surface and was done by putting a few drops of spirits upon an absorbent dressing, igniting it and, while it was still burning, slapping the mouth of the glass on the patient's back. A vacuum is produced and the skin swells into the glass as the blood rushes into its small blood-vessels.

Under cover of these treatments we had many serious conversations, and he gave me advice on how to behave in order to survive camp life. He also explained to me the correct way to begin petitioning for my freedom and to whom to write when the time came – the General Prosecutor of the Soviet Union, the Central Committee of the Soviet Union and also to the Gulag. In those days no correspondence was allowed from the camps, and he told me to memorize not only all that he told me but also the names of my campmates. 'Flora, you are young and you will survive and when you are free maybe you will be able to contact the families of your friends.'

To this day I will always remember this kind man. He certainly saved me from being executed because, had he reported me to higher authorities, my English 'spying' background, plus the 'sunflower sabotage', together with the fact that my name was Kaplan were sufficient to have me shot. He took the greatest risk as an officer responsible for the behaviour of political prisoners in matters of sabotage, arson and any crime against the camp regulations. Had the woman brigadier known that instead of being punished I was now working peacefully in the hospital she would have denounced my friend, but he managed for my sake to appease her in some way. The only thing that distressed me was the fact that I had denied the hungry Soviet people some 500 grams of sunflower oil from the plants that I destroyed.

To explain anatomy to me Dr Lass took me to the dugout shed which served as a morgue and where the post-mortems were carried out. Every dead man had to have his cause of death established in the proper Soviet bureaucratic way, and a report was filled in which had to be signed by Dr Lass. Because of the heat, in summer the corpses had to be immediately buried as there was no ice to preserve them.

When I saw Dr Lass making an incision on a corpse for the first time I did not feel sick in spite of the fact that I had never seen an operation. I helped her, and she cautioned me: 'Be very careful with the scalpel and don't injure your hand in any way because you can get blood poisoning from the corpses.' I would look on fascinated at how the human body was constructed as, holding the organs in her hands, she showed me the kidneys, liver, heart and so on. Looking at that frail gentle woman, I thought it marvellous, and if she could stand it why not I? Medicine was to become the leitmotiv of my whole life.

We were working with a man who had died with tuberculosis, and Dr Lass showed me the parts of his lungs that had been destroyed by the bacillus. Now I understood why my cellmate Natasha had been coughing up blood, and I realised that nothing could have saved her. That was my first medical diagnosis.

Dr Lass, who suffered from kidney stones, was sometimes too ill herself or too tired to make the regulation

71

autopsies, so to conform to official orders I would make the incisions and then stitch them up while Dr Lass filled in the 'cause of death'. As she was a skilled and efficient doctor she established the necessary post-mortem data by guesswork – bluffing, I sometimes used to call it.

As a result of my diligent studying I was allowed to work as a nurse, and someone took my place as a cleaner. As a nurse I began to live the lives of my patients. Every story was sad. One exceptional ward, where I had to summon all my courage to enter with a smile and words of comfort, was that for patients suffering from phthisis (pulmonary consumption). The ward had eight patients aged from seventeen, maybe even younger, to twenty. They were the sons of Kulaks, thieves and other common criminals who had been corrupted by the Soviet system and were all in the last stages of consumption. It was called 'the dying ward'.

The ridiculous regulations of prison camps did not allow political doctors to be on duty at night, so there was only a nurse and a charwoman. One night one of the boys began coughing up blood and standing beside him I felt deep compassion for him as I looked down at the white drawn face with two red spots burning on his sunken cheeks. Every cough brought up a glass of blood. All seven pairs of eyes of the other patients looked on me, wondering what I would do to help him. My immediate reaction was to give him an intravenous injection of calcium chloride, the only medicine we had, and I left him with the old woman, who sponged his face with cold water washing off the blood, until I returned. I managed with great difficulty in spite of his convulsions to place the needle into his vein and injected the drug. The other patients looked on apathetically. It was not the first time they had seen a man die, and they themselves might be dying the same death tomorrow, suffocating from their own blood.

After a few more convulsions my patient spurted out blood like a fountain and died. It was over; he was in peace. I washed the blood away and folded his arms across his chest, and I closed his wide-open blue eyes. His face had such a surprised look as if to ask 'Why?' Sitting beside him all alone with the light of a kerosene-lamp my heart bled for all the other youths doomed to die like this boy, far away from their families.

Our little team of doctor, midwife, nurses and *sanitars* (hospital aids) did everything in our power to help our fellow-prisoners and prolong their stay so that they would not be sent back to work. One unusual case was that of a truck-driver who had had two-thirds of his body burned in an accident. We constructed a hammock for him from strips of blankets and iron bars, made a tent of medical gauze and placed bottles of hot water near to keep him warm. His only treatment was morphia, cod-liver oil and manganese chloride. To our amazement he recovered after six months, but his scars were terrible to see.

We had a case of leprosy in a sixteen-year-old boy, who was isolated from the other patients. He had already lost one arm and one leg, and the ribs on the left-hand side were exposed as his flesh rotted away. The smell was atrocious. His spirit was amazingly strong, and he would curse and swear and demand attention all the time, so that he was a terrible strain on the nursing staff, but we forgave him for his angelic face and golden curls. Though he had spent several years in this hospital, his life-history remained a mystery to us all. He died from pneumothorax (collapsing of the lung).

There was death and there was life. One day one of the hospital aids came to me and whispered that there was a girl outside who wanted to see a nurse. How she had passed through the guards I do not know. It was dusk, and I could not see her face properly.

'What is the matter with you?' I asked.

'I feel sick and I have a pain in my stomach, but sometimes it goes away,' she replied.

I went away and returned, giving her a belladonna pill,

and she thanked me, but I had a strange feeling that there was something seriously wrong and that I should not have given her that pill.

Suddenly in a spasm of pain she held her hands over her stomach and began to scream. The aid, who was much older than me, said over my shoulder: 'Don't be daft . . . she is going to have a baby.' The woman was in the last stages of labour, and we took her quickly into the kitchen and there she gave birth to a healthy baby. It was the first time I delivered a baby.

My second baby was born in the surgery. It was a breach birth, and the little girl had breathing problems. The midwife and I attempted to revive her by putting her alternately in cold and hot water, but when this did not help the midwife took the baby under the arms and threw her up and down. Suddenly she popped out of her hands and fell behind me on the leather couch and started to scream. We stood with our eyes and mouths wide open in terror. But when we quickly picked the baby up and the midwife felt all over the little bones they were all right, nothing had been broken in her fall. She was a healthy baby and none the worse for her flight in the air. Our methods were perforce unorthodox, but working together with Dr Lass and the midwife I became an efficient nurse.

The hospital was short of morphia, and as Dr Lass had an attack of kidney stones Dr Arnov sent me to the veterinary dispensary, which was about ten kilometres away. It was beginning to get dark when I set off and on my way back in the pitch dark I fell into a deep rut. I felt no pain and, lying on my back, looked up into the wide expanse of sky glittering with stars. I lay there totally enchanted and began to recite, 'Twinkle, twinkle, little star, How I wonder what you are?' with a mystical feeling of freedom. I felt that somewhere there was another life, a free life, a happy life with father buying boxes of apples at Christmas, rosy round beautiful apples. I could even smell them as I lay there.

A terrible stabbing pain in my knee brought me to my senses. I remembered my mission and Dr Lass's face twisted in agony, and somehow got myself up on to my feet and out of the rut, still clutching in my left hand the precious morphia, and hopping on one leg I reached the hospital. It was only after I saw that Dr Lass had fallen into a deep sedated sleep that I paid attention to my knee. It was bruised and swollen, but despite this I had to continue with my work.

Now that I was accepted as a nurse I was given the responsibility of seeing that the medical supplies were in order, and I made the most of this part of my work because it made me feel human and took me out of the camp area to the medical depot in the nearby village; but usually my trip was in vain because of the shortage of medicaments. We had a serious case of tetanus and as usual had no serum, so I was sent to get it from another camp. I received my instructions from the civilian medical officer to start off immediately and walk along the road where I would be picked up by a truck. My camp was called Borovoy Women's Camp but it was commonly referred to as 'the Wives' Camp'. It was not enclosed with barbed wire and had only watchtowers where armed guards were on duty all the time. If anyone had tried to escape, she would have been immediately seen and shot. Our women's camp was located not far from the men's camps, know as 'death camps', for they were notorious for their cruelty and sadism. The political prisoners were forced to work in mines under appalling conditions and on starvation rations. On that sunny day I felt it was a terrible injustice to do this to a man.

Kilometre after kilometre I tramped, turning my head to see if there was any truck catching up with me. It was still early morning, and the air was refreshing and I was elated to be escaping from the camp. I felt like a bird gliding in the sky. No one around me, just endless steppes and the whole universe in front. To cheer myself up marching along I sang at the top of my voice: 'Rule,

Britannia. Britannia, rule the waves. . . . Britons never, never, never shall be slaves.'

The truck did not come, and by midday the scorching sun was beating down mercilessly on my uncovered head. Exhausted I reached the camp where I passed my papers to the officials. I received the ampoules and inquired: 'How am I going to return again? I am tired.'

'You get going and hurry,' the medical officer said. 'There is no transport.'

It was about two o'clock when I began to return. I sat down beside the road to have a rest and to eat my piece of bread. I do not remember any more, and I suppose I fell asleep. It was dusk when I awoke. Somebody was saying 'Get up . . . get up,' and a woman's face was looking down at me. She helped me to get on to the horse-cart that she was driving. She was a brigadier called Olga, a handsome woman, who was in charge of the stockroom of a nearby camp and was returning there. Olga took me back to my hospital as more than ten hours had elapsed since I had left in the morning. I brought the serum, but my thirty-kilometre journey had been in vain. The patient had died two hours after I left.

Autumn was complicated by new illnesses: malaria, more brucellosis and influenza. Mosquitoes, flies and fleas pestered our lives, and I was tormented with bites and itches that developed into painful abscesses. Our struggle against malaria was pitiful because we had not a sufficient supply of quinine.

Winter was coming and we were sent out into the steppes to collect the *karaganeka* (camel thorn) which formed part of the scant vegetation of the steppes. In spring the passing camels grazed on the soft tips of the thorn, but in autumn, after the burning heat of summer, the bushes became dislodged from the ground and blew about in the dreaded *sukhovey*, the dry hot desiccating south-east or southerly winds. They were collected and stored in large mounds to use as fuel in the winter. Along with the other women I used to search for camel and

76

goat hair that had become attached to thorn-bushes and spin wool, using the primitive method of a home-made spindle. The guards used to make us these spindles and knitting-needles from the thorn-bush, and in this way we were able to make ourselves warm gloves and hats. We women were very practical about material things, and able to use our hands, so we survived better than the men because we helped one another and were better at feeding and clothing ourselves. Also we could get favours from the guards, who were always looking for girl-friends. On the whole, the guards in Kazakhstan made a much better impression than those in Moscow or Leningrad. Many were recruited locally whereas in the big cities they were drawn from the Army or the security forces and in the unfamiliar environment of the camps felt that the prisoners were hostile to them and reacted accordingly. Every week several babies were born and taken away to the camp nursery. That is how some women survived. I discovered how the human mind adjusts itself so that any event or variation to break the monotony is cherished and remembered, just as real pleasures become happy memories in the free world.

After the harvest we used to go and find potatoes and other root vegetables, which we cooked using cow dung mixed with straw as fuel. We dug a hole in the ground, put the fuel in, set it alight and covered up the top, leaving a hole for the smoke. It made a good oven, and when it was red hot inside we put the vegetables in to bake. They tasted fine after the dreary camp food, and the smell of hot baked potatoes was ambrosia to us.

There were three distinct groups of prisoners in the camps – the professional criminals, the *bytoviks* (the closest translation is 'offenders against the style of life of the Soviet system') and the political offenders. The *bytoviks* were an awful nuisance in our lives as they were given posts in the administration of the camp and were put in charge of the cultural and educational departments. They delighted in preaching propaganda to us political prisoners and felt superior over us 'enemies of the people' for our disloyalty to 'our Beloved Motherland'.

On special national occasions we were shown films of the heroic epics of the 1905 Revolution and of the ledgendary Red Army Civil War commander, Vasily Chapayev. The film was always worn out and scratched, and the screen was made from a sheet from the hospital, but we sat there enthralled in the flickering light simply because it was a glimpse of a world – any world would have done – outside the drab prison one. These films, including one called *The Battleship Potemkin*, had been made by Sergei Eisenstein, the genius of the Russian cinema.

Watching the faces of the women prisoners in the shadows, lost in that other world on film, they all looked alike; the natural features of youth had disappeared. With their hair hidden under a kerchief, and harsh lines etching their wind-whipped skin, they did not even look particularly feminine. They were persons . . . forgotten persons.

CHAPTER ELEVEN

Then came the winter bringing with it the *buran* (blizzard) with slashing winds of almost supernatural ferocity that sometimes lasted for three days. The cruel cold wrapped itself around you, penetrating your very bones. Before venturing out into the storm we women bound our faces with a shawl from chin to eyes to prevent frostbite. Ropes were stretched between the various camp buildings so that prisoners could hold on to find their way in the icy white blackness.

The prisoners from the men's camps were roped together so that they would not be blown away in the winds. There were many stories about lines of prisoners from the men's camps being lost in the blizzards, and during the winter I was there even a whole train of camels and their handlers simply vanished and were not found again until the snow melted.

Many men prisoners were brought to our sick-bay on sledges, often suffering from tuberculosis, pneumonia and typhoid. Why was this 'generous' gesture of sending half-dead bodies made? I can only think that it improved the medical statistics and gave an illusion of 'humane conditions' to the Soviet labour-camp system. Our patients were half-frozen to the base of the sledges, and Dr Lass and I had to amputate their fingers and toes, our only disinfectant manganese chloride. Only the strong survived and, if they recovered, they were soon taken back to their camps. Many had no fingers left at all, but that was what labour-camp life was like in the Thirties under Stalin's 'protection'.

Back in their own world of misery, after our careful nursing, many died from infection, pneumonia or plain malnutrition. The *katorzhnik* had one overwhelming obsession. Hunger filled his whole life. Even so, many of our patients asked me to try to get in touch with their relatives should they die. They were intellectuals – professors, engineers and highly qualified professionals whose lives had been cut off at the peak of their careers. They were now reduced to beasts of burden and forced to dig ditches in frosts that ranged from −20° to −40°. I used to keep a little diary with the names and dates of death, and during one of the regular camp inspections an official found my little book and I was sent to the punishment cell for three days and told that next time the penalty would be worse.

As punishment for my 'crime' the civilian medical officer, who disliked me, sent me to help unfreeze the corpses with old Ospan. This was necessary before we could perform an autopsy. It was so cold in the shed that the bodies were frozen solid, and Ospan lifted them so that they stood erect round the iron stove like statues carved from marble. Once I remember seeing a man moving his arms and legs, then with a thud he fell to the ground. I shrieked in terror and ran away. He was not moving, only unfreezing.

Next, despite the fact that there was a blizzard approaching, the civilian doctor gave orders that I should help Ospan bury the corpses. 'We have too many,' he said curtly. His decision had nothing to do with respect for the dead but was merely a medical statistic. It was perishingly cold and I put on my *valenkis* (knee-high felt boots) and covered up my face with a shawl, then with another nurse dragged out the corpses and placed them on the sledge, the bottom of which had been covered with straw. I sat on the sledge between Ospan and the corpses with my legs dangling on the ground. The cold was so intense that it seemed to eat into my very soul and my mind became a blank. As the blizzard whipped into a crescendo my only thought was to huddle close to Ospan's back, my face pressed against his dirty old coat. I kept grabbing handfuls of snow and rubbing my cheeks to prevent them from becoming frostbitten, and to keep myself awake for fear of falling asleep and freezing to death. Behind me lay the naked corpses under an old grey blanket and a counterpane of white snow. It was not until much later that the dead were given the dignity of being wrapped in white paper shrouds. Could these bodies once have been part of a family pulsating with love and life? Were their beloved ones even now missing and mourning their absence or their fate?

We were driving to a mass trench-grave which had been prepared in the summer. After some kilometres we stopped amid the whirling white snow. 'Here we are, Pilora' – Ospan's name for me, 'Get off. The old horse is tired and we will hardly be able to make it home.' The horse had been battling against the full force of the storm and was now staggering. It was the only joy left in Ospan's life, and he cared for it like a child.

The macabre experience of dragging those stiff bodies into the mass grave tortures me to this day. The grave was shallow, and we covered them up with snow. I tried to say some words of God for the souls of those men. The burial was all over very quickly, and we began the journey back to camp.

It was early spring, and a year had passed since I had been in this camp. I had adapted myself to the camp life and, remembering the kind NKVD man's advice, like the three wise monkeys I had shut my eyes, ears and mouth as that was the only way to survive. 'Every man for himself' was our prison motto. Only the work from morning until night blotted out of our minds the realization that there was any other civilization far beyond the steppes. Women have more strength and adaptability than men, and our strongest weapon was our natural instinct for life, which made it possible for us to rise from the ashes like a phoenix.

During a morning break one day Dr Lass whispered to me: 'Flora, there is disturbance going on. Be on your guard. The civilian doctor is brewing trouble for you about the corpses you and Ospan buried in the winter.' Shortly afterwards I was taken by the guard to the Special Department of the NKVD where behind a desk in the office a stranger sat. My protector and friend was no longer there. The older types of officer of the NKVD, a legacy from Cheka days, were being replaced by a new sadistic Stalin-indoctrinated breed. Again the fear enveloped me like a dark cloud. 'Citizen Kaplan,' the officer asked me, 'did you bury some corpses with Ospan last winter? How many corpses were there? Where did you bury them?'

I answered 'Yes' and explained that I did not remember exactly where we made the burial because it was during one of the worst blizzards of the year. Then I was dismissed and allowed to return to the hospital, where Dr Lass awaited me. The reason for my interrogation was that two senior members of the Secret Police had been making an inspection of the camps in our area. As they approached our camp in an open carriage they had noticed a terrible smell of mouldering corpses. The nearer they came to the camp, the worse it became. They stopped to investigate and found the decaying bodies in a shallow ditch. By mistake Ospan and I had buried the bodies in the wrong place, far away from the prepared site.

Not long after my interview the guard came for me. 'Kaplan . . . quickly with your belongings . . . Etap.' I began to cry. The three or four nurses in our barracks looked at me in pity and despair, but without even saying goodbye I was forced out of the lives of Dr Lass, Dr Arnov and those other decent people who had befriended me during my days working in the sickbay. They had given me not only a profession but also a knowledge of life. They had even risked punishment to do this. Through them alone I could now, on my twenty-first birthday, seven years after I left Glasgow, read and write Russian as well as speak it. Now I could even face the death and hardship of camp life. My only fear was what lay waiting for me ahead.

Trudging in my *valenkis*, which were becoming soaked as the sun melted the snow, after three hours I reached another camp. There I was given hard labour and put to digging ditches with a lot of other miserable women. Sometimes I was so spent that I could barely get up from my hard bunk but forced myself to go on as anything was a diversion from this living hell. Every day was the same and, if we stopped to talk to each other, the guards shouted 'Davai, davai' ('Get on'). We had to break the frozen earth with a crowbar before we could dig with a shovel, and every metre took an age. By any standards it was inhuman work for a woman, but compassion was in short supply in camp life.

Sometimes we were even robbed of our pitiful possessions by the *blatnoi*, thieving gaolbirds who would sneak into the barracks to steal. We were too numb and too worn out to make any effort to protest. The weak could not fight, and the camp administration took no notice so it was useless to complain; even the guards themselves feared these criminals. Life in the hospital was horrible, with all the dying and suffering, but in comparison with my new life it had been a haven. 'Hard labour' was real hell. With my hands blistered, every bone aching and my legs swollen from the cold, in addition to the awful food, I began to become weak again and could feel my strength ebbing away.

Once again vermin was back in my life – fleas and bed bugs – and though we women tried to rid ourselves of them the living conditions and hard work depressed us so much that some of the prisoners could not cope, nor even tried. There is something filthy about insects canni-balising human flesh when you can do nothing about it.

At nights we used to sit huddled on our beds, heads bent close together, as we automatically picked up and crushed the bed bugs or scoured our clothing for lice. In this difficult situation I did everything possible to keep myself clean. Alone with my thoughts I was constantly homesick for my family. The only people free of homesickness were those who had never had a home or family to recall in the dim tunnels of their memory. With my youth, my high spirits and by Britishness I had only to close my eyes and Mamma, Mathilde, Cecile and Sammy were near me. The memory of my family and Britain gave me a reserve of mental strength and saved my sanity.

As I was digging ditches one morning I saw a cart and horse passing along the main road with a woman sitting in it. She was magnificent-looking with strong shoulders, a proud head of thick corn-coloured hair, piercing blue eyes, and a white shawl round her shoulders. I knew immediately that she could be no one other than Olga. She was imbedded in my mind as everything personifying Russian womanhood. She had conquered all the misery of camp life and by sheer cunning and force had turned the situation to her own advantage. I rushed after the cart, yelling, 'Olga . . . Olga . . . don't you remember me?' She pulled up her horse and looked down at the dirty girl calling out to her. 'Flora, what in hell are you doing here?' Mercifully she remembered finding me lying unconscious on the road when I was returning with the serum to the other camp. She immediately handed me a piece of bread and salt cucumber and, crying and laughing, my story came tumbling out.

Then the guard, who had been watching, shouted, 'You get back,' and pushed me back towards the ditch I had been digging.

A month later I was told to prepare for a transfer. Oh God, yet another Etap. I was so ill and sick that for the first time in my camp life I lost the will to live. It made no difference to me what was going to happen. To my complete surprise I found myself on a truck between a guard and the driver and off we went on another unknown journey. After some time I arrived at another prison unit and after presenting my papers I was sent to the *banya*, given clean clothes and enjoyed every bit of this taste of normal living as though it were a miracle from heaven. Next I was taken to a one-storeyed barracks similar to the one where I had lived when I worked in the hospital. It was clean and tidy, and a woman on duty gave me a cup of hot weak tea, the first I had tasted during all my camp life.

Sitting on my bunk, a nurse told me that I was now going to work in the nursery. I nearly fainted from sheer joy. She also explained that the twenty or more women in each barracks were each required to take their turn to clean it in addition to their normal work. You do not need much to be happy in camp life, and I could feel the strengh returning to my tired body.

Next morning at 7 am I was taken to the nursery. Although there was no luxury, everything was sensible and I was told that I would take care of babies from newborn to three years of age. There was a head doctor, a midwife from Moscow (a political prisoner) and Olga was the matron. We worked on shifts of twelve hours a day, and everything appeared to be quite normal as in any other nursery in the free world. I always remember that nursery in comparison with others I was to see in the future. It was all due, I am sure, to Olga's sense of propriety and her skilful organisation. If she had been educated, and not a simple Kulak, there was no limit to what she could have achieved. She was the original Russian *matroshka* (national doll), and when I think of Olga I will always remember her with respect.

Olga was friendly to everybody up to a certain limit as any leniency towards political prisoners was considered a crime. I never became close to her and never permitted myself the curiosity to ask if she had been instrumental in getting me away from digging ditches. I did not know then who helped me get to that nursery and now I never will.

On arrival at the nursery I was curious as to where these babies came from. I learned that they were the children of mostly the criminal prisoners, although some had political mothers. This camp had many male personnel; in addition to the administrative staff there were the blacksmiths, carpenters and other specialist craftsmen whose behaviour appeared to be blameless and who were given considerable freedom to move around as they were a necessary part of camp life.

Privacy was respected when a man crept into the barracks to sleep with his 'wife', even if we were kept awake with the sound of the groaning bed. Sometimes in the night there would be a raid by the guards, and if a woman was caught with a man she was sent to the punishment cell and in the morning at roll call she would be reprimanded and maybe even separated from that particular barracks or moved to another camp. After a while, when the upset had quietened down, the men would begin all over again but this time with other 'wives'. The babies born from these women were taken away at birth and raised in the camp nursery. The mother never saw her child again.

There was one little boy in the nursery who was taboo to the rest of the nurses. He was a most beautiful boy of about three years of age who had been brought up from a baby by Olga and Olga alone. She was like a lioness with her cub and he was her possession although she never showed in any demonstrative way that she loved him. The only affection I saw was when she swallowed him up with her eyes.

Living in my new barracks and working in the nursery in a clean uniform, life became bearable again. I was given drugs for my fever and was recovering from my ordeal in the punishment camp. A woman called Tanya became friendly towards me and when I was not capable of doing something in the nursery, owing to my weakness, she

86

helped me. Prisoners who by luck had been given the opportunity to work in hospitals or the nursery had a much better chance of survival, as not only were the conditions better but also the mental stimulus helped. Had I been forced to continue to do hard manual outdoor work, like millions of Russian women prisoners, I doubt that I would have survived.

Sometimes I sneaked into Tanya's barracks where, because I was now more or less fluent in Russian, I was able to understand what they were saying. They were the wives of important communists and in the camps they were called the CH-SI-IR, the initials standing for Members of the Family Related to Traitors. The second category was called ZHIR, which in Russian means 'fat' but in this connection meant Wives of Husbands Who Had Committed Treason. They had been the 'golden people' of the Soviet Union, living in luxury in the Kremlin before Stalin's purges. They had their dachas on the south coast of the Black Sea, luxurious motorcars, caviare and sumptuous furs; but they had been hidden from the eyes of the ordinary workers and had never ever thought that anything could intrude into their cosseted lives.

They were 'honest' communists, descended from generations of revolutionaries. They were the wives of executed communists, even Bolsheviks, now themselves deprived of freedom and living worse than beasts. Yet they could still believe in their beloved Stalin. 'It's all a mistake. . . . He doesn't know about us. . . . We must bear with him. . . . He is surrounded by enemies.' For me it was incredible and pitiful to see these deceived women who still worshipped Stalin and Yezhov ('the bloodthirsty fanatic' who directed terror until he was removed in 1938 and disappeared for good. His period was called Yezhovshina. *Yezh* in Russian means 'hedgehog', and the analogy was that people were trapped and held in his spikes).

My mind was beginning to expand and I was beginning

to ask questions. Why were these innocent people sitting in camp? Why were they so dirty and underfed? I was rebelling against it.

'Why don't you rise up and bash their faces in? Why are intelligent people sitting here and submitting to so much degradation and not doing anything about it? What have they done to you? In England this would never have happened. Do you really believe that your husbands were shot because they were traitors to your country? You can't all be spies. Have you all been brain-washed?' I hissed my questions at them, angry at their plight.

They listened with resigned vacant expressions. 'Shut up,' they said. 'You are too young to understand and you don't know Russian history. We have to go through it like others before us. Forget all about it. It will all come right in the end . . . all come right.'

CHAPTER TWELVE

My clandestine encounters with my new friends, running to and from their barracks, brought a new and dangerous excitement into my life. I looked forward to joining them, realising full well that this was strictly against camp regulations. Many times they cautioned me: 'Flora, be careful. We understand that you are lonely but you can get not only yourself into trouble but also us.'

During my visits to their barracks they would sing songs, and one of their favourites was a parody of the famous popular song by the composer Lebedev Kumach which begins with the words

> Wide is my native land with rivers and forests

and ends:

> I know no other land where a man breathes so freely.

As they sang I often wondered whether they really believed in their country or hated it as I did. If so, they were never frank with me and would never admit their hatred even if there were no ears of the NKVD to hear. Even my new camp 'friends' were frightened of me, because I was a foreigner in their eyes.

One of the women had been an actress and she would get up and with wicked irony impersonate the camp commandant, declaring: 'You are the enemies of the people but despite this you are now being given the chance to atone for your crime against the Soviet Union. You must redeem yourselves by heavy work. Therefore you must make more bricks of mud and dung, dig more ditches, irrigate more hectares of our Beloved Motherland. What are food and clothes compared to patriotism? Our loyalty surpasses all hardships for the glorious future of the Soviet Union.' She always ended her oration with 'Hurrah, hurrah, hurrah for Stalin, the Saviour of the People'. We giggled and laughed at ourselves in our rags . . . and then wept. They were women of strong will and all intelligent, and had lived full and interesting lives before their imprisonment. That was the beginning of my political education, and it gave me the whole pattern of Russian hypocrisy. This hatred and flame against injustice, to myself and these women, would remain in my mind and soul for the rest of my days.

Miracles come in many guises, and the arrival of a parcel from Mamma remains one of the most treasured memories of my life. The marvel of my mother, who against overwhelming odds managed not only to trace my whereabouts but also persuade the authorities to let her send me a parcel. Only a woman with an almost superhuman driving force could have cut through all the Soviet bureaucracy and evil intimidation of the Gulag regime and achieved what she did.

It all began with a letter from Mamma from her camp at the canal to Uncle Abraham. He then contacted Cecile, who wrote to Mother and told her that I had been put in prison. Although mail from camp was strictly limited, somehow my mother wrote letters and got them out to the chief of police of the Kresty prison in Leningrad where I had been, to the commandant of her own camp, to the Prosecutor of the Soviet Union and to the head of Gulag (Chief Administration of Camps). How long it took and how she achieved it, to this day I do not know as in later years Mother spoke little of her life in camp.

Camp prisoners were allowed to receive parcels from their relatives from time to time, but I never expected any. Only Cecile seemed in a position to send me one, and I had moved so often that I believed the sheer bureaucracy of the Soviet system and her own poor knowledge of the Russian language and ways would defeat any efforts she might make. So imagine the shock when one day a parcel was given to me by a camp official. It was wrapped in hessian and sewn up with firm stitches, and looked grubby and travel-stained, but my name and the address of the camp were written in strong letters in purple indelible ink. When I opened it there was a small note from Mamma, a little dress she had made by hand from some bright material, a pair of exquisitely patched pink knickers and a pair of stockings. I did not even know that Mamma was still alive and wept with joy. Memories of the last time I had seen Mamma when we said goodbye and vowed to love each other for ever came flooding back. Despite my loneliness and ill health I knew that Mamma and I would survive and that one day, God willing, we would meet again.

Although I enjoyed my work with the babies my health was beginning to deteriorate. My coughing was worse and my legs were troubling me, especially my knees. All the deprivations, bad food and harsh living conditions over the years were beginning to tell. My teeth began troubling me and, though there was a camp dentist, his methods were primitive and he did his extractions without any anaesthetic. The roots of most of my teeth were extracted by cutting through the gums to get a grip before he could remove them with forceps. It was a painful and final treatment; there was no attempt to save teeth, and drills were nonexistent.

December had come, the time for the European Christmas, but in camp any religious celebrations were strictly forbidden. It was touching to see how some of the older women clung to their Orthodox faith amid the godlessness of communism even though they knew they were taking risks. In this unholy place people still believed. I saw old women kneeling to make their heads touch the ground in obeisance according to their childhood religious beliefs.

Even Olga, so tough, so strong, nurtured a respect for a Christian belief instilled into her by her parents. She secretly organised a little Christmas party for us in which I took part in the preparations. From the dry wood of the *karaganeka* I made a little Christmas-tree and painted pictures which I hung on the nursery walls, and toys out of papier mâché. Some of the old women managed to get some paper and transformed it into chains, just as they had done in their childhood. Our Christmas was only on display for an hour, but for me it was a glorious glimpse of forbidden fruit and brought back memories of the happy days of my childhood in Glasgow. There was added delight in the fact that we had fooled the guards and got away with it!

New Year, always a most sentimental time for me, passed with tears and memories. Everyone felt – and prayed – that with the coming of a brand-new year something must happen to change our lives. Even prisoners who were staunch communists turned to the God they had once ridiculed. Among the political prisoners in those days there were many Baptists and Pentecostals who had been persecuted for their religious beliefs just as they are today. God was everywhere that New Year's Day, 1941.

My health deteriorated quickly. Even on the days when, too weak to work, I was given sick leave I could only drink hot water. On 13 March 1941 a guard came shouting: 'Kaplan . . . come on.' Everybody looked at me as I asked fearfully: 'With belongings?' 'No' – and that was all. I was taken to the office of the Commandant and waited outside the door until I was called in. He scarcely looked up from his desk as he asked: 'Surname? Father's name? Birth? Date of arrest? What city do you come from? Name of prison?' He then handed me a paper and said: 'You are free.' It was as simple as that.

I was dismissed, and a guard took me to another barracks where I met three other girls – Katya, Tanya and Lena – who had also been freed. I was completely numb, and the thought of freedom and all that it stood for had not yet sunk in. We were ordered to go to the *banya*, and for the first time I began to realize what had happened to me, and we began joking and laughing as only young people can. 'Who are you and where do you come from?' they asked as they heard my bad Russian. They also explained their 'crimes'. One was a prostitute, another a common thief, and the innocent blue-eyed blonde accused of light criminal charges had a very ill baby with her, so small and sickly that it was no bigger than a doll wrapped in a huge shawl. They were strong good-looking girls and had all served five years' hard labour.

We were given a cheap new 'wardrobe of clothes' smelling strongly of disinfectant which consisted of a pair of more or less wearable *valenkis*, a faded plain blue cotton skirt, a padded coat (second class), long grey knickers and a pair of coarse brown stockings. The only way to keep the stockings up was by tying them with a piece of rag. We were also given grey shawls that smelt musty, and I wondered who had last worn mine and what was her story.

The only real thoughts that concerned me were: Where am I going? What are they going to do with me now? I had been told that I was being sent to Karaganda, but had no idea where that was. All that I remembered was that I had arrived at a place called Karabas, but I was not aware that there was actually a town called Karaganda.

We were given a loaf of black bread, and dried herring and a rail ticket. Today I have no memories of actually walking out of the camp gates, only of leaving the camp early in the morning and climbing into a small cart which took us to the small station at Karabas. The guard left us there and we waited in a low wooden building. It was only then that we all fully realized that we were free, when we saw the other passengers waiting for the train. The other girls had large suitcases, but I had only a small bundle with the clothes that Mamma had sent me. We waited excitedly until finally the train arrived.

It was packed with people as this was a branch of the main line from Moscow. We scrambled up the high steps to the 'hard section', which was filled with peasants on their way to the Karaganda market, and there was a smell of cabbages, sweaty bodies, *makhorka* and the rank smell of ancient sheepskin jackets. Peering at us through the smoky atmosphere in the carriage, the peasants began talking among themselves and I heard the word *lagerniki* (camp prisoners). They were not malicious, merely curious, and accepted us as part of the life of their country.

A few hours later the train stopped and we stepped out. So this was Karaganda. We had arrived at a much larger railway station and there was a hustle and bustle, shouting and cursing as the train emptied and people pushed and shoved with their belongings. We were bewildered; the emotions, faces, noise were so different from those we had experienced in camp. As we stood there a withered old Chinaman, wearing a coolie hat and with a long pigtail down his back, approached us and, speaking bad Russian, asked: 'Want sleepie?' Slightly bewildered, and because there were four of us for safety, we decided to accept his offer and followed him, walking with our belongings to the outskirts of the town, which was quite some distance from the station.

We arrived at what looked like an underground village; only the roofs of the houses showed above the ground and chimneys with thin spirals of smoke. Going down some clay steps and passing along narrow passages we came to a maze of little mud huts just high enough to stand up straight inside. The Chinaman went in first and beckoned us to follow. We found a gloomy little room

94

with a bench, battered plain wooden table and two little stools. There was nothing else except an iron stove that was filling the room with smoke as well as passing some up through a chimney in the roof. We asked where we were going to sleep and he replied showing a mouthful of yellow fangs, 'Rightee, rightee . . . .' and returned with four wooden planks. Using the girls' suitcases as supporters we made them into a bed. Katya had brought a tin kettle with her and put it on the stove to make some hot water. Nearby we found a pile of prickly bush and some dried cow dung and stoked up the stove to keep the baby warm, as the ground was bare clay and the air damp.

The Chinaman watched us making ourselves at home, nodding his old head in agreement with a smile that never left his face. We shared our bread and fish with him and drank a cup of hot water. Then we fell asleep from exhaustion and excitement despite the fact that the poor little baby cried all night. So passed our first day and night of freedom. In the morning the old man, who had been curled up in the corner, told us: 'Payee . . . payee . . . workee . . . workee.' He was incredibly ancient, bent and wrinkled like a yellow apple, but he was human. Hungry for kindness and affection, his words fell sweetly in our ears.

Quite clearly the baby was desperately ill and needed medical attention and proper care. We asked the Chinaman to give us directions to the nearest hospital and police station where it was necessary for us to check in before we could even begin to find work and earn some money. Cleaning ourselves as best we could, and putting on our prison finery, we set out for the Old Town of Karaganda, which had one main road, oddly named Maxim Gorky Street, and was lined either side with low mud whitewashed houses. There were little gates and gardens, a few trees and a lot of dogs barking everywhere. After the drab grey world of the camp it seemed like Wonderland to me. In the distance we could see the mines and the derricks silhouetted against the sky.

Groups of miners talking to each other freely, and even laughing, walked along the road on their way to work. We passed a post office where I posted a letter to Mamma, and I was overwhelmed with joy when I saw a library where I knew that I would find books again.

I looked at my new 'friends'. Camp life is a great leveller, and now I was beginning my new life with three girls who had been complete strangers twenty-four hours before. Now something intangible bound us together.

The hospital was a series of whitewashed barracks with signposts to various medical departments. I was feeling so ill by now it was decided that I should return to our new 'home' while Tanya would stay with the baby in the hospital and Lena and Katya check in at the police station and look for work.

When I returned to our new home the Chinaman was kind to me and boiled me some water as I lay shivering on the hard makeshift bed. Freedom seemed to have come for me too late as I thought I was dying. The pains in my joints were so intense that I was indifferent to any sense of being free. My subconscious kept telling me, You are free . . . free . . . free, but mentally and physically I could not cope. Even if I was free, the knowledge of what I had seen in the camps would haunt me for the rest of my days.

Always present in my head was the agonising thought that Mamma was still in camp, and thinking of the fate of my sister, and my brother, whom I still did not know about, was torture. I lay and sobbed on the bed while the old Chinaman looked on with sympathy.

The three girls got work at once and moved closer to the mines, but I remained on my hard bunk for several days. I could not eat anything and was running a high fever. Clearly my health was deteriorating daily, and when one of the girls came back to see me she immediately decided that I was too ill to be moved and that they would have to call in a doctor. With the help of the old Chinaman the girls found a kind and elderly doctor

96

who came to the dugout to see me. He diagnosed pleurisy and said that both my lungs were infected; I must go to hospital for treatment.

There were no ambulances in Karaganda Old Town but somehow the doctor managed to get a horse-cab and, supporting me in his arms, took me to the hospital where I arrived almost unconscious. I noticed, however, that as I was carried into the hospital I was put into a separate room, a luxury only reserved for desperately ill and dying patients. I did not know that the old doctor had suspected typhoid and had risked his own health to care for me in the horse-cab. My only thought was: Thank God I am going to die in a real bed with a sheet on it.

Days and nights passed in a haze. I could not move without screaming with pain, but through the mist I could feel loving hands caring for me. As they had no X-rays the doctors were baffled as to the cause of my extreme pain, and when I felt myself slipping into unconsciousness my one thought was: I want to die . . . now. Days passed. Weeks passed. How long I do not remember, but when I regained consciousness I noticed that the last of winter was passing. I had grown so thin that I was a bag of bones. My medical history baffled the doctors as I had a combination of many illnesses and my body was in such a weak state that only time could heal me. With the drugs available today the toll on my body would not have been such a strain and my recovery would have been more rapid, but this was the Soviet Union, 1941. I remember one morning when a jolly-faced professor came to see me and smiled: 'Well, you certainly gave us some trouble. We began to think that you did not want to stay with us here.' Then leaning closely over my bed he said softly: 'In your delirium you always spoke English. When you leave here be careful.' By now I understood what he meant. The Russians have a saying, 'Nado zheet' ('You have to live'). My life was not finished and all my love and duty lay to Mamma – that one day we would find each other again.

During the time I had been lying in bed my clothes had been destroyed because of the typhoid scare and because no one had thought that I would survive. Though I did not have any intimate friends among the nurses, the head nurse told me that she had asked among the staff if they had any clothes they could spare.

She brought me a bundle of darned and worn-out garments, but they were warm and clean. Today I wonder why, when I was well enough to leave the hospital, with my nursing experience I did not ask if I could stay on and work there. My only explanation is that they did not offer me a job and I was too shy to ask.

On leaving hospital I had nowhere to go other than to return to the Chinaman. I had lost touch with the other three girls. They had not once come to see me during all the months I was in hospital.

While looking for work I found a workshop where men were doing all kinds of repairs. It was a filthy dirty shed with a cement floor, reeking of kerosene and hardly the place for a twenty-three-year-old still miserably weak. They took me on as a cleaning woman, and despite the fact that it was a hopeless task to clean the floor I took a delight in arranging the workbench with all the precision of an operating-theatre. Spanners, screwdrivers, hammers were laid out in order.

'Don't wash the floors, for God's sake. Just take a broom and sweep it up. You have to be careful of the sharp iron filings and not to cut yourself.' The instruction came from an old man who sat in one corner mending clocks. I became fascinated as he showed me how to clean them and how to change the coil in the electric plates which people used to cook on. After my work I returned to the Chinaman's house. Now one of the girls, Lena, came to see me, bringing me some biscuits made from carrots and told me not only that Tanya's blue-eyed baby had died but also that all of them had been married within three weeks to miners. She offered me some advice that was to open up a whole new chapter in my life.

'Flora, go to the mines. There are plenty of jobs there and the money is good. Who knows, you may even find a husband.'

In my loneliness I was grateful for her visit, but I knew that I had no place in her life nor she in mine. I was on my own again. True, I was a free woman, but my living conditions were miserable as I could only afford bread and macaroni after paying the Chinaman the money I owed him for the rent. But while I was deciding how I was going to exist and how I could change my circumstances I continued sweeping and cleaning at the workshop. By now it was summer, and one day, 22 June 1941, we heard a tremendous excitement outside. An important announcement was being broadcast from the loudspeakers in the street: *War is declared*.

CHAPTER THIRTEEN

In the autumn of 1941 I left my kind old Chinaman and found accommodation with a doctor, a man of sixty who offered to let me live in one of the rooms in his small flat on the condition that I helped with the cleaning and in winter stoked the tiled stove. For the first time I had a little room with an iron bed, a table, a chair and wardrobe. It was my first normal comfortable room.

Remembering Lena's advice I immediately applied for a job to the administrative office of the mines. I knew that I should in any case be called up for some kind of war work, so why not make my own choice? At least in the mine I would get better food rations and higher pay than in a workshop.

My first day at the mines I got up at five o'clock in the morning and with the other women I went to the cloakroom to put on the rough mining clothes. They were made from tarpaulin and consisted of a jacket and trousers, but as they were so stiff with grime we wore underneath our own warm clothes. We were also issued with heavy canvas boots. At the entrance of the pit we were given a small miner's lamp called a Wolfe lamp, the only kind used in mines where methane gas was present. These lamps lasted about three hours, and women were employed as lamp-carriers to supply the miners with additional lamps when required. The best part of the day was using the *banya* at night.

The horizontal pits were very old and in the 1940s mining technique was backward. To reach the shafts we had to walk down a deep slope one and a half metres wide and four kilometres long. It was also the ventilation slope, and was terribly cold and draughty. As there were no lavatories the places where the miners relieved themselves were covered with a growth of white fungus like huge white mushrooms.

My job was to shift the coal from the shafts where the cutter and shoveller worked either crouched on his knees or in a semi-reclining position as the ceiling was no higher than 98 centimetres. It was really very hard work. When I had loaded the small wagons I pushed them with my back and shoulders, digging my heels in the ground. Once several wagons had been filled the pit-horses would take them to the main junction. The galleries were badly lit, and the beams supported by pit-props were often broken in half by the weight of the earth above. You had to be careful all the time, looking under your feet and protecting your head against the jagged edges.

Once when I was on duty the miners would not listen to my request to carry an injured man to the surface. I was met with a torrent of foul *Mat*: 'Go fuck your mother.' In a rage I shouted back: 'Fuck your mother yourself.' The men were dumbfounded, and immediately we all burst out laughing. I had made friends with the miners and from then on was treated as one of them.

I had been used to hearing swearwords from the day I stepped on Russian soil. It began with the pupils abusing us at school. *Mat* or *Matershina* dates back to long before the time of Peter the Great. The nucleus of this 'foul and obscene language' is the word 'mother'. The Russians worship, kneel before, their beloved Motherland just as long ago they worshipped their God and Faith, but the *Mat* they use to express indecency is incredible. You can 'fuck your mother' in anger, in irritation, in depression, seriously, playfully. It is used by the lowest intellect and the highest. The Russian *Mat* that I have heard competes on equal terms with that of the Hungarians, who are also artistic in using the word 'mother', but their obscenity is nothing to the miners' *Mat*. If my ears could have withered, they would have fallen off that autumn in the Karaganda mines.

After a year as an auxiliary worker in the pits my good doctor friend managed to get me a job in the underground sickbay as a nurse when I could be spared from pushing the wagons. It was terrific to be again working as a nurse despite my lack of a diploma. The underground sickbay was situated deep down in the mine. It was a small room dimly lit and equipped with a telephone, a first-aid shelf and a canvas stretcher. There were many traumas, and I often had to run in the dark with my Wolfe lamp, first-aid kit, stretcher and aluminium-wire splints.

Later, when I worked in the surface sickbay beside the railway track, I had a dream one night. I was going to work on a cold blizzard morning and was crossing the lines to get to the sickbay on the other side when I saw big black wagons moving towards me without an engine. In fright I started to scream and run from one snowbank to the other, looking for the steps that had been cut out to get to the top of the drift. Suddenly the wagons were on top of me. I saw myself carried legless to the sickbay, blood flowing from my body on to the white snow and faces looking upon me with despair. Then I saw myself lying on the table in strange surroundings and a voice calling out to me: 'Flora . . . Flora. . . . Oh my God.' I woke up. All the next morning the dream kept coming back into my mind, and I could not get rid of it.

My friend Lena dropped in to see me and I offered her tea with lemon, which was a luxury in those days, and of course I told her about my dream.

'Did you see a lot of blood?' Lena asked, and I answered 'Yes.' 'That means you'll find some blood relations.' She knew my life and said: 'Maybe you'll meet your niece Marina from Leningrad.' During the war the pastime of women in Karaganda was to tell each other's fortune with playing-cards and to interpret dreams.

Drinking our tea she told me about how she had a

rendezvous with her lover, a miner, at five o'clock. Something which I could not explain warned me that she should not go, but all my remonstrations were no use. She was determined and she went. It was only thirty minutes after she had gone that I heard a commotion in the street and her children came in, screaming at the tops of their voices: 'Mamma . . . come, Auntie Flora . . . Mamma.' I stood frozen. Rushing out with the children I came just in time to see the bloodstained remains of my friend covered with a sack lying on the railway line. What happened in my dream had happened exactly to her.

There was complete silence as we stood and watched them carry her body and take it to the morgue at the hospital where the old watchman and I tended the mangled body as best we could. I made her a little cap and prepared her so that I could take her two sons to say goodbye to their mother. They never suspected what lay beneath the sheet and saw only the sleeping face, serene and at peace.

We buried her in the Karaganda cemetery. Her husband had been killed in action, and now the children were orphans. I knew that there was an uncle somewhere, but until I could contact the family the boys were left in my care.

The social workers of the mine had organized a special committee to help the evacuees who were flowing in from the occupied regions of the west, providing them with accommodation, food and clothes. The only station at Karaganda became an important railway junction and it was overcrowded with evacuated plant and machinery. Since the beginning of the war food-supplies had disappeared from the shops and prices of food in the market had soared.

When we women began to help unload the train one day I noticed that all the boxes came from the British Red Cross. When I returned to our depot and began unpacking I was delirious with excitement when I saw the lovely English clothes that had come all the way, thousands of miles, to Karaganda. They were part of the great drive of Bundles for Russia which had been organized by Mrs Churchill. Nobody in Karaganda had ever seen such clothes in their lives and in distributing them among the needy we women could not resist taking a few things for ourselves. I took for my 'sons' Valerie and Boris navy-blue reefer coats. It was not long before the market was full of people selling these English clothes. At that time a coat could cost over a thousand roubles and that meant three loaves of bread, while tobacco was about 200 roubles. Food was more important than finery. These clothes helped people not to die of starvation. If they did not sell them, they would exchange them for provisions. I used to go by train to the countryside, trudging from one peasant house to another exchanging these clothes for potatoes, *shzpik* (salted pork) and whatever I could get my hands on. I was twenty-three years of age by now, and the boys called me 'Little Mother' as I packed them off to school every morning.

After school they would always come with me to get the water. The shortage of water in Karaganda was a pressing problem and it was sold for two kopeks a pail from a pump which was enclosed in a little shed with an attendant. I used to carry the pails with a wooden yoke balanced on my shoulder, and the boys carried small pails or jugs to share my burden. Sometimes our journey was in vain as there was no water. In winter it was much more complicated. The boys were dressed warmly and muffled up to their eyes because the temperature was −40°. Around the pump ice would have formed and people slipped, spilling the water, which caused even more problems; it formed into ever larger areas of ice − to the delight of the boys, who used it as a skating-rink. I had traced the boys' uncle in Tashkent, and he was coming to collect them. Parting with them was very painful to me, and memories of them always stayed with me. They were the first children who made me feel a mother whom they loved and needed, but I knew that they would be better off with their own family in Tashkent.

In the winter of 1942–3, when Russia broke the circle of Stalingrad, German, Romanian, Hungarian and Polish troops surrendered and were taken prisoner. We heard rumours that many of these prisoners of war were coming to Karaganda to work in the mines, and when we saw the commotion as barracks were hastily constructed in the steppes outside the city we knew it was true. The mood of the Karaganda population towards the prisoners of war was aggressive as they were the ones who began the war and had brought death and devastation to the Russian country. Everybody also resented that we had to feed them as the shortage of food was the main problem.

From the window of our sickbay one summer's day I looked out and saw a troop of war prisoners led by an officer under a guard of Russian soldiers. With excitement we nurses crowded to the open windows, and I heard a babble of different languages – German, Romanian, Hungarian and Polish – as they stood at ease. They all wore their national military uniforms and were all young beardless boys. How could they kill?

The head of the sickbay gave us instructions that the prisoners of war were to be treated under the rules of the Geneva Convention and we were to give first aid to any prisoner requiring it. The attitude of the miners looking on at their enemies was not very friendly. Russian *Mat* was thrown into their faces without limit, but with the presence of the Soviet guards there were no incidents.

With the return of Russian prisoners of war who had been treated atrociously in German camps, there was naturally great friction between them and the Germans. Every day there were fights and killings, and blood was everywhere. War for these men continued underground

105

to such an extent that the mining authorities were forced to appeal to the Communist Party and the NKVD for support in solving this new and complex situation. Finally the Russians were sent to a different mine.

My knowledge of a little German and my English helped me to get on with my new patients and I was often called to act as an interpreter. Thus I met Jouanel, an officer of the Romanian army who escorted the injured for treatment in the sickbay and spoke to me in German interpreting the soldiers' complaints. He was tall, fair and a little older than me, and I felt that he was a very considerate person by the way he treated his countrymen. I was fascinated by his gentleness, in contrast to the Russian men I had met.

Our fates were so different. He was a prisoner of war, and I had been a prisoner. I was a victim of one system, and he a victim of war. But we had both been torn from our native lands through different causes. This was sufficient to create a deep sympathy towards each other, and as we were so young it was love almost at first sight.

The more we saw of each other the more I yearned for him. I thought about him, dreamed about him, and the memory of that unexpected and gentle kiss on the nape of my neck as I bent over him to bandage his finger aroused my emotions. I was sleepless. I was aware of his passion towards me, but a rendezvous was so complicated. We discussed this problem several times, but how, where and when could we meet when every evening after work he was confined to the prison barracks surrounded by barbed wire and watchtowers?

To keep our secret meetings was dangerous for both of us. It was wartime; he was the enemy and I was an ex-convict with a British background. For me to walk through the village and out into the steppes was in itself humiliating as everyone watching knew that the direction I was taking led to nowhere. I could only be going to meet someone who could not be met anywhere else. But I was not alone. It was common gossip that for many

Karaganda women the steppes were the only place they could find solace and love.

Jouanel also had his problems. He had to confide in somebody in the camp to help him. The other prisoners not only covered for him during the time he shaved and cleaned off the day's grime but, even more important, they also had to place a dummy in his bed to fool the guards on their round of inspection during the evening.

We met about three kilometres from the town, which took each of us, walking from different directions, about thirty minutes. When our paths finally converged and we saw each other we ran together. Jouanel used to pick me up in his arms and whirl me around from sheer happiness. In the clear atmosphere of the steppes in the early evening we could have been seen clearly from the outskirts of the town, two specks of humanity silhouetted against the skyline.

As I lay in Jouanel's arms under the constellation of Ursa Major one night he made a romantic pledge: 'Flora, this war will soon be over and the world will return to sanity. I love you with all my heart, body and soul, and I want to be together with you for the rest of my life. You must promise not to move from Karaganda for the next two years so that I can return and find you again.'

We managed to meet several times a week during that long hot summer. I picked up a few words of Romanian and he of Russian. It was the most romantic pure love I had ever known, but I had been hurt too much to believe in a future together. I lived only for the present.

Our love-affair continued until late autumn when one night Jouanel failed to appear. This worried me immensely as it had never happened before. He could be late but he had never failed to come. To ask anybody from his camp was dangerous and our meetings were kept secret from my friends. I just had to wait. Somehow he would try to get in contact with me. I was right. One day one of his countrymen, whom I knew and trusted, came for first aid. How to begin? How to ask about Jouanel? Even in my distress I was always on my guard as I never forgot the ears around me.

To my immense relief the Romanian handed me a letter from Jouanel explaining that he had been held by the guard. He had become careless and was noticed shaving and making himself tidy and followed when he went to the place between the barbed wires which he used to escape from the camp. He was caught red-handed and interrogated but he did not give my name away. He was placed in a punishment cell from where he had been transferred. I was heartbroken.

In front of the two-storey building in which I lived there was a stone quarry about 300 metres wide and twice as long. The part of the quarry which was already worked out was then used for domestic waste as Karaganda Old Town had no lavatories. Carrying my waste out to throw into the quarry I looked down and watched the wretched prisoners working there. About five metres down on a plateau a group of prisoners under guard were staring at me. Among the emaciated ashen faces I recognised the face of Jouanel. The shock was so great that I ran away, only to return in a minute to look down into his loving, speaking eyes. I could not stand there any longer without being conspicuous but I felt that he needed my help. I used every opportunity to try to get into contact with him, and he managed by dumb signs to convey his need for tobacco and bread, and with his foot he indicated where to hide it.

I rushed to my room to find something I could barter for a loaf of bread and a packet of tobacco, a box of matches and newspaper to make the cigarettes. That night with my bundle on my arm and in my oldest trousers I went to the exact place above where they were working, considering every dangerous step which would take me down to the spot where I was to leave the parcel. Lowering myself down the side of the quarry, trying not to make any noise to alert the guard dogs of

108

my presence, I made my dangerous descent. Groping with my hands I found the two rocks Jouanel had left, and lifting them up found a cavity in which I placed my precious parcel and covered it over with the rocks.

I had changed duty to be free next day and early in the morning I went to the quarry and stood far away on the opposite side from where they were working and where I could still observe their movements. I was delighted to see Jouanel picking up the parcel and hiding it in his tunic under his coat. To my surprise he turned his head searching for me and when I thought he was looking in my direction I took off my deep red scarf and slowly and casually put it back on again, the signal that I had seen him. He in return with his fellow-prisoners took off their caps and bowed. The next day snow covered the ground and the quarry was not worked. I made many visits back to the quarry again looking for Jouanel, but after a couple of weeks I gave up. We had lost each other.

Not all the prisoners of war worked in the mines. Skilled specialists were used to build the New Town, and the élite of Karaganda exploited tailors, shoemakers and even house decorators for their own purpose. As a consequence many war prisoners made friends with the girls of Karaganda. In spite of the strict regulations there was jealousy and fights, but human nature was bubbling over, leaving a trail of flaxen-haired blue-eyed babies who today are loyal citizens of the Union of Soviet Socialist Republics.

CHAPTER FOURTEEN

The war was finished and the European prisoners of war had been repatriated; now small, slightly built Japanese prisoners were building the roads and opening up the steppes. I was surprised but indifferent when I received from the Supreme Soviet of the USSR a medal for 'distinguished merit during the Second World War 1941–5'.

I still did not know anything about the whereabouts of my mother. Now that there was no necessity to earn extra money in the mines for food, and I had a little put by, when a friend told me of a vacancy in the sickbay of the main metallurgical plant I applied and was given a job.

I was on duty in the sickbay there when the security guard at the entrance telephoned and told me that I was wanted at the main gates. He said that a man was asking for me, and I immediately asked to speak to him on the telephone.

'Flora Alexandrovna Leipman, may I speak to you?' a strange voice asked. (In Russian the second name used after the Christian name is the father's.) 'Will you come immediately to the main entrance?' I was surprised and apprehensive as this was a situation that I had not met before.

'I can't go away from the plant as I am here on duty,' I told him at the gate. I was still in my nurse's uniform.

'I must speak with you privately,' he replied.

'Who are you?'

'That is not the question. I must see you. I can't speak here.'

'Why couldn't you tell me your business on the telephone?'

'Listen – you have no time. I have no time. I have your address and I know you receive money from the British embassy. If I report you to the authorities, you will be put back in prison where you belong.'

'How can I receive money from the British embassy when I only came out of camp five years ago?'

'Shut up. When do you finish your shift?'

'Tomorrow at nine o'clock in the morning.'

'At ten o'clock I will be at your place.'

I wanted to say more but thought better of it and kept my mouth shut. I was looking at how he was dressed: he was clean and had the air of a foreigner about him. He did not seem to be a local man, and I had the suspicion that his jacket was English because of the good cut. I returned to my work, but my sixth sense told me to tell the security guards, because everybody knew me at the plant.

'I wonder who he is?' I asked them.

'We are also wondering who he is!' they replied.

Next day at the appointed time he came to see me at my rented room. There was nobody in the house as they were all at work. I had not relaxed during the whole night as I was worried and puzzled as to why the man had spoken to me about the British embassy. If he knew that I was Flora Alexandrovna, what the hell was he doing approaching me at work, where he would be seen by everybody, when he could have sent me a letter or come quietly in the night to the house? Or was he really a Russian agent trying to frighten me and to test my allegiance to the Soviet Union? To assure the NKVD of my loyalty, despite my background, my fitness to work in such a plant? If he was a man impersonating an English spy, why was he dressed so ridiculously like Sherlock Holmes in that tweed jacket?

I thought it all out and decided that the moment I had spoken to him I would report the whole incident to the

NKVD as this was my only chance of self-preservation. Another idea came into my head: Where did he get that English jacket? It was all too obvious that there was something wrong and that I must stick to my decision: keep quiet and listen to what he had to say. I was only twenty-eight, but I had been through too much by then to make a mistake.

When he came at 10 am he knocked on my window, which was sinister as it meant that he knew not only my address but also the exact location of my room. I crept along the corridor to let him in, and he followed me silently to my room, where he came to the point immediately.

'If you are going to co-operate with us, the British embassy will give you a lot of money.'

'Do you speak English?' I asked quietly.

He answered in Russian: 'What did you say?' His reaction was so spontaneous that I realized he did not know the English language. He was bluffing me.

He continued to question me, saying: 'We want you to tell us everything about the plant. Get us figures on the productivity and how many people are working there. How many different workshops. We are going to meet privately once a week, and you will feed us with the information you have gathered. If you don't co-operate, you will know the consequences.'

I made myself look very frightened and began to cry. 'I don't know anything about industry. Leave me alone. I am only a nurse there.'

'If you don't co-operate, you will have a nasty accident in the street.'

On leaving he made an appointment with me to meet him on the corner of one of the streets in Karaganda in a few days' time to deliver my information. I agreed. I had right from the very beginning decided to denounce him but I did not go out that day or make any connections with the NKVD as I was afraid that they might be trailing me. But that night about 11 pm I went to the

na – Marie Leipman – with Cecile
Mathilde, Glasgow, 1915

Mama with Cecile, Mathilde, baby
Samuel and nursemaid, 1917

er – Alexander Leipman, Glasgow,
5

Father in Glasgow, 1928

Cecile at the High School for Girls, Glasgow, 1928

Flora aged six, Glasgow, 192

Flora and her class at Garnet Bank School in Glasgow, 1928

Samuel and his class at Garnet Bank School, 1928

Flora, Dunoon, Scotland, 1929

The Leipman family. From left to right:
Samuel, Mathilde, Cecile and Flora,
Troon, Scotland

Mama with Mathilde, Flora and Samuel

hilde, London, 1930

Cecile, London, 1930

Flora, Hyde Park, London, 1930

Mathilde and Samuel on board
the *Feliks Dzerzhinsky en route*
for the Soviet Union, 1932

Mama, 1934. Taken in the labour camp
when Flora was visiting.

...el before his arrest, Leningrad,

Flora and her first husband Karl Kredgi, 1936

...r in Yalta, 1956

Flora in Karaganda after her release, 1941

Flora with her mother in Yalta

Flora with the Americans in Kiev, 1

Flora with her mother at the Russian
Museum, Pushkin Square, Leningrad,
1960

Flora, Leningrad Winter Palace, 19

Chukotka, 1963

Brigid Edge and Flora outside an old
people's home for women in Leningrad

r at the First of May
nstration in Vilnius

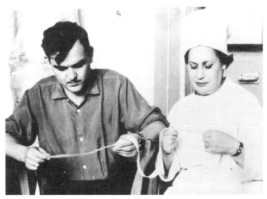

Flora, ECG nurse in Vilnius

Jennie Barrie and Flora, London, 1985

Flora at Gordonstoun School, Scotland, 1985

police headquarters. It was risky because there were no proper roads and no street-lights, so the nights in Karaganda were pitch dark. Stumbling along in the black I felt my way, but somewhere in the back of my head I kept asking myself if I was doing the right thing.

Though nobody had ever mentioned it to me, we all knew where the dreaded NKVD building was, a branch office of the main one in the New Town. I went to the door of a small building, knocked at the door and said to the guards: 'I have something of importance to say to you.'

They told me to stand outside. Finally the door was opened again and I was taken into an office where a fat man in military uniform, with a bored face, was sitting behind a desk.

'I am very worried and I don't know how to explain it to you,' I began.

He listened to my bad Russian and became interested as I explained how a man had approached me and that I didn't know his name, but he had wanted me to work for the British intelligence service.

'What is his name?' he asked.

'I don't know.'

'Why are you telling me all this nonsense when you can't even remember his name? You've let a spy get away. Take her out.'

I was put out in the corridor, and as there were no seats I had to stand. By now I was really frightened – terrified that they could send me back to a labour camp. Had I done the right thing in denouncing an English spy? To denounce my own country made me a traitor to my birthplace. But somewhere very very deep in my head I felt that this was all a trick. It was an NKVD trick. I had been living so peacefully the last few years, and now this had to happen. How I wished that I could have spoken to someone kind and wise who would have advised me what to do.

After a while I heard a motorcar arrive and was

bundled out into it with two uniformed NKVD officers. Nothing was said, but I was pleased at last to sit down in the jeep as I had been standing all that time. We drove to the New Town where the main NKVD building was. There was the same procedure and I was left to stand until 2 a.m., when I was again interrogated. I went through all the same questions and answers, and told the officer about my proposed rendezvous with the man in a few days' time.

'How was he dressed?' they asked. 'Had he a foreign accent?' And always the same question: 'But why didn't you find out his name? You are not leaving before we find him,' the officer announced.

I was taken to a cell for the rest of the night. Dawn was arriving, and still I could not sleep. During that day I was left alone in the cell and brought only a plate of soup and a piece of bread. I was interrogated again that night, and the main question they threw at me was always: 'Why didn't you report at once when he first approached you? You gave him time to escape.'

Apart from the questioning I was worried about my work and my friends who did not know where I was. I had been missing for twenty-four hours, and the Soviet law insists that you cannot neglect your work without a valid excuse. I had been told not to worry about that as it would all be fixed for me, but it still nagged my mind. Before I was released one of the officers said: 'Don't worry. You did all right. We have informed your plant of the reason for your being absent.'

When I returned to my work I found that I was quite a celebrity. The head of the medical unit and my colleagues told me: 'We have been told that you caught a spy.' They were proud of me as the security guards blurted out the incredible story so that the news had swept through the whole plant and everybody knew about the spy scare. As the cat was out of the bag I had to make some explanation as to why I had been held, and to make good the whole ridiculous situation the officials of the plant congratulated me on my courage and loyalty to the Soviet Union. The NKVD had not foreseen the consequences of their blunder. About half a year later I went to the New Town on business and I saw 'Sherlock Holmes' passing in the street chewing an apple. When he saw me he turned green and looked the other way.

During the whole of that year I had no information about Mamma, but now I learned that after twelve years at Belomorsk camp she had been evacuated to the Ural Mountains, where she was then in exile, and again by God's will and her persistence traced my whereabouts through the Karlag (Karaganda Camp Administration) and got a letter to me. Now that she was an invalid she did light work sewing and earned a small wage. I immediately sent her one thousand roubles. To get the money I sold a three-metre length of green chiffon that I had bought from one of the Moscow evacuees on the black market, and as inflation was sky high – a loaf of bread was 200 roubles – that was sufficient for her to buy at least three loaves of bread.

Mamma wrote to me that if I appealed to the right sources I could get her an exchange of exile and have her moved to Karaganda. During the next two years I wrote dozens of letters to the various authorities pleading Mamma's cause. In 1948 I succeeded in getting an answer from Moscow, an official paper giving permission for her exchange from exile near Perm to exile in Karaganda and I would be allowed to go and collect her.

After great difficulty, because of the disorganization in transport after the war when for years great masses of people flowed across Russia, I managed to get a ticket to Perm. People who had come from Moscow and Leningrad, Gorki, Kazan and other cities during the war were now going back to their homes. Apart from these families there were political prisoners who had been detained, ex-political prisoners, ex-criminal prisoners and all the scum of the Soviet Union who had been released from prison during the bombings. Everybody wanted to go home.

I was caught up in this boiling cauldron of human beings. There were only two trains a week between Moscow and Karaganda, and when I arrived at the station with my two heavy suitcases – one with clothes for Mamma and the other with food – it was bustling with people shouting, screaming, pushing, shoving, and children crying. You could not get near the train. At last I managed to climb up on to the couplings, where I stood with several other people since the door of the carriages on either side was locked. The train began to move, and people with sacks on their backs began grabbing on to anything they could clutch on the train like grapes on a vine. They were even lying on top of the roof. Only at the next station was I able to force myself into a carriage and get a seat.

And so our long journey began. It took three or four days to get to Perm, almost suffocating in the overflowing carriages, and I cannot remember now how many changes I had to make. I had made a little pocket in my bra to keep my money and the precious documents. If I lost Mother's papers I would have lost everything and our only chance to be together. At Perm (now called Molotov) I was faced with the same commotion as I had seen in every station we passed through. Every bench was occupied. People sat on benches, under the benches, on top of the benches, and the place was filled with the acrid smell of *makhorka*. The air was nauseating and stale.

My next problem was how to get from Perm to Krasnovishersk where my mother lived. I had first to get permission from the NKVD to be allowed into the camp. Walking with the two heavy suitcases, I at last, with immense difficulty, found the NKVD building. I stated my case, showed my papers, and asked permission from the office.

116

'Wait,' the man told me, 'wait . . . wait.' And that was all. I stayed in the corridor sitting on my suitcases for some time before I was able to get an audience with a senior official. His office was sumptuously furnished and typical of every other NKVD office; the only light came from a lamp on his desk. I showed him the papers from Moscow, and he took all the information about Mamma's place of exile. Trying to make himself look important, he began turning over the pages of a big file that a man had brought in, though he may well never have seen it before. 'Who is Samuel Leipman?' he asked and then, turning over another page: 'Who is Cecile Leipman? When was she arrested? You are all spies.'

He pushed the file towards me and showed me my brother's signature – Samuel Leipman. The recognition of my dear brother's writing and the confirmation that Cecile had been arrested were too much for me and I became hysterical. He began a cat-and-mouse game and told me that I could not go to Mother as Moscow had not sent the papers through. The disorganization of the system was then, and is today, so chaotic that his explanation could have been true.

'You were all a dirty lot of British spies. Why don't you go back to Karaganda and repent by doing some good work? Then you will be able to justify your family's crimes.'

'I'll never denounce my mother. I never believed that she was a spy nor was my brother. My mother is old. She is deaf. She is dying. I haven't seen her for fourteen years. I have not come all this way to receive that answer. If you don't give me permission, I will go all the way to Moscow and I will report you.'

Threat for threat. That was the only language they understood. I think he took pity on me. His face somehow changed and he shouted: 'Take her out.' I then waited in the corridor with my bags for about two hours. A guard came out and handed me my permit. I stood outside the building not knowing what to do next. It was

117

late and dark, and the only place that I could spend the night in comparative safety was at the station. I trudged back there. Slumping in a corner I tied both my bags to my wrists as I knew about 'night thieves' who robbed people sleeping in public places. I waited until the dawn, talking to the people around to keep myself awake.

I needed to get to Solikamsk, which is in the heart of the Ural Mountains. This region owes its tremendous mineral wealth to massive deposits of important ores such as nickel, lead, zinc, silver, gold, cobalt and rare metals, potassium salts, malachite, bauxite, marble and many kinds of precious stone.

There was no motor transport so I found a cart going in that direction, and at Solikamsk we had a break and I remember to this day a beautiful little church there. I had then to look for different transport. 'Go to the market,' somebody advised me. 'The peasants will be able to help you.' My suitcases had become like lead and hindered my walking. I was desperately tired but I could not leave them with anyone.

I managed to come to terms with an old peasant who lived in the region where mother was. He told me to wait until two o'clock when he had finished selling his products and then for a certain amount of money I could go with him on his cart. I knew that I was taking a risk as he could kill me *en route* and steal everything from me, but luckily there were three more peasants travelling with us.

The road was an unkempt mud track leading through the forest. It was late autumn and the most beautiful drive: nature in all her grandeur. The fir-trees seemed to reach the sky, and the smell of the sap was delicious. Gazing up into the canopy of green I remembered the Ural legends of the famous writer, Vasili Bazhenov, who told of the Queen of the Mountains, stories I first heard with Dr Lass and my friends in the camp. The Queen lured a young peasant boy, a stone-cutter, into her mountain to work on a malachite cup. A copy of this tulip-shaped glorious cup can now be seen in the Hermitage in Leningrad.

The scenery changed from mountains to valleys as we followed the sparkling Kama river. I did not speak with the other people. Nature had calmed me and I felt at peace and happy. We passed villages of low wooden houses, the old Russia of long ago, and then, coming to a small settlement, the driver said: 'This is Krasnovishersk.' It was already dusk. I paid him, thanked him and picked up my suitcases. The village of primitive wooden houses had a street pavement covered with wooden slats because of the mud. I began to walk with my suitcases, knocking at houses to ask if they knew where Mother lived. There were no street-names, no house-numbers, no lights. Nothing.

The nearer I felt I got to Mother, the more my strength returned. Leaving my suitcases on the planks I ran from door to door. After I had asked at numerous houses someone pointed out a very small house at the end. I knocked at the door, and Mother was standing in front of me in a plain faded blue dress and with grey hair. I recognised her immediately. She looked very young but strange. She did not recognize me and looked confused. The shock was so great for her as I was only sixteen when we last saw each other. I embraced her and held her to my bosom and prayed that she would never disappear from my life again. I would cherish her to the end of my days.

CHAPTER FIFTEEN

Crying we remained locked in each other's arms, until at last we were interrupted by a woman's voice.

'Shut the door, for God's sake, Come on, you two. Stop all this dampness. Let's have some tea.'

Elena was a little younger than my mother. She had a beautiful face but had developed elephantiasis, and I felt sorry for her. The friendship between Mother and Elena had sprung up during the difficult dreary evacuation from the canal to the Vishera camp. She had been a leading actress in the Moscow theatre. She was a good actress and amused Mamma, and she was the only one of our friends who had the patience amd compassion to cope with Mother's deafness. During my stay the three of us got on wonderfully together and I took part in the preparations for the anniversary of the Great October Socialist Revolution, which was to be held in the small Palace of Culture where Elena was the paid organizer for the drama and choreography. To pass the time she offered me the chance to dance in one of her productions as a Cossack, and Mother made the costumes. It was a comforting diversion while we were waiting for permission to leave.

It took two to three weeks to get all Mother's papers in order. We had to return to Solikamsk to get them signed, but nothing mattered as we were together again. Mamma's face was glowing with happiness, and she spoke to everyone we met, telling them: 'My daughter has come. She has got me free.' I used to whisper to Mamma to be quiet and not talk so much, but the people who surrounded us had all been through it, too, so we were safe. The only questions ever asked were: 'When did you get free?' 'How was it?' 'Where are you going to live?' We were sharing the past together and our hope for the future.

Once settled back in Karaganda with me Mother began with all her determination to plead with the authorities in Moscow to learn the whereabouts of Cecile and Sammy and to exonerate us all from guilt and restore honour to our family name. Trying to contact Cecile, both Mother and I persistently wrote to the addresses we remembered and to the Address Bureau in Leningrad, but it was useless as Leningrad had been mercilessly bombed. She wrote to the Praesidium of the Soviet Union, to the Supreme Soviet and to the Procurator-General of the Soviet Union and the Military Tribunal. These high-ranking offices were familiar to everyone who had been in prison or in camp. She even wrote to Stalin several times.

To our astonishment the wheels of state machinery began to work and we received official letters from Moscow notifying us that our case was being reconsidered and that enquiries were being made to search out the children. Whenever Mamma received the envelopes with their official stamps she would boast to me: 'See – you said they would not answer me. I am going to continue writing to them until they are sick to death of me.'

Writing petitions, waiting for answers to letters, sewing new dresses for me, keeping the room tidy and cooking kept her fully occupied. Soon after her arrival at Karaganda we had gone out to the market and bought her a secondhand Singer sewing machine. It cost 900 roubles, at a time when my pay was about 600 roubles a month.

In camp Mamma had been able to make herself a corset, meticulously sewing it by hand out of scraps of material, to replace the one she had neglected to wear on the day she was arrested. Now that she had the time and a sewing machine she made herself a very fine corset indeed, which gave her immense satisfaction and the feeling of being well dressed again.

Mother's health improved, but she was deaf and the only means of communication between us was by using our own kind of sign language or paper and pencil. Mamma wore round her neck a piece of cardboard that I made and when I wanted to 'talk' to her I wrote the words down. I got the idea from a book I had read about Beethoven. I had also made a horn out of papier mâché which was helpful, because Mother would ask millions of questions and she wanted an answer. In front of people we spoke Russian to each other, but when we were alone we spoke English, even though it meant shouting to her.

The gulf of fourteen years could not be bridged, because I was only sixteen years old – a child – when I last saw my mother. She remembered me as her little girl but now she was faced with a grown woman of thirty with my own conception of life and my own point of view about what had happened to our family. Her poor mind was so confused that she could not cope with the reality that I was an adult now. The strong link of maternal instinct had been obliterated during those fifteen years of repression in forced-labour camps of the Gulag. She bitterly resented my new authority and my repeatedly telling her to be careful what she said and did. I was against her continuously nagging the authorities, because at last we were free. The syndrome of fear was still strong within me, and my only thought was to protect her.

Mother in the isolation of her deafness now had only the newspapers from which to glean her knowledge, and she believed what she read and took everything for granted. She could not read between the lines as I did and lacked my cynicism. During her long detention she had been deliberately denied any knowledge of the outside, free world. The world stopped for her in 1933.

122

The memory of Cecile and Sammy was so hurtful that we could not even share this. We each suffered in our own way in silence, trying not to discuss anything that brought back memories; Mother could not even look at the photographs of them which we had sent with our letters and which she had preserved all through her camp life.

Pre-Revolution Karaganda was inhabited by Asian people – Mongols, Tartars and Kalmyks – and in the nineteenth century about 100,000 Russians emigrated there. Foreign capital, French and British, was used to exploit the minerals for the metallurgical industry and the coalfields. After the Revolution the mines were nationalized but the site, which had been honeycombed with mines, was not suitable for development. Now fifteen kilometres from the 'Old Town' a 'New Town' was under construction.

It was well planned with broad tree-lined streets, parks and impressive blocks of apartments. There was a sports stadium, cinemas, restaurants, schools, little cafés and even a theatre (the Palace of Culture) and department stores. When I took Mother there in the train, even if we could not afford to buy anything she would delight in window-shopping and looking at everything she saw. She was like Alice in Wonderland. Gradually she became more and more dissatisfied with our life in the Old Town and she grumbled about the place, having in mind to move to the New Town.

'How can we get out of here?' she would ask. 'What a terrible place this is to live in. Can't go anywhere . . . can't even go out in the evenings. And you can't walk anywhere because of the mud, and the cinema is a dirty shed. Why can't we live in a proper town?'

'You can't live there yet because you are still under police control and you have no passport; even if I could get us a room we should not be allowed to be registered there. You can't go out in the evenings, you know, because of the Black Cat jumping about.' The Chernaya

Koshka (Black Cat) were gangs of criminals who robbed, killed and terrorized pedestrians in the streets. They were dressed in black and had constructed on their feet strong springs which enabled them to jump out of the darkness like cats. This explanation pacified Mamma for a while.

The New Town was already overcrowded with mining and civil engineers, teachers and many intellectuals. As there were several polytechnic colleges there were also many students. The whole population of Karaganda in those years was evacuees, exiles and ex-prisoners and as many nationalities – Koreans, Chinese, Germans and many others. It was a lively progressive young community.

Mother and I had made a few friends in the New Town whom we used to visit. They all had nice apartments as they were all leading communists and occupied important positions. One of them was Eugenia Alexandrovna, who, after finishing her degree in medicine in Moscow, had been sent to Karaganda by the Communist Party as head of the Health Department. She lived in a beautiful bungalow of four or five rooms and had a large garden where she made her own vegetable patch and grew cucumbers, tomatoes, potatoes, strawberries and a small orchard. Eugenia lived in a region where all the top officials had bungalows. They all had official transport with a chauffeur, and during the day the wives would exploit the drivers by using them to take them shopping, to the hairdresser's or to visit friends.

Despite all her connections and our friendship she would not help me to get a place in the new medical institute, which she could have done by pulling a few strings. She excused herself by saying: 'You cannot enter the institute because you have no certificate stating that you have completed your secondary education in a Russian school.' I had only a paper saying that I had come out of the labour camps, and that was not likely to help! The director of the institute was a Kazakh and he was more concerned to get places for his fellow-countrymen, who were absolutely illiterate and could not speak two words of Russian. But that was the hypocritical communist ideology – that they had to give education first to the backward Kazakhs of the steppes.

Anybody could have education except me, but I was determined to get higher qualifications. I now had a certificate that I was a nurse but I wished to have wider knowledge. When she saw me reading books from the library late into the night Mother used to say to me: 'Why are you wasting your time? Why don't you get married like other women? We could do with a man in the room.'

Annoyed that she was interrupting me, I used to explode: 'I don't want to be married. I want to study. Since I was fourteen I have been denied education, and all my friends are highly educated and I am not.' I was determined and managed to get a four-year correspondence course in English from the Moscow University of Foreign Languages. This made it possible for me to study my native tongue. The courses were very difficult, and the only time I had to study was between my nursing shifts and looking after Mother.

In 1952 it was necessary to go to Moscow to sit for my diploma. I had nowhere to stay because all the hotels were filled with delegations of top people from all sixteen republics of the Soviet Union, a situation which still exists today. However, my friend Zhenia had an aunt in Moscow, and as she had not seen her for some time she decided that she would go with me and that I could stay with them. I had to leave Mother behind, and she was very angry and would not accept being left out of the fun. With the greatest patience Zhenia and I explained to her that it was impossible for her to go because she was still under the surveillance of the police.

I had not been in a big city for fifteen years, and I was excited and fascinated by the hustle and bustle of Moscow. Arriving by train we took the Metro, which

125

was so beautiful in its Russianism. The walls were covered with dazzling mosaics depicting historical achievements in agriculture and industry, and portraits of farmers, country folk, miners and others. As I looked in awe, open-mouthed, Zhenia grabbed me. 'Come on, come on, stop dawdling: we've got lots to do.'

At last we arrived at her aunt's house. She was an old white-haired woman of eighty, highly intellectual, and loved to play bridge. Throwing our luggage down, we rushed out again to Gum, the State Department Store not far from the Red Square, where Lenin lay in his glazed brown-red granite mausoleum in front of the high brick Kremlin walls. In Gum the crowd was overwhelming, and pushing our way through the crowd of comrades all bursting to get in I had the impression that the whole world of the Soviet Union was here to shop. There could be nobody at work!

We were looking through all the departments when I saw some exquisite porcelain. 'Look at these *bludso* [saucers],' I said to Zhenia, but as my pronunciation of Russian was not perfect I said *bladso* instead, which means 'whore'. People turned their heads to look at me, laughing when Zhenia grabbed me by the arm and dragged me out of the crowd, whispering: 'For God's sake, shut up!'

Taking a bus to the Institute of Foreign Languages I arrived just in time to receive my examination papers, which I did as diligently as possible. There were a few complications with the tutors but I managed to pass and received a certificate that I had completed my four-year English course. Back at Zhenia's aunt's house we celebrated my success with vodka; even the old lady joining in. My day ended with sending a telegram to Mother.

Returning home to Karaganda, walking along the platform to the train, I saw a couple ahead of me. An elderly porter was carrying a suitcase and with his other arm gently supporting an old lady. Her figure and gait

126

reminded me of my mother. I turned to Zhenia and said: 'Look at that woman. Doesn't she resemble Mamma?'

'You silly ass, that is your mother.'

I could not believe my eyes. I was stupefied. I knew it was no use shouting to attract her attention as she was deaf, so I ran past her and confronted her and, looking calmly into my bewildered and furious face, in her most coquettish way she said: 'Don't be angry with me. I had such a lovely time.'

Mother felt so hurt when she was left behind, and was so eager to see Moscow, that she disregarded all caution, the possible complications of being without a passport and the dreadful consequences it could lead to if she was caught. She had packed her bag and with the help of friends bought a ticket to Moscow. In her usual amiable way she made a friend of the train attendant and explained that she had no place to stay in Moscow. A kind middle-aged man, he took her home to his family, where she lived for three days as a paying guest. Only fate or destiny, or call it what you will, could have arranged that Mamma and I should be travelling on the same train back to Karaganda. The only difference was that she travelled first class and we travelled third.

With my new diploma I was able to get a position as a teacher in English, something I had always hoped to do, but I was restricted to the fifth, sixth and seventh classes.

Four years passed, and Mamma was quite different, much healthier and savouring her freedom and grabbing life by the handful. Every day she needed some kind of excitement and would rush off whenever possible to the New Town and go to the cafés, to the cinemas and look at the shops. She had her sewing machine and now in her new independence she was determined to support herself and not rely on me. After all, she had brought up her children on a sewing machine and she had also all her skills in sewing by hand. She could not live without sewing.

127

One day in the New Town we saw hanging in the big department store racks of silver-fox furs and that no one was buying them. Suddenly Mamma ran away from me and I heard her asking for the manager of the store. I stopped her and asked what she intended to do. She was so excited, saying: 'I have got an idea. Be patient with me. Listen, I am going to offer the manager to make hats and muffs out of these fox furs.'

'They will never let you. Don't you know everything is state controlled and they do not allow any private enterprise here?'

She charmed the manager, a bright young man, and he arranged to give her some fox furs to make some samples. For a whole week our room was filled with fur, as everything had to be cut and made by hand. But Mamma's hands had lost none of their skill, and with her flair and taste she made two beautiful hats with muffs to match. She took them back to the shop and everyone was so delighted with the result that Mamma was now in the fur business with regular work. How Papa would have smiled and been proud of her.

Since I was working as a teacher and still continuing with my nursing one evening a week, with Mother's money coming in as well, we now at last had a better standard of living. We were not only able to eat better but Mamma also bought material and made clothes for us both so that we were considered to be well dressed.

Nobody wanted to work at the school where I got a job as it was far away from the mines and every morning I had to walk three kilometres on the muddy roads with the bitter winds blowing in from the steppes. The children were a mixture of all nationalities: Russian, Kirgis, Kazakh Tartar, Chechen-Ingush, German, Chinese, Korean, Kabardin and others. Every one of these children had parents with their own ethnic tradition, and the mothers were always interfering with the education. One little girl of about thirteen was kidnapped from school by her future husband. The

128

Mongoloid families predominated and they were charming-looking children; all the eyes were slanting in a different way, and they had little noses like blobs of dough and ink-black hair. The children were wild and jolly, and they spoke Russian as badly as I did and we got on wonderfully well together. Whenever they got a chance they would chatter each in their own language, and the classroom was like the Tower of Babel. Their behaviour was outrageous, and I used to shout at them and usually caught the wrong one. I would push a child in the corner for punishment and smack his bottom only to be told that I had the wrong boy. I could not differentiate one face from another.

These children had never heard English in their lives, and their ages ranged from twelve to fourteen. They were fully grown boys, wore their national costume and carried knives, but it was not long before I had them singing 'Five Little Pigs Went to Market' and 'Sing a Song of Sixpence'. I taught them by phonetics, and they picked up English remarkably with a clean accent.

At the teachers' conference we used to speak about their abominable behaviour and talk about what we could do to harness all that energy to something useful. We had no educational games and no normal school equipment. I decided that as it was the end of the year we must have a New Year carnival and that it would be nice to have masks.

'Where are we going to get masks from?' one of the teachers asked.

'With the children I can prepare moulds out of clay, which is plentiful, and make animals' heads – wolves, tigers, bears, foxes – and we will make the masks from papier mâché and when they are dry the children will paint them.'

The carnival was a brilliant success, and our animal masks were realistic and most amusing as the children cleverly took on the characteristics of the various beasts. It was a comical sight to see all the animals singing and dancing together and hear the joyous sound of the children's laughter. All our hard work had not been in vain, although making the masks had messed up the whole school. The boys were so enthusiastic that they brought in pails of clay. The corridors were covered with the wet clay footsteps of the children. Everything was in disorder, and the pupils made excuses not to prepare their homework because Flora Alexandrovna had given them errands to do.

In addition to the carnival I wanted to put on my own production of *Cinderella* and have the children speak the lines in English.

'And where will you get the costumes from?'

'We can ask the parents to bring any kind of material and old clothes they can spare. And if somebody could get some gauze that will be very helpful. We can dye it, starch it and make the costumes.'

Some of the teachers were enthusiastic but others were boring killjoys. However, I was determined to have our party and my play. Everything was complicated, and only through the black market and using my own money was I able to buy some dyes.

With the help of Mamma and keen mothers we made costumes from dyed gauze which were really marvellous. The dresses were starched with potato flour to make them stand out like crinolines. They were in various colours – light green, yellow, pink and blue – with different-coloured sashes. From silver paper we cut out stars and stuck them all over the skirts. Every dress was different. For the role of Cinderella I chose a little Chechen girl with a Madonna-like face with huge brown liquid eyes.

My prince was a good-looking blonde Russian boy. His costume, and that of the other courtiers, consisted of long brown stockings, pairs of women's dyed black knickers gathered at the waist and on the thighs, which made fine pantaloons, puffed sleeves and a ruff folded out of paper at the neck. But their costumes were not complete without feathers for their caps. We were all quite upset about it. The boys wanted feathers. Suddenly I suggested: 'Can't we use cock feathers?' Everybody was so relieved at this solution to the problem that it was agreed.

One day an irritated mother came in swinging a featherless cock, and shouting at me in front of the children that the pupils had stripped the poor bird of its tail. Hearing the noise, the headmaster came out of his office and joined in the confusion. He was furious. 'See what you have done,' he said. 'You have upset the whole school, and now parents are complaining.'

But in spite of all the antagonism my play was a smashing success. The caps with the cock feathers were admired; the dresses were like out of a fairy tale, and the girls and boys danced the minuets, curtsying and bowing against the scenery that I had painted with stunning effect. As a result of our success I was invited by different schools to share my method of teaching English not only in the classroom but also by organizing hobby groups to enrich the pupils' interest in the language. In this way I introduced the *Golden Nursery Rhymes*, Perrault's *Fairy Tales* and the Brothers Grimm into the dead lives of the children of Stalin's Kazakhstan.

CHAPTER SIXTEEN

On 5 March 1953 all the loudspeakers announced that an important statement would be broadcast at eleven o'clock that morning. Crowds of Karagandians stood in awe and uncertainty looking towards the loudspeakers attached to the telegraph poles in the streets. Punctually on the hour it was announced that Stalin had died and that this would be a day of mourning. Everybody was stunned. Complete strangers began crying and embracing one another in the streets. 'What are we going to do? Our beloved Stalin is dead.' Their grief was so intense it was as though they had lost someone dear to them in the family.

After my experiences in the camps I felt that it was Stalin who was responsible for their fates, and could only explain the hypocrisy of their behaviour as mass hysteria. But what I was told happened in Red Square in Moscow was unbelievable, as hundreds of people were crushed and trampled to death trying to catch a glimpse of the body as it lay in state. No king or queen of any nation, except perhaps Queen Victoria, could have received such lavish tribute. The headmaster at my school had received orders from the Party and we hung a large black and white photograph of Stalin on the wall of the hall. It was draped with black material and paper flowers made by the teachers.

Pioneers and Komsomols were organised in shifts to stand on either side of this portrait-in-state. Every ten minutes different children marched into the school hall and, approaching the portrait, saluted one another by raising the right hand. They then changed places with those who had been on duty, who, with straight back, lips firmly closed, left the hall intent on showing off the importance of their honourable duty. The austerity of the ceremony brought back memories for me of the Changing of the Guard at Buckingham Palace. In deep silence parents, eyes red with endless tears, passed by this portrait to pay their last respects. The sense of despair at the loss of their idol was so great that they seemed to think that Russia herself had come to her end. One evening when I was on duty one of the teachers, who could not leave her three-year-old daughter at home, had put her to sleep on two chairs in the corner of the hall while parents and pupils stood around in mournful groups smothering their sobs. The silence was depressing, when suddenly light footsteps were heard pattering across the hall, and the little girl rushed towards her mother crying: 'Mamma, Mamma, *ka ka, ka ka.*'

We could not keep from laughing. Some of the boys, quivering with suppressed giggles, were unable to brave it out and ran away, leaving their posts. Peals of hysterical laughter echoed through the cold corridors, releasing the tension of the whole melodramatic situation. I let them have their laughter.

In not many years to come the schoolchildren would be told to blacken Stalin's pictures, blot out his words from their history textbooks and erase him from their memories. They would witness the obliteration of his name from the cities, factories, schools and streets, and the removal of his body from the mausoleum in Red Square where Lenin lies. But that generation would never know the whole truth of Stalin's monstrous crimes, the mass arrest of millions of innocent people including women, children and old people. Although Khrushchev exposed those atrocities at a special closed session of the 20th Party Conference in February 1956, they have never been made accessible to the ordinary people.

Soon after this the headmaster, whom I thought a

friend, denounced my mother and me as ex-political prisoners, and in consequence I was invited to the local Education Board and there told that I was not sufficiently qualified, or politically educated, to teach Soviet children. Thank God I was only dismissed for that!

Mother began nagging me again: 'Now that you have been kicked out of that job at school, get those silly dreams of teaching out of your head. You will have us starving again.' I listened to her as I still had my nursing to fall back on and summer was on its way bringing a breeze of fresh air.

We had received Soviet citizens' passports and our exile came to an end. It is the custom in Russia to celebrate any event as the excuse for an extra drink. As the Russian saying goes: 'Even purchasing a pair of shoelaces is sufficient reason to drink a bottle of vodka.' So as this was really a great event in our lives we drank *zveraboy* with our friends – ex-prisoners – sitting round the table. A vodka drink with a terribly strong pepper flavour, the word *zveraboy* translated means 'to fell a bull', and with home-made pies, pickled cabbage, salted cucumbers and hot boiled potatoes it was a feast for the Gods.

Mother floated round the room holding her precious document in her hand. She was a clever woman, knew the price of her freedom and realized the privileges that she was now entitled to. 'I am free . . . I am free,' she shrieked. My friends smiled as they were very fond of her and sympathized with her as she had suffered so much in the loss of her children. It was a happy night in our lives and one to be remembered.

One of my close friends, Julia, who lived in our house, had come all the way from Moscow to Karaganda to meet her husband, who was in the camps and was soon to be freed. She was crushed and broken-hearted when her husband came back with a camp wife on his arm, and we friends had helped her through this crisis. These situations were not new and happened to many; war and prison camps broke up families, bringing deep distress to the cast-off wife or husband.

Karaganda had a small library with not a bad collection of books. During the next few weeks Mamma spent hours there. I did not take much notice of this new hobby of hers, but something was brewing in her mind. The explosion came when she told me: 'We are going to the Crimea, to Yalta. It is a lovely place and I was there when I was a little girl with my mother. I've read all about it in the library and I am sick of your Karaganda. I am going to work hard and save money.' And she did.

Now that her fur business was finished she went by day to nice people, sewing and repairing, and would have breakfast and dinner with them. She was so helpful in a family that they recommended her to the élite of the New Town where the wives were lonely and Mother was an adorable companion. She would laugh and joke about her Paris life with Papa, how they went to the Moulin Rouge and the Folies Bergères, and how Papa gambled at the Casino in Monte Carlo where he loved playing roulette. They were spellbound at Mamma's stories and totally ignorant of the other side of the Iron Curtain and the glittering free life of Paris, London and New York. Her memory would go back to those days, but her fifteen years of agony in camp, her dead child, her lost son and daughter – these memories she kept to herself. They were wounds that should not be touched.

Most of our evenings Mother and I spent with the Pospelov family whom I had made friends with in the train coming back from Moscow the year before. They were always glad to see us, and a close friendship sprang up between us. Comrade Pospelov was a leading engineer in the coalmining industry, and in spite of the political differences between me and the head of the family – he was a Communist Party man – he never made us feel any different from them or referred to the fact that Mother and I had been political prisoners.

Comrade Pospelova (in Russian the feminine names

end with the letter 'a') would accompany herself on the piano singing arias from the various classical operas. Mamma would sit wistfully by as I shouted the tune into her horn and then, as she had a good musical memory, it was sufficient for her to catch only one or two notes for her face to brighten up and she would join in the singing.

Though he was a communist, I could confide all my troubles in Comrade Pospelov because I knew that ideologically he was against the system. I told him that Mother was restless and wanted to leave Karaganda for Yalta and that I was hesitant as to whether I should listen to her or not. 'The quicker you get out of here the better,' he responded. 'I will help you to get the rail tickets and also, if you will allow us, please accept a little money from all our hearts.'

Kindly, compassionately, he said to me: 'Flora, you are too good to live here, and you have the responsibility of making your mother happy. You must help her to cope with what is left to her and if she wants to go to Yalta so be it. You must give her time to readjust herself to her new free life.'

When the time for our departure from Karaganda came I had no regrets. Apart from some good friends made and lost during the fifteen years I had spent there, it had been a complete waste of my personal life; but I had seen a modern city grow where once had been only a wilderness. In my heart the very name of Karaganda even today brings only the memory of a vast kingdom of human suffering and degradation, a graveyard of lost souls.

Yalta is the most popular of the resorts in the Crimea and is famous for its wines and tobacco, tourist industry and health resorts in the former palaces of the tsars and nobility. The sea was shining and the sky was blue and the air seemed wonderfully fresh after our long journey from Karaganda. It was the early summer of 1953, just after the death of Stalin. We had with us only our personal belongings, a little money we had saved and, of course, our precious passports. In one of the seaside hotels we rented two beds in a dormitory of six people for about 60p a week, which was very cheap for that time. Later we were able to rent a room not far from the beach. The difficulty in renting rooms was the *propiska* (registration), which cost a thousand roubles simply for the privilege of having our papers stamped. Mamma soon got herself a job in the repair shop in the hotel lobby, but it was a problem for me to get work in one of the sanatoriums as there were no vacancies for nurses.

The other people in our hotel room were all very nice elderly people on holiday. Mother soon made friends with an intelligent Jewish woman from Leningrad and, of course, told her about my trouble in getting work. The woman's name was Eva, and she was interested and helpful. She told us that her son, a doctor, was soon coming to Yalta and she felt sure that he could pull some strings to help us. Nevertheless, I continued to look for work at all the sanatoriums along the coast, and high in the hills I came across a special one for tuberculosis.

When I managed to get to the director and showed him my nurse's diploma and my workbook (every Soviet citizen has an internal passport and a workbook which gives the history of his or her working life) he told me: 'You are a very efficient and good nurse, but all the places are occupied. Our sanatorium is strictly for military personnel.'

I began to understand that there was something wrong and that they did not want me. 'Can't you do anything for me?' I pleaded.

'I'd like to,' he explained, a little confused, 'but, you see, you were born in England and you were in the camps. I am sorry.' Clearly he was not going to risk his position for an ex-convict.

I did not tell my mother that I had not found a job as I did not want to upset her and instead said that the director had asked me to return next day.

But you could not deceive Mamma. 'You are lying, Flora. They won't have you. I feel it in my heart that you resent this life, but what can we do? You must be strong, Flora. There is no other life.'

For the next few days I helped Mother with her sewing in the little workshop. The fashion for men's trousers kept us going because in that year baggy trousers were not the style and we were kept busy making them narrow.

There was plenty of activity in Yalta as a film company from Moscow was making *Othello*, and in our free time we went and watched them on the outdoor set. One morning Mamma got up very early leaving the keys of the shop for me. Time passed and she did not return for breakfast or lunch. I became worried and asked the porter, who told me that Mamma had got herself a job as an extra in the crowd scenes.

Eva's son arrived and he helped me to get work at last. In the process of my Russian upbringing and my camp 'education' I had become quite efficient in a few Russian tricks such as *znakomstvo* and *blat*, synonyms meaning 'pulling strings'. These 'arts', and many others, I would have to employ to survive in the Russian jungle where I had to protect my mother from the adversities of life. As a result of this *blat* I got a job in one of the most beautiful sanatoriums, the Palace of Livadia, where in 1945 the Yalta Conference was held with the three top men of that time – Churchill, Roosevelt and Stalin. There I met in 1953 in late summer Burma's leader U Nu and his entourage and many American delegations with whom I had my first English conversation with foreigners.

It was so pleasant for me to work in that beautiful palace where so many historic events had taken place. The room for the nurses overlooked the sea, and the lawns were covered with red and yellow roses. The food was awful as there were no vegetables, and I had to report the complaints of the patients to the director, who would only say: 'If you had been here ten years ago, there was not even that. Tell them they are lucky to get food at all.' For distinguished guests like Nehru and U Nu there was, of course, a different menu. I received as my salary 400 roubles a month, which today after the devaluation is forty roubles. The rent of the room was 300 roubles, and a pound of carrots cost ten roubles. Mamma made about the same amount of money as I did, and somehow we made ends meet.

During my work at the sanatorium I had to attend the political seminars which were held in 'the Red Corner' (conference-hall) where a large portrait of Lenin hung, together with many slogans, one of which was 'Study . . . study . . . study . . . and again study.' There we studied Marxism and Leninism. These lessons were compulsory, and it was a serious offence not to attend. There I learned that, because of the capitalistic system, English and American children were starving and millions of unemployed and homeless slept in the parks and streets. Only the communist system was good.

After being on duty at the sanatorium I was returning home one day when Mother came screaming out of the house to meet me. She was waving a paper which stated that my sister Cecile had died from pneumonia in 1948 in a Sverdlov labour camp. I held Mother in my arms, comforting her, but I knew from those who had received information of this sort in answer to their requests that where it was stated that the prisoners had 'died of pneumonia' they had in fact been shot.

Mamma lay on her bed for days, not eating and with empty eyes. Her drawn face was too much for me to bear. It was not fair; it was so unjust. Stalin's crimes had no ending, and they were inhuman and merciless. Mother's new friend, Berthe, did the best she could to be with her and help her because I had to go to work. Months before Mother had sent a letter to her friend Elena, with whom she had shared her exile in Krasnovishersk, inviting her to stay, and now we received a reply that she would soon arrive.

Elena completely changed Mother's mood. They had been friends for so many years and understood each other and had shared so much. Together the four of us came to a decision that it would be better for me to go with Berthe when she returned to Kiev.

'Go with her, Flora,' Mother encouraged me. 'She lives in the centre of the city, and you will meet nice people. The people in Kiev are more educated, and you will probably be able to give English lessons.'

So far Mother had done well for me, and so I agreed to go. After all, without her persistent search to better our living I would probably be in Karaganda today. To get my *propiska* (residence permission) to live in Kiev we thought out the ruse that as Berthe, who was my age, was disabled she must require the services of a nurse.

CHAPTER SEVENTEEN

One of Berthe's relatives, her cousin, was head of a poly-clinic in Kiev, and another, Clara, worked in the ear, nose and throat department there; with their help I got work in the outpatients department and settled down with Berthe to enjoy the ambience of a big city. Among our neighbours in a communal house was a Ukrainian family. The father was a professor of skin and venereal disease, and his second wife, a woman so fat that she had to have two chairs to sit on, was from Poland, extremely intellectual and a wonderful dressmaker.

From the first wife the professor had a son, Dimitri, who was studying constructional engineering in one of the universities in Kiev. Dimitri was married to a lovely girl called Nastia, who was in the last stages of pregnancy when I arrived, and we used to meet each other in the communal kitchen, although she had her own room in the centre of town. The other family in our building was Jewish with three small boys, and then there was an old aristocrat who lived by herself. This meant eleven people sharing one lavatory, but this was considered superior accommodation as in some communal houses twenty families lived together.

We had two gas-stoves, one sink, and each household had its own little table with its own cupboard. There was a rule in those houses that nothing should be touched from other people's tables, but as we were a happy quartet of families there was no conflict. Each house had a list hanging on the wall with the duties for cleaning the lavatory, taking out the rubbish, washing the floors and cleaning the bathroom, and each person did one week per month. Sharing duties is so indoctrinated into the Russian mind that nobody shirked. It was hell for the old people, however, and as they could not afford help we took turns to do their work.

All the news and events were exchanged in the kitchen, but when the husbands came home every door was closed and there was no more friendly gossip. We all heard that Dimitri's wife was due to go to hospital to have her baby but one day when I came home from work everyone was crying, and I felt instinctively that something terrible had happened. Nastia had died giving birth to a baby girl as the doctors could not stop her haemorrhaging. The house was filled with sadness.

After three weeks the baby was brought home, and all the women of the house were concerned with the motherless child. I became her nurse for the next three years. Her name was Vera. I remember her first steps, first words; and the name she gave me was 'Fofa', which was to stick with me for many years to come.

In the early summer of 1957, Mother came to see me. I knew before she came that she would never understand my love and fondness for that family. She would be jealous. That was one of the streaks in her character which had developed after her ordeal in the camps.

'Why on earth are you wasting your time with that child?' she would say. 'You don't go to the theatre. You don't go to the cinema. You come home from work and the first thing you do is take the child in your arms. Why don't you go somewhere where you will meet someone and get married? If you are running after Dimitri I can tell you he will never marry you. You are making a fool of yourself. He is a Party man and he is going to be a professor and it is only two years since his wife died.'

'But I don't want to marry him. Why do you think that I want to marry him?'

'I see all your tricks, holding the baby in your arms and smiling at him. All you talk is baby-talk with him.

What she did. What she doesn't do. What she is going to do. And the whole lot of you paying court to that child. Spoiling her.'

Mamma showed antagonism towards this child and other children because she was covered in an armour of pain and pity for herself – but when nobody was around I caught her playing with the baby. Her apparent hatred of children, and difficulty with people in general, was due to her deafness. This suffering made her nervous all the rest of her life. Her hopelessness in her deafness made her very strong-willed, hiding her natural kindness. She was so hurt by fifteen years as a political prisoner, her deafness, the loss of her children and the guilt that she felt for taking her children with her to her homeland. But was she to blame? At the same time her remarks about Dimitri and my response made me ask myself what my real feelings were towards this man. We had known each other for some years, and it became clear to me that a feeling stronger than friendship had developed which I now had to admit to myself, and I knew that his attitude towards me was the same.

Kiev is a beautiful city on the banks of the River Dnieper. Third largest in the Soviet Union, it has been described as the 'mother of Russian cities' as it was the capital of Kiev Rus until the middle of the thirteenth century. That summer the city was busy preparing for the first Word Youth Festival, and the streets were filled with young people of all nationalities. On our walks in the First of May Park, Mamma and I would meet people of all nationalities, and as most of them spoke English it was quite natural for the Russian students and people who knew English to speak to them. It was so jolly and everyone was happy and the tide of excitement was so overwhelming that we, too, got carried along.

Through Dimitri's family I met many students from the Foreign Language Institute and we used to gather and talk about this festival. Several of them were getting jobs as interpreters and suggested that I do the same, but

Dimitri told me: 'You can't do that, Flora. You don't speak Russian well enough.'

There were always a lot of foreigners standing outside the Kiev Intourist Hotel at this time, and one evening I noticed some Scotsmen in kilts talking in a group. I thought how I would like to speak to them but was too shy to approach them, when I heard a voice saying: 'I'm from Scotland. I'm from Bonny Scotland. My daugher was born in Scotland.'

At the nucleus of all this vibrating excitement was Mamma. She was laughing and telling the men about her life in their country. They were entranced with her, but despite the colossal old-fashioned hearing aid she held in her hand – everyone trying to speak at the same time into the microphone – she did not hear a word. Even so, her face was filled with joy.

'This is my mother,' I said as I joined the group.

'This is my Flora,' she whooped with pride, and we waved goodbye to them and they shouted, 'Come to Scotland.'

Returning home through the park I laughed at the improbability of their invitation. It was as easy to go to Scotland as to the moon. The realization that I could never go back made me want to scream in despair and beat my head against the wall. And I had a distinct feeling of premonition. That hilarious meeting with my countrymen only heightened in my mind the gulf between me and those plain young Scotsmen, innocent of any of the atrocities we two women had been through: mud, dirt, lice, degradation.

About seven o'clock in the evening there was a ring on the door and a militiaman came and asked if Marie Samuelovna Leipman was staying there.

'Yes,' I said.

'We want to speak to her.'

The corridor was suddenly filled with eyes as I took him into our room. Berthe was lying on the sofa and jumped up, with a 'What's the matter?' Mother as usual was sitting quietly and smiled at him. He started to speak to her and asked her for her passport. He looked through it and said: 'You have no *propiska*, and tomorrow you must return to Yalta; if not, you will be put in prison for violating the law.'

I tried to explain that she was an old woman, that she had only come for a few days. It was no use arguing with the law. Mother was deaf and was repeatedly asking, 'What is the matter? Why don't you tell me?'

'You have no *propiska*,' I shouted into her ear. 'You are being sent back to the Crimea.' The whole house must have heard.

Next day Mother was off. While everybody was rejoicing my deaf sixty-eight-year-old mother was deported: a mother whose only crime was to come to see her daughter during that lovely time, when she could have been so happy speaking not only English but also French with all those glorious young people, was pushed out of the city like a tramp. The insult of it. Were they afraid of what Mother might have said about the Soviet system of labour camps?

A few days later Berthe and I were in the First of May Park when we heard a man saying loudly in English: 'Do you want to see a nickel? Have you ever seen a nickel?' People were passing by trying to ignore him. He was dressed in a red sports jacket with a loud bow-tie, tall, thin and obviously American.

As we passed he offered us an American magazine and involuntarily I answered in English. We made acquaintance and sat down on a bench. 'Why won't the Russian people take the magazines from me? I'm friendly. I only want to speak with them. They pass by and look away. What's the matter?' he asked.

At that time I did not think that a conversation with a foreigner could cause trouble. Quite naturally he explained that he was a delegate from America with the first American Medical Tour, and they had been in Moscow and Leningrad. Then he told me that he was a doctor of the near-blind and asked me what I did. I told him I was a nurse and we immediately had something in common. 'Where do you work?' he asked.

We exchanged formalities and he offered us two tickets for the opera. His name was Dr Ronald Clark. Berthe and I were wildly excited. I had nothing suitable to wear so as Berthe had an old piece of satin, the lining of a coat, we made a lovely dress on her machine with a flirty flared shirt, a décolleté neckline and little scraps of silver fox round the cuffs as was fashionable at that time.

The Kiev opera-house is one of the oldest and most beautiful in Russia, and we marvelled that our seats were in the stalls. When Dr Clark and his friends came in to take their seats he waved to me, calling, 'Hi, Flora!' and during the interval we went into the foyer and I met the whole group of twenty-five, including five wives and one good-looking black doctor. Their kindness was so touching that I immediately had a warm feeling towards these people. Their manners were such a contrast to the *Kievlany* with whom I was surrounded. I wondered what these Americans would have thought if they had known that I had been in labour camps.

A few days later I was working in my office when there was a knock on the door. It opened and, with a Cheshire Cat grin, Dr Clark said: 'Hullo, Flora . . . I found you.' I nearly fainted. He was not alone as he had the whole group trailing behind him with chocolate Eskimo ice-creams, armfuls of books and lots of chatter.

The doctor sitting opposite me, a loyal Party Member, was dumbfounded. His immediate reaction was to order us out of the office. I went into the corridor and asked the Americans: 'What are you doing here?'

'We wanted to see how you work,' Dr Ball, head of the delegation, said. 'Introduce us to the director of the clinic, Flora?'

'Please sit down for a moment,' I replied.

Dr Clark was offering ice-cream to everyone and trying to communicate with the other nurses. In the confusion I went into the head doctor's office. He was already furious. He had been informed by one of the charwomen, who had rushed into his office shouting 'Americantsy . . . Americantsy!' I was in a mess. The Americans should not have come without an appointment, but how was I to know the inquisitive nature of these happy-go-lucky people? They were already poking their noses into any door they found.

Meantime I was having it out with the head doctor. He was scared stiff, saying: 'What are we going to do?'

'Please don't be so cross,' I answered. 'Dr Ball is one of the most respected professors in America. These are not ordinary tourists. They are prominent doctors and they are our guests.'

Every few minutes the door would open and Dr Clark would pop his head in. 'Flora, what's going on? What are we waiting for? We have to leave soon and haven't much time. When can we see the head doctor?'

The director wrung his hands in agitation and addressed a member of the local Party committee who happened to be present in his office. 'What are we going to do? We have no sanctions from above to receive these foreigners.'

'Let's contact the Central Committee,' she answered, 'and you, Flora, get out of here.'

Outside the director's door everything was bubbling with confusion. Patients and young students were quite happy to greet the Americans while the staff hid in their offices. The few nurses in sight were being forced to accept the ice-cream from Ronald Clark, who said to me: 'Flora, why are they not taking the ice-cream? It's not poisonous. I'm a doctor. I wouldn't hurt them.'

'Why don't you take it from him and stop this nonsense?' I asked the nurses. 'He's not going to bite you.'

The Americans still insisted on meeting the head of the poly-clinic. I was called into his office.

'Let them in,' the Party committee lady, her lips in a thin line, snapped.

Dr Ball, Dr Clark and the others came in and we began a little conference with me acting as interpreter. Ronald offered the director some fine medical books, which he refused to accept. Ronald Clark was a man with a strong personality and very erudite, and he was amazed to be confronted by such blatant inhospitality. He was so offended that he threw the books out of the window.

It was typical of the suspicious mentality of the Russians to turn what should have been a friendly exchange between America and Russia into a political problem, and a farce!

CHAPTER EIGHTEEN

Our conference was at its peak when the door opened and *he* came in, and I guessed immediately that he was a representative from the Secret Police, even though he was in plain clothes. He walked straight up to the director who was sitting at the top table and shook hands, nodding politely in acknowledgement of the Americans. Then, saying something quietly to the director, he approached me and asked me to step out into the corridor. Trying not to attract the attention of the Americans, I slipped out with him.

The man introduced himself as Comrade Ivanov from the police, and then he said to me: 'We will talk about this matter later, Flora Leipman, but meantime try to get the Americans out of the clinic as quickly as possible, and if they ask questions about me tell them that I am a doctor.'

We returned to the room, and the Americans sprang on me: 'Where have you been, Flora? We are lost without you and who is this man? Introduce us please.'

'He is a doctor,' I lied. I was on guard throughout the conversation that followed because I did not know whether the KGB man understood English or not.

'Who in the hell is he, Flora?' Ronald asked. 'Don't kid me. He's no doctor. He's a cop.'

'Translate what the doctor is saying,' the KGB officer said. Either he did not understand English or he was playing a game.

But Dr Clark continued and had his final word: 'Tell the director, Flora, that if he and his colleagues had

149

come to America I would have shown them everything in our hospital. Also I would have used my car to bring them home to meet my family. Poor Flora cannot invite us to her home, she has no place to take us. And why are the nurses running away and closing doors in our faces?'

I managed to get the Americans out of the poly-clinic because in any case it was time for their lunch back at the hotel. They were pleased with their visit and had no complaints about their reception with the exception of Dr Clark, who was still grumbling as they went out of the door. They could not possibly have known the uproar that their spontaneous friendly visit caused in our clinic, which was quite unprepared for receiving guests. The clinic was not at its cleanest, the white uniforms were old and shabby, and there was no luncheon to offer. The infamous Prince Potemkin stunt of making a fake façade (for Catherine II he built a sham Crimean village with only the front of the buildings) could not be repeated. Russians are very boastful by nature, but our clinic was denied the opportunity to show off. Instead my Americans had seen the real Russia.

Saying goodbye to me, the Americans invited me to go to their hotel for a farewell party the next day. I returned to the office of the head doctor where the KGB officer asked me to sit down. The director was flushed, uncomfortable, furious that this should have happened at his outpatients department, and I suppose he was sorry that he had been persuaded by his relatives to take me on to the staff and that he had turned a blind eye to my past. He was still influenced by fear of the Doctors' Plot of 1952, when many leading doctors, most of them Jewish, were arrested and accused of attempting to assassinate Party leaders and commanders of the Army.

'How do you know these Americans?' the KGB man asked. 'How long have you known them? Why did they come to *this* poly-clinic?'

'I met them in the park and in our conversation naturally they asked me where I worked. I was proud to

150

tell them that I am a nurse and working in this lovely poly-clinic.'

'But you must have known that it is forbidden to tell foreigners where you work.'

'I didn't know that. Why can't we speak to foreigners? What is wrong in that?'

It made me indignant. Why should he interrogate me when Moscow, Leningrad and Kiev were filled with foreign guests? But I told myself, Flora don't forget where you have been, and adopted a different attitude, smiling and making myself look foolish. 'I'm very sorry if I have made some mistake,' I cringed.

'Please don't contact the Americans in future without our permission. You will be given instructions, so be at this address at nine o'clock in the morning. Your director will give you a few days off from the clinic.'

I could have kicked myself for getting involved with these Americans. I should have known better, but it had been such fun to be with them and to speak English. I had been proud as a peacock.

Next morning I went to the address, which was situated not far from the centre of Kiev in an ordinary housing estate. Comrade Ivanov showed me into a room that was empty except for a desk, two chairs, a telephone and, on the wall, a portrait of Lenin. His attitude to me was amiable and he addressed me in the Russian style of 'Flora Alexandrovna' and asked me to sit down.

'We should like you to proceed with your acquaintance with the Americans,' he continued. 'If you are co-operative, no harm will come to you. We should like you to find out why they have come to the Soviet Union. What do they say to each other? You know English well. They are your new friends, but they must not become suspicious that you have anything to do with us. You must understand that, Flora Alexandrovna. You have a mother and you would not like anything to happen to her or to yourself. So be sensible.'

I was disgusted and began to cry. 'My poor mother,

who came to visit me from Yalta, was kicked out like a tramp and she is not allowed to live in Kiev; and now you want me to do something for you. You are using me.'

'You don't need to cry. Just do what we say and everything will be all right. If you do well, I will help you to get permission for your mother to live in Kiev.'

I knew that they had men and women everywhere watching people like me. My future and that of my mother depended on how I handled the situation. In short they wanted me to become an informer. I agreed. I had no choice.

Dismissing me, Ivanov said: 'You have our permission to continue to be the Americans' interpreter. You must not say anything against the Soviet Union or your former life. Try to avoid getting into any political discussion with them. If they persist in asking awkward questions, divert the conversation into another direction. Report everything you hear back to us.' He gave me a telephone number which I had to memorise. Immediately on leaving the house I wrote the telephone number down in my notebook as I have no sense for remembering numbers. Then I set off for my new adventure as Mata Hari, in high spirits, and glad to get off so easily.

It was a hot summer's day and I went to the party which was held in the Ukrainia, the Kiev Intourist Hotel. I put on the one suitable dress I had. It was made of Chinese silk printed with flowers, the only material available in every shop. All the women of Kiev were wearing this silk. I wore no stockings as nylons were problem number one, and I had no make-up.

It was a typical American reception complete with a bountiful bar where we all helped ourselves to drinks. Mingling with the American doctors were a few Russian ones whom they had met on the tour. My new 'happy snap' friends had laid on a photographer to

152

record the event for 'the folks back home' and even produced a tape-recorder to make personal messages.

This was my first social encounter with English-speaking people for so many years. I should have felt joy at being with these people, but I was only depressed. 'What's that long face about?' Ronald Clark said, interrupting my reflections.

Then Dr Ball joined us: 'Flora, what happened after we left you? I do hope that you didn't get into any trouble. I warned Clark that we should not go there without permission.'

Overhearing the conversation, one of the American wives said in a naïve way: 'Flora, you will not be sent to a labour camp for speaking to us, will you?'

'How do you know about the camps?' I answered.

They all burst out laughing. 'We know all about your camps, about the Soviet system, from the press and other media; and in America a lot of books about the labour camps and prisons have already been published.' This gave me food for thought.

After the reception we all went into the restaurant where the mayor of Kiev was host at a banquet for these distinguished guests. Besides doctors many prominent citizens of Kiev had also been invited. I was placed between two Russians: one was Comrade Ivanov, and on the other side was a representative from the Ministry of Health. Everyone was enjoying themselves. There were the usual toasts, and the tables were loaded with vodka and food. This was not *pakazukha* (showing off). This was real.

I had no time to eat as from every side people were calling out, 'Flora help . . . translate: what did he say?' And from Russian into English and from English into Russian. The Americans and the Russians all became a little bit tipsy. There was a lot of confusion, laughter and fun, and during this commotion one of the Americans came to the back of my chair and, swaying a little, said to me: 'Flora . . . these are for you. You are a good guy.'

153

Dozens of packets of nylon stockings tumbled from his hands on to my lap. I was frozen stiff.

'What's this?' Comrade Ivanov whispered, 'And what is he saying to you?' I did not interpret that he said I was a good guy, merely that the nylons were a present for me.

The table became silent. I had this gift of nylon stockings in my lap and I did not know what to do with them. I was in front of all the crowd sitting there and with a KGB officer on my left side and the Man from the Ministry on the other. To give back the present was rude and to accept was not feasible. But how was I to get out of this dramatic situation? With a fierce determination I jumped to my feet, gathered up the bundle of nylons and forced them back into the hands of the American, saying: 'Thank you, but couldn't you have been more discreet?' Two of the group came forward and guided the drunk American away from me, saying: 'Come on, John. Stop it. Let's have a drink.'

I looked with regret as the stockings disappeared out of my life. How I would have loved to have those stockings and how I needed them. But a voice at my elbow interrupted my dreams:

'What did you say to him?' the KGB officer asked.

'We Soviet women do not accept presents from strangers,' I said.

'Very good . . . very well done.'

The party broke up and I said goodbye to those wonderful Americans who had given me such a good time.

A letter saying that the American Medical Association appreciated my interpreting was left at the poly-clinic with some gifts of books and magazines, but to my deep annoyance I was told to take them all to the KGB office and they were never returned to me.

On my next encounter with Comrade Ivanov we discussed the Case of the Nylon Stockings. I reported that Dr Clark expressed his views that Russian women were too fat and did not 'inspire sex'. That the meals in the restaurants did not include vegetables and in general were very unhealthy. That Soviet doctors were not interested in his medical books and refused to accept them despite the fact that he had brought them all the way from Massachusetts. If the director and his colleagues had gone to America, he said, the doctors would not only have opened the doors of their hospitals to them but also invited them to go sightseeing and taken them to their homes to show them their family life.

He dismissed me, and going downstairs I crossed paths with the other interpreter from the banquet and knew for the first time that interpreters were all informers of the KGB. Comrade Ivanov was not very smart because what I reported to him was nothing in comparison with what really happened. Bethe and I had invited Dr Clark to the flat of one of her friends, where we sat late into the night talking freely and frankly about everything in Russia and my yearning to return to England, which was never suspected by the KGB.

Before he left Dr Clark proposed to me that I should go to America, where he would pay me 400 dollars a week to work in his hospital. Even such a clever man as Dr Clark could not understand that it was impossible to leave the Soviet Union. The Iron Curtain would not allow it. This was a police state, and if they disliked foreigners coming to their country they even more disliked Russians leaving. I was in correspondence with Ronald Clark for more than thirteen years. He wrote that his tape-recordings and the movies he had made in the Soviet Union were the top show of the university where he lectured, and 'Flora, you were the star.'

To return to my routine, after my American adventure the director of the poly-clinic turned against me and his relative, Clara, with whom I was working in the ear, nose and throat department, was angry with me because she had got the job for me. There were no more friendly talks with her. I tried my best not to excite her because if she got on to her hobby-horse of communist ideology and that I was not grateful for what was being done for me she could make my work hell. And, even though I suffered from the resentment of my colleagues, work had to be done.

CHAPTER NINETEEN

Word of Khrushchev's 'secret speech' exposing Stalin's crimes in February 1956 leaked out, first to Party Members and Chekists and eventually trickling through to the masses. The name Cheka stood for Extraordinary Commission for Struggle with Counter-Revolution and Sabotage. It was the agency of political terror until the early 1920s when the functions were taken over by the NKVD or OGPU and later, in 1956, by the KGB. These old Chekist Bolsheviks, any who by chance had not been arrested during Stalin's purges, were now retired and received generous pensions and got their 'Kremlin rations' at special shops.

I heard that in Moscow there was a special commission for 'rehabilitation', which according to a standard Russian dictionary means 'to be fully exonerated or to prove oneself in the right'. So began the investigation and rehabilitation of millions of innocent victims and their relatives who, under Stalin's paranoiac brutality, suffered up to twenty years and more in labour camps, and also of those who had perished and whose graves remain unknown to this day.

But even in the late Fifties Stalinists still believed in their dead leader and that his condemnation of these victims had been justified, that it was actually true when he proclaimed in the Thirties: 'The enemy is among us.' Nobody really knew how to react, from the KGB to the man in the street, what side to take – Stalin's or Khrushchev's. But certainly there was a general feeling of relaxation and everybody was talking about rehabilitation.

Berthe had a friend, a Chekist, who had retired, and she told him my story and the tragedy of my family and asked him if he could help to hasten rehabilitation for Mother and me. She introduced me to him, a man of about sixty-five, grey-haired and refined and immaculately dressed. His name was Gregory Antonovich. He invited me to lunch in a small restaurant in one of the parks in Kiev and there I told him how I had been writing to the State for many years, but with no results, to find out the whereabouts of my brother. I also explained to him that my mother was living in Yalta and that we were separated as she was not allowed to live in Kiev.

He was kind and considerate and was trying to hold my hand during lunch. 'I am going to help you. Don't worry,' he said. 'It's all in my hands now.' It was becoming dusk and on the way home he began groping with his hands all over my body and said: 'If you are going to be nice to me, I am going to help you.' He was strong and well built, and after some struggle I managed to put my hands on his chest and, with all my strength, shoved him away.

'You dirty old dog,' I shouted. 'How dare you take advantage of me? I am a fool to have confided all my troubles to you. I should have known better than to have believed in a Chekist.' I turned round and walked away. I forced myself to forget the incident and could not even tell Berthe because I did not want to destroy her illusions about her dear friend.

A few months later I received a letter from Yalta in which the Chekist apologised for his bad behaviour and thanked me for not telling Berthe. He wrote to me that I should go to Yalta as he had something very important to tell me, and inside the letter was a cheque for my travelling expenses. I wondered what it was all about, and as it was an opportunity to see Mamma I asked for a week's leave and off I went, notifying Mother that I was coming to see her. On arriving at Yalta, Mamma and I were wildly excited as there was so much to tell each other about the new reconsideration of the cases of political prisoners.

My dear mother was still working in the hotel and we were pleased about that because the job was not difficult and she still had to work another five years to add to the fifteen years she did in prison to make up the twenty years of service that were necessary before she could receive an old-age pension. She would receive from her 600 roubles a month (before revaluation) 50 per cent as a pension.

Out of the 600 roubles my mother earned she paid 300 for rent, including electricity and water rates and use of the kitchen – the lavatory was in the street – and that left her with ten roubles a day for food, half of which bought a loaf of bread and a bottle of milk. A box of matches cost one rouble, and vegetables were only sold in the markets at sky-high prices. Mamma could not possibly have lived without working on the side, and I also sent her money.

I did not tell Mamma anything about Gregory Antonovich as I first wanted to hear what he had to say. He had given me his telephone number, and we arranged to meet. Sitting in the park, I told him: 'I am curious to know why you asked me to come and why you sent me money and I would like to give it back to you.' But he refused to take the cheque back.

'Listen to me and don't ask questions, and don't interrupt until I have finished. I feel very foolish and deeply regret the incident at our last meeting, but it is possible I can facilitate your rehabilitation.'

He was staying at a sanatorium especially for Chekists, top Party Members and the KGB. All the men were dressed in plain white baggy suits, a kind of pyjamas that gave a sense of anonymity to the guests staying there. Part of the cure for the patients was sleeping in tents by the seaside to breathe in the sea air. During one of these evenings of relaxation the discussion revolved around

159

the latest political changes in the Kremlin and in the tragic fate of faithful communists who had been treated appallingly. They also discussed their own experiences. When it came to Gregory Antonovich's turn he spoke with compassion and concern about a little English girl who had been brought to the Soviet Union in her early teens. He told how her mother had spent fifteen years in prison, two sisters and a brother had vanished into the abyss of the Gulag and she had spent five years in a labour camp. The whole family had been accused of being English spies.

When he finished there was silence and he thought that the other men were dozing when a voice said: 'Do you know them? Is she still alive? How could one so young go through all that unbelievable horror?' Gregory Antonovich explained that he did know me and how cruel it was that even now we were not allowed to be together because Mamma had been forbidden residence in Kiev. 'Can't you do something about it?' he asked one of the men.

That 'voice' had been so touched by the whole story that he wanted to meet me.

'You must go home and immediately write a petition to the Public Prosecutor of the Soviet Union,' Gregory Antonovich explained to me. 'State all the facts, dates and details and tomorrow at ten o'clock in the morning deliver it to this man, who will approach you in the grounds of our sanatorium on the first bench to the right when you get into the park.'

I went home and began writing my story. Mother did not say anything as I was always studying something or other. I wrote page after page, and late in the evening I finished my treatise. Early next morning I walked high up into the hills. The air was fresh, and I had a feeling of expectation that something really nice was going to happen. Then my usual scepticism crept in and warned me that it was a good job I had not told Mamma anything in case nothing came of it.

160

I sat down on the first bench in the grounds of the sanatorium as I had been told. At the correct time three men came into view. One was my fat friend. They walked past, looking at me. Then one of them returned, sat down and greeted me.

'Good morning, Flora Alexandrovna. Excuse my taking the liberty but I have heard so much about you from Gregory Antonovich. Your story is extraordinary and shocks me profoundly, and I really think I can help to expedite your rehabilitation. Even now I can't believe that mother and daughter are not allowed to live together.'

Despite his kind words I was on my guard and with some hesitation I asked: 'Where are my papers going to? I have written hundreds of times already for rehabilitation for my family but had no success and I want to clear my mother's name.'

'I work in Byelorussia in the Supreme Soviet of the BSSR,' he explained to me, 'and my brother is in the office of the Procurator-General of the USSR as an assistant prosecutor. If you give your papers to me, I shall be going to Moscow to see my brother and I will hand him your petition.' With a feeling of fatalism I handed over my sacred document. He shook hands with me and said, 'You will soon hear from me, Flora Alexandrovna,' and we parted.

Just inside the gates of the sanatorium Gregory Antonovich was waiting for me. 'How did it work out?' he asked. 'I know that he will help you, Flora, because his brother has a very top official job.'

I did not tell Mamma about my strange encounter as I did not want her to go through any more disappointments. But back in Kiev three weeks later I received an official letter from Moscow stating that my petition for rehabilitation was being reconsidered. The year was 1959, and a month later I got an urgent telegram from mother: 'Rehabilitated. Coming to Kiev.' So the Chekist officer did help me; he fulfilled his promise. He was a real Russian and behaved the way people should to help each other, and perhaps his conscience provoked him to want to do something good and better than the system. The miracle had really happened. The notification that Mamma had received from Moscow stated that she could return to Leningrad where she would receive her official papers.

Mamma had a wonderful time in Kiev as Berthe took her to the opera-house and all the operettas. But meanwhile I had to work even harder and take on an additional nursing job and give a few English lessons to save money for our jouney and have sufficient to pay the rent and buy food when we arrived until we settled down permanently. We had no savings, no pension, nothing except my small salary.

When I told Dimitri that my family was going to be rehabilitated, to my surprise he responded by giving a little party in celebration. Russians always seek some kind of excuse for an extra drink. I did not really believe that he was happy on my account, but it was an event in the family. We were all sitting round with little Vera's *babushka* and Mother in the centre, her face shining with happiness. She had at last come through the pain of realising that her oldest daughter was dead. But she would not put to earth her son Sammy. She waited for him all her life, and I kept up the myth of Sammy being alive all through those years to give her something to live for. She lived until she was ninety, flamed by the fire of hope.

I had my own emotional problems to sort out as I knew it was not going to be easy to leave Dimitri and the baby behind. For the three years that I had been together with Dimitri I really thought that he would marry me, and I knew that Vera accepted me as her mother. Like any other woman I wanted a baby and a husband. When the day of our departure came and the train was leaving Dimitri embraced me for the last time. I looked into his eyes and thought that I needed only one word from him and I would not leave Kiev. He remained silent as he enfolded me with his arms and we stood entwined. Only when somebody shouted from the platform did he let go of me just in time to jump from the moving train.

Sitting with Mamma in our compartment I was deeply distressed, puzzled and hurt. I loved Dimitri very much, but ours had been a strange relationship. Sometimes he was very near to me, at other times far away, holding me at arm's length. I had always been aware of his reticence but could not help wondering why did he not propose marriage to me. It was three years since his wife had died, and from what I heard from his friends he had never loved her but it had been a marriage of convenience because she had her own room in the centre of the city and this was the most golden dowry of all. In Russia everyone wants to escape at some time from the family's cramped living conditions, and it was not uncommon to marry for the convenience of gaining your freedom.

I knew that I was not a good investment as a wife. I had nothing to offer – no 'home' of my own, no money and an invalid mother whom I would never abandon. There was nothing to love me for except myself. Apart from admiring Dimitri for his vitality and his physical attraction, the hours we spent together talking about art, literature and life in general were infinitely tender. There were moments when I sensed that he really loved me, too, but the circumstances were too overwhelming for him to admit it, possibly even to himself. That I was Jewish he found hard to accept in the anti-Semitic climate of that time, but even proof of my mother's innocence as 'an English spy' was unacceptable to him.

This highly intelligent, intellectual man was a real son of the Soviet system and he symbolized the brainwashed attitude of his generation. Just to admit his love for me, because of my past, was a crime in the eyes of the Communist Party, and he was not making one false step. On hindsight I now realize that Dimitri distanced himself from me and denied me the final commitment of making me his wife because I might have hindered his promising career – 'Caesar's wife must be above suspicion.'

Meantime I had written to my friend Annie in Leningrad and asked if she would put us up until we could get something more permanent. The nearer the train came to Leningrad the more I thought about Annie with whom I had been corresponding from time to time since 1941 when we were both in Karaganda. Annie and I worked together there in one of the nurseries for a time, though by profession she was a pianist. She was tall with large spectacles and a stern expression. The complete opposite to me. Stalin's tentacles had reached her when she was living in Leningrad with a violinist whom she was going to marry. What on earth they were sent to prison for I will never know. They went through hell. 'He was the most beautiful violinist,' she told me, 'and he died from hunger, neglect and cold, digging ditches with his hands in Siberia.' Annie had been exiled to Karaganda where she met a man, became his mistress and bore his child, but through her relatives in Leningrad she managed to get permission to return there and had taken up her former career as a pianist.

I had also written to Aunt Mary, whom I had not seen since 1937, and to my cousin Zoya. I had to make my own decision about whether to meet Zoya again or not; so much had passed since our vagabond days together. However, there was a much more important thought in my mind and that was to see my niece Marina, the daughter of my poor sister Cecile, who was now about twenty-four. All these thoughts were popping into my head and vanishing again, and there were other more pressing and practical problems to settle. How were we going to live with so little money and how was I going to manage with Mamma? All that responsibility before me. Could I cope?

I had sent a telegram to Annie, and as the train neared Leningrad I wondered if I would recognize her. I had not

164

seen her for more than eighteen years. The station was crowded as they always are in Russia. Mother was quiet and lost in her own thoughts. She was returning to Leningrad for the first time after twenty-seven years. She had been born there and always remembered the city as St Petersburg. She still remembered all the prices of food during the Tsar's reign, and over the years had constantly recounted to me that you could buy in any shop then bacon at twelve copecks a pound. I did not need to ask what her feelings were now as she returned to the city where she had not only met her fate but had also lost her three children. Her feelings were all in her face.

There was no difficulty in recognising Annie as she saw us and ran towards us. The same Annie, the same spectacles, the same stern expression and the same kind eyes. Arriving at the house a little boy rushed forward and shouted: 'Aunty Flora . . . Aunty Flora . . . *Babushka*.' These words made me feel so good as it was like coming home.

Annie lived in a communal house and we shared her one room, which was not large by any standards. It was divided by two curtains into three living-areas. At one end Mamma and I camped in cramped conditions; the centre area was the communal 'salon' and housed the piano, some bulky furniture and a dignified centre lampshade; and Annie and her son shared the remainder of the room with the door opening on to the passage. There was not one inch of space wasted as under every bed suitcases and bits of this and that were stored. Everything that was said in that room was shared, and what with trumpeting into Mamma's hearing aid and Annie's son practising the violin it was not exactly a haven of peace when I came home from work. But through years of communal living the Russians have come to accept the lack of privacy in their homes and have found a way to make it work. There is simply no other solution for thousands of people who still live in communal houses.

While I was living with Annie little Kiril was studying the violin as she was ambitious to give him a musical education. In Russia nearly every house has a piano and 85 per cent of the population insist on a musical education for their children, whether they are talented or not. Annie was no exception and she paid no heed that her son had no inclination to play the violin. Mother and son were always quarrelling over his practice, which he clearly hated. I noticed that, as soon as Annie went out, hidden under the bed he had a big box of screws, plugs and various-sized batteries. All his stolen leisure was spent soldering something together, and the smell in the room was awful. There were enough ordinary smells without that, but I knew that it was important for him and encouraged him in his hobby. In secret he made me a little crystal radio, and when we were found out there was a big row and Annie was very angry with me. I regretted interfering.

Not far from where we were living, there was an institute of engineering where it was written on the noticeboard that boys interested in radio technology would be accepted for training. Later on I had many discussions with Annie about trying to get a place for her son in that school, but she always insisted that he was a poor scholar and was behind in all his school subjects. It took a month of quarrelling and persuasion to make her change her mind. The institute took Kiril into the school, where he not only received expert training but was also better nourished. Today that same backward child is not only one of Russia's brightest stars in the technical world of science, but is also one of the most eminent scientific researchers in Leningrad. It is sad that, even though he is not a communist, for security reasons I cannot give his name or where he works.

At that time, despite the fact that he was almost illiterate in other subjects, his potential was recognised and he was admitted to the institute as the country was in dire need of technical specialists in every field. Today this would not happen. He would have had to pass a stiff entry examination or bribe the selection board. I doubt that this brilliant man even today knows that his mother was exiled to Karaganda. The relationship between the Leningraders and those poor ex-political rehabilitated prisoners was never easy, and the latter made every effort to conceal their past history because they realised that talking about it could only antagonize the more fortunate citizens. Stalin's shameful past had to be hidden. Annie had also accepted this attitude and was always anxious to protect her son and herself from the lifetime stigma of the Gulag.

CHAPTER TWENTY

On arrival at Annie's place I received a letter from Zoya. It was now 1960, and it had taken me twenty-five years to return to Leningrad. My cousin related that she and her mother had survived the Leningrad blockade; she had worked as a German interpreter and Aunt Mary as a nurse orderly in a hospital. Zoya had married a soldier, an alcoholic, and was bringing up his children. Throughout all the terrible years, the First World War, the Revolution, Stalin's monstrous purges and the Second World War, Aunt Mary had managed to save some of her beautiful old furniture, and her one-roomed flat was in the typical Russian style which has a grandeur of its own. Many less fortunate Leningraders during the siege of 1941–2 had to burn their furniture to keep warm or barter it for food. Because she had remained at the same address Aunt Mary's name was still in the telephone-book and so it was easy to contact her.

The reunion between Aunt Mary and Mamma was sad as she had lost her son Yura in the war and my mother three of her children. The tears flowed. I had always loved Aunt Mary because not only was she the first wife of Uncle Abraham, and knew all the family, but she had also helped me in times of crisis. Aunt Mary symbolised for me all that was Russian and aristocratic. It was not only the furniture that she had preserved but also herself and her beautiful manners. The years of suffering had only enhanced Aunt Mary's serene elegance with her white hair and classical profile.

Now Aunt Mary prepared the tea in the Russian style

from a chubby copper samovar which I recognised as an old friend. This same samovar had got me into a great deal of trouble soon after we arrived from England as one day Uncle Abraham asked me to add water to the samovar. As this was the first one I had ever seen I poured the water into the place where the coke was burning and a burst of dirty steam shot out of the ventilation-holes soiling the white lace tablecloth. My uncle was furious at my stupidity.

The table had been prepared in the Russian style just as Aunt Mary had done for years, with fine porcelain and the specially lipped little saucers for the jam. As we sipped the hot Russian tea we took jam from the saucers with a small teaspoon. Aunt Mary never served tea with lemon but always in this old traditional way with her home-made jams and home-baked small cakes and biscuits.

Now she proposed to take Mamma to live with her, while I remained with Annie. I knew that this was the right decision as Mamma would be more comfortable and she and Aunt Mary had much to talk about covering a lifespan of memories. With her practical approach to life, Aunt Mary advised me that the first thing we must do was to go to the District Soviet of People's Deputies where we must queue for registration and get our names on the housing-list for the rehabilitated.

The first day I went to the office without Mother as she was too tired to stand the strain of those endless queues. This building was situated not far from the Alexander Nevsky Monastery at the end of Leningrad's most famous boulevard, the Nevsky Prospekt. As I was about to enter someone roughly pushed me aside and said: 'Nothing doing.' He was a burly fellow, poorly dressed with a drawn and weathered face, and he continued: 'As if you don't see there is a queue.'

I was embarrassed and explained: 'I am so sorry. I am a stranger here and I don't know the regulations.' It was only then that I looked around at the tired lined faces and realised that they were all ex-prisoners like Mamma and myself.

I put down my name on the list hanging outside the entrance, and my queue number was something like 150, which meant that over the next two days I had to return twice a day to check my number on the list. If I was not present at the exact time my number came up, I would be cut off the list. I do not know how many persons they could accept a day, but these queues were there every day for many years. Standing in the queue speaking to people I found out all the documents that I needed for the first application. I looked at them and thought: Oh my God, what a lot of unnecessary trouble we still have to go through to get one small room.

Whenever I am standing doing nothing waiting in queues I have the habit of counting: the telegraph-posts, the number of people in the queue, the windows in a building, the cars that go by. This silly game releases the tension of waiting. That day I counted about three hundred in the queue, and this was only in one district. In Leningrad there are anything between ten to twenty districts and these queues were not only in Leningrad but, I suppose, all over the Soviet Union. So approximately 300 multiplied by 200 equals 6000, multiplied by, say, 15, which adds up to the grand total of 90,000 ex-prisoners a month in need of housing, pensions and other social welfare. I will always remember those queues of sad grey people who had nowhere to sit for hours on end and only the food they brought with them. It had been declared by law that all rehabilitated people would receive compensation and the return of property which had been confiscated. But that was only on paper. My mother never received a copeck for her fifteen years of slave labour nor for her three lost children.

When at last my turn came in the queue I was admitted into an office. The inspector took our papers and examined them and then asked many questions. 'Where is your mother's birth certificate? Where is your

170

birth certificate? Were you owners of a private house in Karaganda? How many square metres of space did you occupy?'

I answered her quietly, holding back my impatience. 'How can my mother have a birth certificate when she was born in Tsarist Russia, and please let me remind you that she was sitting for fifteen years in prison and all our documents were lost.'

The only reply I got was: 'Why did you come here if you have no documents? Until you get these documents I will not begin your case.'

She went on and on and I could hear the thumping of my heart for sheer exasperation and rage. 'Where am I to get my birth certificate from?' I shouted. 'I was born in Glasgow, in Scotland.'

When I arrived back at Annie's home I sent a telegram with a pre-paid answer, which cost me a fortune, to Karaganda asking the Deputy to confirm that my mother and I had no private house there. I also went to the Foreign Office to ask them to get a copy of my birth certificate from Glasgow to prove that I am the daughter of my mother; but my mother also had to prove that I was her daughter. When all the documents that had been asked of me were ready I took them back to the woman in charge of our district. She told me that they were all correct but she could not give me a *propiska* for Leningrad as I had more than 7.6 square metres in Kiev. She was correct. I did have more than 7.6 square metres but it was in Berthe's room, who had been kind enough to take me in. They were not my 7.6 square metres. The official was clearly bored and in a flat voice continued: 'You must give me a paper proving that you had less than 7.6 square metres.'

I wanted to answer her sarcastically but I checked myself. If I had put her against me with my facetiousness, my future life with Mother would be hanging on a thread at the whim of this woman. Instead I discussed the whole incident with Mother, who told me that I must go back to the Housing Department in Kiev to get it all straightened out. Returning to Kiev – and my money was melting like snow – I had to go through all the different authorities until finally I got to the top Executive Deputies, where I was shown into the office of the head man.

He sat impassively as I explained that I had enjoyed more square metres than allowed by law when I lived in Kiev and because of this Leningrad had refused me a *propiska*. I handed him my petition. He read it and then answered: 'We can't do anything for you. It is the regulations.'

It was then that I lost my temper. 'Why can't you do anything for me? The question is about point six square metres, which prevents me from living with my mother who is sick and in need of my care. Fifteen years she was in prison and now, when we are rehabilitated and should be happy, you are making a fuss about such a small amount. You occupy such a high position but you cannot solve such a small problem.'

I could not control myself. Tears were running down my face and I became hysterical, choking as I sobbed. Again I had not succeeded. Mother and I would be separated because of .6 square metres. Somebody came into the room and before I had time to look two militiamen (police) took me under each arm and pushed me out of the room. When we arrived downstairs one of the men said to the other as they let go of me: 'Let her go to the devil.'

I returned to Berthe exhausted and broken in spirit, until she reminded me of my friend Tamara, who was the wife of the Minister of Culture and a leading interpreter in Kiev. During my stay in Kiev I had given her lessons in English. She was a woman of great authority and had a lot of friends and *blat* (ability to pull strings) and knew everyone of importance in Kiev. I had been too shy to approach her before but now I braced myself and telephoned her and we made an appointment to meet in her home.

When we met, with tears from nervousness I told her my whole story. She listened and then said: 'Why didn't you come to me before? What the hell is all this about? Wait a minute.' She took the telephone and called 'Ivan Ivanovich'. (This name in Russia represents the ubiquitous 'Mr Smith' in England.) Tamara was at her most charming: 'Ivan Ivanovich, how are you? I have been thinking of you a lot lately. We must meet again soon. Do you think that Sidorova is still working in the Council Office? Ah, she is. Will you put me through to her?' There was a slight pause, then Tamara continued in a silky voice: 'Hello, darling . . . what a pity we have not seen each other for such a long time . . . have you got some nice new clothes . . . ? Can you do something for me?'

Tamara put down the telephone and told me to come back tomorrow when she would have some news for me. Next day when I arrived we took a taxi and drove to a large office block. I sat in the reception hall while Tamara disappeared. She returned and took my application and within a few moments arrived back with a signed paper. The document confirmed that I had only seven square metres of living-space: I had been within the regulations all the time!

During my short visit to Kiev I met Dimitri several times. He was getting on very well with his scientific dissertation, and little Vera had grown into a lively little girl. When I left to return to Leningrad they both saw me off and again we embraced and parted but nothing was said. How I loved him, but again I knew in my heart that he would never ask me to marry him. Mamma had been right all the time. It was hopeless and, if I was ever to be happy, I must dismiss the thought of marrying him from my mind.

I returned to Leningrad and was happy to be back with the precious document. The next morning I rushed to the Department for Rehabilitation and once again stood in the queue. When at last it came to my turn I almost danced into the room, flourishing my document triumphantly. The same woman official looked at it and then said: 'This paper is not addressed to me. It is written in your name.' Trying to keep cool and under control, I replied: 'But what is the difference? The paper is from Kiev and the right office. It proves that I had less than the formal requirement.' She was silent for a moment before replying: 'That's all true, but I can't put the paper in the file if it has "Flora Leipman" on it. It has to be addressed to the Council in Leningrad. Get out. Next, come in.'

As this was the days before the copying machine I made a copy by hand as I was frightened to send the original back to Tamara in case it got lost. It meant queueing at the notary's office for his signature as to the copy's authenticity. Then I wrote to the official in Kiev asking her to send me a new document addressed to the District Soviet of People's Deputies. I had no work, and the days seemed endless waiting at Annie's for the reply. I also began to sense that I was becoming a nuisance to them; somehow I had to find a place of our own.

Despite all our problems Mamma and I had a lovely time going to concerts with tickets which Aunt Mary provided. At that time her job was collecting the money from all the kiosks selling theatre tickets, and in this way she was able to get some free. The best concerts in Leningrad were given by the Leningrad Philharmonic Orchestra, and we were always there. During the concert Mother used her hearing aid, which gave out a high piercing screech. Mother did not hear it, but the people around us did and became furious!

At last we received the blue stamp of the *propiska* which allowed us to live in Leningrad. It made us feel proud that we had climbed up the social ladder from Karaganda to Leningrad. Karaganda was awful, Kiev was not bad, but Leningrad was the ultimate of our dreams. Mamma opened her internal passport every few minutes to look at the blue stamp and check that it was really true.

The *propiska* is the key to the whole of the Soviet housing sytem. Without the right *propiska* your life can become hell, destined to live far away from your friends and family in the big cities. It is an accepted fact that many students marry just so that at the conclusion of their studies at one of the big institutes they can remain in that city and not be sent thousands of miles away at the whim of the State. The going rate for a 'marriage of convenience' to get a *propiska* runs into several thousands of roubles, and can cost as much as a year's salary, but the young do it all the time and if they cannot afford it their parents help them. There is another way to live in a big city without having the inconvenience of a phoney marriage and that is to find someone with a private house on the outskirts of a city. For a fee – and in the Sixties it was 300 to 500 roubles – you paid the landlady, who wrote you down on her documents as a relative.

To lose one's *propiska* is like a death warrant. It is a punishment and the loss of all hopes to get good food, better facilities for study, to do research work, see films, festivals, concerts and art exhibitions – all the culture and entertainment to be found in a big city. I have tried many times to imagine what would happen if the *propiska* system were annulled. I can only think that flocks of people, dissatisfied with the dreariness of country life with its bad roads, shortage of interesting food, desirable clothing and entertainment, would flood the cities in a great wave. Moscow and Leningrad suck from the whole of the Soviet Union delicacies like tinned food, chocolates, luxury cakes, delicious sausages and salamis and imported clothing. The vast Russian countryside survives only on mountains of cabbages and potatoes and eternal boredom.

The room we finally received on Nevsky Prospekt was about fourteen square metres, maybe less because of the Old Russian stove jutting out in the corner. The house contained seven separate families, all as usual sharing the same kitchen and bathroom. The corridor was stuffed with everyone's surplus belongings – suitcases, bundles, old wardrobes and unused furniture. To get to the kitchen you had to pass through this corridor, struggling with your shopping through the narrow space. The front door was covered with letter-boxes, bells and instructions. 'One ring for Ivanovich', 'Two rings for Leipman', and so on. The kitchen was very large with a plain wooden floor which I found a curse when my turn came to scrub it. Each family had their own table and cupboard for provisions, but we shared the gas-stoves. Mamma and I had constant difficulties with the lavatory as the door of our room opened on to the outside corridor and collided with the opening of the lavatory door when anyone went in or out. Life in a communal flat is never easy – but, then, only the strong survive in Russia.

CHAPTER TWENTY-ONE

In 1963 I had made a decision, which I had been keeping back as long as I could, to contact my niece Marina, my sister Cecile's daughter. I had written to the different authorities to find out her whereabouts and through the Address Bureau had managed to track down where she was living. The most important and sensitive aspect was how Mamma would react to meeting her only granddaughter for the first time. Cecile's husband Innokenti had married again after her death, and I made an appointment with his sister to visit them. The day came, and I was very nervous. I had not seen my niece Marina since she was two years of age, and by now she was in her late twenties. I took poor Cecile's rehabilitation with me as I wanted to prove her innocence to her daughter.

From the reply I had received I had a strong feeling that my brother-in-law and his sister did not want me to see Marina but had merely submitted to my request because of my forceful letter. For days before I was nervous and tense as I gathered my thoughts. It was not easy to accept that somebody else had brought up my sister's daughter rather than a member of our own family. And, worst of all, that Cecile had died in prison separated from her child and her family. What would Marina be like? Would she accept me? All these thoughts kept racing through my head as I travelled to a beautiful part of Leningrad where she now lived. *En route* I passed 'The Big House' (KGB Headquarters) and brushed back the memories of those wretched people standing in the queue waiting to know about their relatives. When I finally arrived at the house I braced myself as I walked up to the door.

It opened, and a woman I did not recognise stood there. I felt instinctively that she was Cecile's sister-in-law, and my throat choked and my eyes were blurred with tears. Without showing any emotion she invited me into the sitting-room, which was well furnished in typical Russian style. The first item I noticed in the room was my mother's English Singer sewing machine and I began to cry. I could not control myself. I was spluttering with grief. 'Please, Flora, stop it and try to control yourself because Marina is coming now,' the woman said crisply.

Into the room walked a slender young woman, the living image of my sister Cecile. She had the same oval face and large wide-set blue eyes, silky blonde hair. The resemblance was extraordinary.

'Hullo, Aunty Flora.'

'Hullo, Marina.'

Just two words of greeting to span the tragedy of three lives. We sat down in silence, and then in a quiet composed voice Marina said: 'I have some photographs. Will you take them, please?' With that she handed me the little bag that Cecile had once embroidered and that had become faded, crumpled and soiled with the passing of the years. Inside were some sepia-tinted snapshots of my family that had been taken before we went to Russia. There was Mathilde the ballerina with her elegant young feet standing on points, we three sisters looking so happy in our smart cloche hats and fur-trimmed coats, me as a schoolgirl leaning against a tree in Hyde Park, Mamma and Papa who had blessed us with such a fulfilled childhood, and Sammy with his irresistible charm waiting to get to grips with life. Memories came flooding back as I looked at them, of that innocent and happy childhood we had once known in Glasgow.

'Have you got a portrait of your mother?' I asked through my tears.

'No.'

178

'Why?'

'I don't know her.'

Such bleak cold words coming from the mouth of my sister's child. I was shattered. 'But, Marina, she is your mother. You know that Cecile was in prison and died there, but now she has been rehabilitated and proved innocent of any crime. Aren't you happy to see that you have a real aunt? Don't you want to know something about your grandmother?'

'No, I don't want to meet my grandmother. She was a spy.'

'Who told you that? What have they said to you? Haven't you any respect for your own mother?'

'No, because Grandmother was a spy and that is why my mother was arrested. She should not have left England and brought her family here.'

Again there was a deathly silence. I was numbed. I did not know what to do. The situation was so dramatic, so incredibly embarrassing for both of us, that nobody wanted to speak. Marina seemed so far away from me, and I knew that she was repeating not what her heart dictated but what she had been told to say. I tried to reach out to her and brighten the atmosphere. 'Do you like the English language?'

'Yes, I have finished my preliminary English course.'

'Would you mind if I spoke English to you?'

Marina did not speak English very fluently but she had good pronunciation. I said that I should like to come sometimes and help her with her English studies at the Pedagogical College. Her timid reply, 'Yes, Aunty', gave me a warm feeling that she was human after all and that I should be patient. This was only our first encounter. We fixed a day when she should visit us, and back home I prepared Mother for the meeting which must surely be a terrible ordeal for her. To my amazement Mamma was quite calm and my distress was far greater than hers.

Marina arrived at the appointed day and the meeting

went off quite naturally. We had a cup of tea, and Mother invited her granddaughter to go to the cinema with her. Marina answered Mother's questions, and we learned that she had been married and divorced but now had a new fiancé. Mother promised to make her a little dress, and we took her measurements. She appeared to be enjoying herself, and either she was being kind and generous, because of my imploring her to meet her grandmother, or she really was happy with her new-found family. At the end of the afternoon she left and promised to come and visit us again very soon. Mother showed no especial emotion. To her Marina appeared to be just an attractive young woman who had come into her life.

By now I had a situation in one of the poly-clinics in our area as nurses were in great demand at that time. Marina telephoned me at work one day and suggested that I meet her at the Moscow Metro station. I asked her why, but she said that she would tell me when we met. I was slightly puzzled but could I do nothing but wait and see.

Marina and I met as planned and she told me that her father insisted that she should not see us any more. Clearly she was embarrassed, and I really think she was sorry about this decision, but she had been brought up indoctrinated in the Russian way of life with Pioneers, Komsomols, political propaganda. Her first baby-word was not 'Mamma' but 'Uncle Lenin'. At school she only heard 'Long Live Lenin', 'Glory to Our Great Motherland', 'Long Live the First of May', 'Long Live the Great October Revolution', 'Long Live the Soviet Union', 'Long live . . . long live . . . long live', etcetera.

How could she possibly cope with this bolt bursting from the sky? Suddenly to be confronted with a grand-mother and an aunt from the murky background of labour camps. I do not blame her and hold no resentment in my heart that she went out of my life, but I had lost my only close relative, my dear sister's chid. It was the system that had made her reject Mamma and me.

Though we lived in a communal house and had no proper furniture, the shops were stocked with sensible food, and even if my wages were low we managed to get along. It is quite impossible to compare the standard of Russian living with any Western country as the values are so different. Transport was very cheap and in the late autumn Mother was able to return to her beloved Yalta to see her friends. I could afford it, and she deserved the trip to help her forget Marina's betrayal.

In winter, when Mamma returned, without my permission she took on any kind of manual work she could find to help our finances, such as cutting the bread for the restaurant of the October Hotel. In those years, under the Khrushchev regime, there was less discrimination towards ex-convicts. Dr Sananovsky, whom I had met in Yalta and who had previously helped me get a position there, suggested that I work with him as his assistant in the functional diagnostic laboratory at an important scientific research institute. But first he told me that I would have to study on one of those special courses held to train nurses for higher positions. 'You will learn to work on an electrocardiograph and do pulmonological tests,' he explained. 'The work will be very interesting and complicated, and after you have studied for six months or so you will be able to work with me in any department.'

I was not sure that I would like the work as it was far away from where I lived and I told him that I would need time to think it over. But when Mother heard that I had been invited to work at the Institute she was overjoyed. 'Oh, how wonderful! You will meet nice people and all the professors.'

I explained to her that it was far away and that she would be alone for a long time. Her face lit up as she replied: 'Don't worry about me. You have to go there and maybe you can use your English and give lessons to these nice people.'

My main worry was leaving my mother alone for so

long. She was a very ill woman and suffered heart attacks and fainting fits. I was always anxious that she might one day fall down in the street, and who would take care of her? But Mamma, with her indomitable courage, was insistent. She was not afraid to die and often said to me: 'What's the difference where I die – in the street or in my bed? You can give my body to the Institute because we have all died without graves.' That was said in her black moods, but on good days she lived with the belief that her son Sammy was still alive and that one day they would be reunited. I never denied her this hope.

The Institute was situated not far from the blue and white Smolny Institute, which was designed as a boarding-school for the daughters of eighteenth-century Russian nobility. Lenin lived and worked there during the Bolshevik Revolution, and the building is the present headquarters of the Leningrad Communist Party. It is on every tourist's sightseeing tour.

When I arrived at the Institute I took off my coat and was given a uniform, because in those years no one was permitted to enter a hospital without wearing a white coat. I was in awe of the whole situation and felt intimidated as to whether I would be taken on the staff. Everything was worrying me. Had I the right shoes? Was my hair all right? How was I going to behave and what was I going to say? I was excited beyond belief. People bustled around me, nodding acknowledgement to each other with an air of quiet professional efficiency. I had never been in such a place before. I went into the secretary's office, and behind a typewriter sat a woman of my age, well dressed and with beautiful manners. I introduced myself and she asked me to sit down. We immediately began to talk as woman to woman and she plied me with questions. 'Are you Jewish? Where do you come from?' I was careful in my answers, but like all Russian women she immediately began to tell me all about herself and in ten minutes I knew her life-story. She was the wife of a military officer and had moved

182

around a great deal in her army life. She assured me that the director, whom I had come to see, was a marvellous man and that she knew I would be happy working with him. I told her quite frankly that I had never worked in such a place before and that I was desperately nervous. She assured me that I had no need to worry and that I would be taught everything. When the telephone rang she turned to me and said: 'You can go now . . . and good luck.'

I entered what looked like a small conference-room and was greeted by the director. There was no smalltalk and no smiles; it was all very businesslike. I was told that the work was of a scientific nature and that I would have to study hard. At the conclusion of the interview the doctor signed my application. My relief was immense, but I knew that I still had to go through the Otdel Kadrov (Personnel Department). The conversation finished, he said goodbye and I returned to the secretary, who was interested to know the result of my interview. She passed me on to the Personnel Department where I received all the application forms, which I took home to fill in.

I sat with Mother a whole day and night quarrelling about what I should fill in and what I should leave out. I had to give my curriculum vitae, and there were so many awful and difficult questions. Were you ever arrested? What were you arrested for? Were you in prison? When were you rehabilitated? Are you a member of the Communist Party? Have you ever been elected for any position in the Party? Have you ever been abroad? And still more and more questions that drove us mad, as, because of our past, we could not take advice from anyone. We just had to work it out for ourselves, wondering what to admit and what to omit. These questionnaires are perfectly normal procedure in the Soviet Union, and it is only when they apply to oneself that their full importance is realized. They are a curse. I have seen Russian friends of mine struggling with them, and they knew the language well and had no past to hide as we did. If our friends found it difficult, what chance had Mamma and I?

I returned to the Personnel Department sleepless and worried and handed over my papers, my internal passport and my military document. It took several days before my papers were checked and I could hold in my hand again my precious passport, with a new stamp stating that I was now an employee of the Institute. Mother and I almost crushed each other as we hugged in delight.

Next day Mamma starched and ironed my little nurse's cap until it looked brand new, and with an immaculate uniform I arrived for my first day's work.

I worked with five laboratory assistants and one head doctor. The only male was a little man with huge glasses called Gleb who was to become my best friend over many years. My other friend was Galina, and the three of us together made a little circle of our own. We were the smokers and we were always ordered out into the corridor. For the first time in my life I felt able to speak freely with people I worked with as we had complete trust in one another.

Most of the work with our patients was done in the morning, leaving us free in the afternoon to work out the readings and make our reports to send in to the doctors. During this time we used to talk, and they used to laugh their heads off at my bad Russian. I was fluent, but my grammar was shaky and I spoke with a noticeable Scots accent. I used to try to turn the conversation away from my British background, but gradually it began to leak out from the Personnel Department that I had been born in Scotland. I was looked upon as a freak, but this also gave me a kind of special standing because many doctors in the Institute were postgraduates and English was a necessity for their work. Because I could be of assistance to them, all the leading personnel in the Institute – doctors, professors, postgraduates and so on – became interested in me. Out of respect I helped them with their English and I took on teaching the children of some of the laboratory assistants. I felt greatly honoured to help these doctors at a time when Russians were beginning to take an interest in the English language, and it was the first time that I could speak my native tongue among people without a feeling of fear. Though the advanced nursing studies were rather difficult for me, because I had to learn mathematics and physics from scratch as I had never done these before, I felt fulfilled and happy to be part of this Institute. The head of the laboratory used to shout at me when I was doing something wrong, but I knew that she respected my intelligence and curiosity and that it was done in kindness.

The Institute had a large conference-hall where we attended all kinds of medical meetings and of course the usual study of the Soviet Party. Most of the two hundred people who attended these meetings hated them, but I used to enjoy them as it was a way of getting to see people talk. They all had families to go home to, but I had only a deaf mother. I used to look around during the meeting and notice that nobody was really listening. There was always a rush for the back seats where the women sat knitting as wool had just begun to appear on the black market. The men studiously read books tucked inside a medical journal. Some people were even more blatant and just sat muttering to each other. Every now and then there would be a stern call for 'Silence . . . silence.'

People more or less listened to the medical discussions, but when it was a political meeting the time had to be changed from after work until an hour before lunchtime so that there was a captive audience. At these meetings we were told about world events and sometimes there would be a disciplinary discussion about some doctor somehow, somewhere and some time who had done something wrong. Attendance was compulsory, but for most of the women it was just an excuse to have a gossip. I was also allowed to attend the Mestkom (Local Trade Union Committee) but not the Partkom (Local Party Organisation).

But, if Party meetings were only for Members and always held behind closed doors, nothing was secret to non-Party communists because there was always a leakage. The female Party Members gossiping in the kitchen at the Institute could not resist confiding in their best friends the latest Party news, and the best friends of course told her best friends. The male Party Members spilled hints and thoughts to their drinking companions as they knocked back their vodkas!

My wages at the Institute were very low, sixty new-style roubles a month, as I was classed only as an assistant laboratory worker, but with my English lessons bringing in twenty-five roubles a month and Mother's wages of forty roubles we were able to live better than we had done before.

Mother used to bring vegetables, bread and, even more important, pieces of meat home from the restaurant, which she told me the head waiter had given her as a bribe to keep her mouth shut. It upset me tremendously and I used to say to her: 'But, Mamma, why are you bringing these things home? If you are caught coming out of the hotel and they ask you to open your bag and there sits a big fat piece of meat, the authorities will think nothing of your grey hair and your seventy-four years. You will be put into prison and I will be kicked out of my beautiful job.'

'But everyone steals there,' she protested. 'Besides, they give it to me. I don't steal the stuff.' It was no use arguing with her. She was deaf, her hearing aid was not working then, and my comments only annoyed her. Conflicts with Mamma only complicated my life.

CHAPTER TWENTY-TWO

After a while Mamma did not work any longer, because of her declining health, but when she was well enough she went to the Nevsky Prospekt and sat in a little square which was dominated by a statue of Catherine the Great surrounded by her lovers and courtiers. There Mamma would sit dreaming about Old Russia beside other old-age pensioners like herself, talking the hours away and exchanging their experiences of life. She became acquainted with the mothers of Nina and Dasha, friendships that were to last for many years.

The men pensioners occupied themselves playing chess, dominoes and draughts. Summer gave them life, and the possibility to exist in reasonably good spirits, but the winter was an ordeal as living conditions were so cramped that they felt unwanted and a nuisance in the family flat and there was no escape outside because of the bitter cold. To justify their existence, and to help the family, they stood for hours in queues for food. Most of the queues you see in Russia are composed of grey-haired pensioners. They are reviled and cursed by many of the workers simply because they buy all the best provisions, leaving the shops empty by the time younger people go to shop after their work.

Nina and Dasha had graduated from the Institute of Foreign Languages and were both working in publishing, translating Russian into English, and when we were together we always spoke English. They advised me to buy a radio so that I could hear the BBC. Mamma was against buying one as it meant almost three months' pay, but I was stubborn and bought one on instalments. As my mother was deaf, and she was oversensitive in her jealousy that I could listen and she could not, I invited a younger engineer to install a special device with an earphone so that Mamma could listen, too. Because she could not hear the doorbell I arranged that a red lamp would flicker on in our room which she could see.

The World Service of the BBC broadcasts three hours later than the Russian programme. Though the jamming was a terrible nuisance, the later I listened in during the night the clearer it was, and I was in seventh heaven.

But meeting English-speaking Russian people, going to the library and reading English literature and with my radio listening to London made me even more aware that I did not belong here. Even if my life in Russia was now more bearable, I still had nothing in common with the Russian people and the environment. Even so, it never once entered my head to apply for an exit visa for England – first, because I knew that they would never let Mother go and, secondly, because I felt that it was too risky a venture to expose myself when life was at last reasonable.

In the early 1960s many posters appeared in the streets of Leningrad inviting medical workers and members of other professions to go to the Soviet Far East to the Chukot National Area. The conditions were for a three-year contract which included money in advance for travelling expenses. The wages were higher in the ratio of one to five the farther east and north you went and, most important, your residence permit in Leningrad would be reserved. I used to joke about it, and the girls would say: 'You are daft. As if you haven't had enough of the cold in the camps.' But the more they teased me the more determined I became. I was sick of living in communal flats sharing the lavatory and the bathroom; I needed money to put into a co-operative building so that Mamma and I could buy a one-room flat.

Some of my friends were living in much worse conditions. Gleb, who worked with me in the Institute, lived in an attic where the water streamed down the walls when it rained. There was only room for a bed, a chair and his books, and clothes lay on the floor. And he was a *scientist*. My friend Galina lived in a basement flat which was damp, dirty and cold, and the walls were black with grime. She had to go out into the courtyard to get water from the only tap available to keep her four children clean. She had worked for twenty years in our Institute and she had no hope of receiving a flat from her work or from any other authority.

I was not going to live like them. I resented that life and I was determined to live decently in a normal flat like that in which my parents had brought us up in Glasgow.

After nights of uncertainty I came to the conclusion that I would tell Mother of my decision. She was delighted because one of our neighbours, with whom Mamma was very friendly, had a daughter who had come back from the Far East, where she had been working for many years, with a pocket full of money – big money, but not easy money. Besides, Elena from Yalta was coming to stay with us as she had not seen Leningrad for many years. My mother would be taken care of as these two women got on very well together, and the three of us living together in one room would have been too much; an impossible situation.

I went to the office of the 'Voluntary Society for Work in the Far East' where I met a nurse and a doctor whom I knew, as we had worked together in an outpatients department in Leningrad. We received our papers and instructions for our journey and living in the Far East, and a few days later I collected my ticket and money.

So I was really going to the north, and Nina and Dasha began joking about my new wardrobe. 'You need to make fur-lined knickers and bras,' they said, 'and a fur mask to cover your nose because it is always blue when it is cold.' They brought out an encyclopaedia, and with maps and rulers we explored the Far East. This occupied us for days, besides shopping for shawls, *valenkis* and warm underwear. Mother lined my coat with padded cottonwool.

I had to apply to my director for leave of absence from my work. He had no objection to my leaving but he was a little surprised that a woman turning forty years of age should undertake such a dangerous venture.

Everything in my life seems to happen in April. I was born in April, my mother was arrested in April, I was arrested in April, and now it was early April and I was going to the end of the world. I suppose I am a romantic, and I am certainly a great lover of nature. I always wanted to have the experience of seeing the wonderful lights of the aurora borealis of the North Pole.

With a rucksack on my back and bulging suitcases, Mamma and the girls saw me off at the Moscow station. The girls had pinned a funny little donkey on my back and, wishing me good luck, they shouted: 'Come back with a millionaire husband but do not run away to America.' As I embraced Mamma and Elena I looked into my mother's eyes. It was as if they were saying to me: 'Sorry, Flora, I am always pushing you into something.'

Our journey was long, boring and monotonous. During the journey all the people did was eat, drink vodka, smoke their heads off and play *durakee* (an old Russian card game). Seven days is a lifetime together in a train. There was no past, no future, only the present. The conversation stuck to one topic only: that life was dreary and unadventurous on the mainland – which was how the people living in Alaska referred to the vast continent of the Soviet Union – and of how they were going to work in the Cold North and return after three years bulging with money. My only diversion was the interesting cities that we passed through: Kazan, Sverdlovsk, Chelyabinsk, Omsk, Novokusnets, Irkutsk, the famous Lake

Baikal with its blue waters shining in the sun. It is the deepest lake in the world, over 1400 feet above sea-level, and fed by more than 300 tributaries tumbling from the mountainside. Then Birbydzhan, Chita and finally Khabarovsk.

On the seventh day we arrived at Khabarovsk on the banks of the Amur river, and there were no complications in getting to the hotel where we had to stay for further orders. The hotel was of the usual standard with six to seven people sharing one room and a lavatory and washstand in the corridor. The situation for me was horrible. When we went to the restaurant it was full and all the men were drunk and many of the women also. These people seemed to be outcasts from society. The women were looking for men, the men for gold and women to feed them. They were the flotsam and jetsam of life, all longing to escape from something. Money was in their blood with the same fever as in the old Gold Rush days in the American Wild West in the 1880s.

The woman who was sleeping next to me was called Catharina. She told me that she had a baby who was mentally handicapped. Her husband had abandoned her and she was here to get away from her ill baby and to earn money to support herself. She was a nursing orderly, a typical plain Russian woman. She had a coarse face with a blank expression but she was young and strong. For two nights she did not sleep in her bed, and returning in the morning she looked soiled and worn out. She would flop on the bed fully dressed and immediately fall asleep. Men would come into the room looking for her and I had a great deal of trouble fending them off to allow her to have any sleep at all. She was one of those women who make themselves always accessible to men, like a bitch in season. This was my new friend.

From Khabarovsk we were told that we were going to fly to Magadan, which was still farther north. The weather was still cold, and I was glad to get away from Khabarovsk with all those drunkards. I cabled to

Mamma to tell her that I had arrived safely and that I was on my way to Magadan.

Our flight to Magadan was in a small plane with about twenty-five seats. Catharina and I sat together, and she made eyes and flirted with all the men in the plane, not omitting the two pilots, who were walking up and down the aisle seeing to the passengers as there was no stewardess. During our flight Catharina went to the 'loo' situated at the front of the plane. She did not come back for a long time and I was worried. When she did return her face was flushed, her shawl dishevelled and her hair tousled as with cast-down eyes she took her place beside me. The male passengers were grinning and hurtling dirty words at her. I felt squeamish when she laughingly told me bluntly that she had had sex with the radio operator on top of the mailbags.

The flight was terribly bumpy, and it was five hours before we arrived at the airport at Magadan. The city is situated on a bay of the Okhotsk Sea and is a port. This spot was chosen in 1933 as the future capital of the entire north-east of Siberia. It was built by thousands of prisoners – Siberian farmers, Don and Kuban Cossacks, Ukrainian and White Russian peasants. When the labour needs of the rising city were filled the new arrivals were sent into the *taiga* (wild fir forests) to build the long motor highways to the Kolyma goldfields. Magadan was called 'The Capital of the Slave Empire', and the prisoners were transported there packed in the holds of ships in conditions similar to those of the cargoes of black slaves exported from the Ivory Coast to the American ports a century back. Nowadays the city has large modern blocks and wide tree-lined streets, and the population is half voluntary and half ex-convicts. They work in coal and gold mining, fishing, fur farms and administrative services.

Settling into the hotel Catharina and I went shopping in the town. We saw tomatoes and cucumbers at from five to ten roubles a kilogram so early in the year and were amazed to see the housewives buying plenty, which showed that they had a great deal of money to spend.

I had a letter of introduction from a doctor of our Institute to her sister in Magadan. She was married to an engineer and had three children, and they had been living there for many years. Her husband's average monthly pay was about 800 roubles and his wife received about 600 roubles doing office work. Every three years they got six months' paid leave which they spent in Leningrad. They had a luxury modern flat with fine furniture and every convenience and enjoyed comforts they would never have had if they had remained in Leningrad.

The first night with my new friends we talked for hours. They were thirsty for news of their relatives, and I threw a lot of questions at them about life in the north. They tried to persuade me to stay in Magadan, but I was determined to go on with my mission.

Catharina and I went to check our documents at the Centre for Volunteer Workers where our passports were returned with a new green stamp, a border visa, and we were given air tickets to our place of destination and 'an assignment to work' in a children's sanatorium in the Chukot National Area.

April was the worst time to fly in that part of the world because of the uncertain weather conditions, but we managed to take off between storms. However, we had only been flying for a few hours when the plane had to make an emergency landing. From the airfield to the transit barracks was a long way, and we were made to carry our two suitcases. It was dreadfully cold as, dragging our luggage behind us on the snow-covered ground, we saw two low buildings banked with snow and out of one a chimney with a spiral of pale smoke that showed it was a dwelling.

We opened the door with great difficulty to a shout: 'Shut the door, you bastards; you are letting the warmth out.' Exhausted and dispirited we came into the building.

About a hundred people of the same type as I had seen from the beginning of my journey were lying on bunks, and the barracks was thick with smoke. Catharina and I squeezed in between some men who made room for us. There was a kettle on the stove in the centre of the room where we could make tea. The lavatory was outside, a wooden hut divided by a partition: I suppose meant for men and women, but the doors were missing. Inside the shack was a wooden platform with two holes cut out, and from there frozen excrement stood up like two stalagmites. No one used the lavatories and people crouched down anywhere, as far away from the barracks as they could, nobody paying any attention to this normal function. The lavatory probably still stands there today as a monument of Soviet socialistic technology.

In this polar cultural centre of Nicholaeyvsk we were trapped for ten days. There were days when in the early morning about six o'clock, or even earlier, we were woken by the pilots and told: 'We are going to fly now.' Out we piled, pushing and shoving and carrying our suitcases. We would just get settled down in the plane, everyone saying, 'Thank God we are leaving,' as the sense that we were going to fly into the unknown gave us a great thrill, when suddenly there would be a shout from the pilot: 'Out you go . . . all of you.'

We would look at one another in amazement. 'Why? . . . Why?' some brave voice enquired.

'Get out . . . that's all.'

Everyone ran as fast as they could back to the barracks, lugging their luggage, to get there first and grab a place near the stove. Sometimes I used to steal out of the barracks to get away from the fetid atmosphere and breathe some clean air. What amazed me, and was to continue to amaze me during my stay in the north, were the skies. The clouds whirled by like a kaleidoscope and at such speed that it was impossible to say what colour they were. There was a mystical quality

194

about that vast canopy above. Some days the skies were El Greco, grey, black and menacing; and at other times they were luminous with brilliant colours. It was a feeling of awe, fantastic in the sense that you were at the end of the earth and if you went any further you would fall into space.

CHAPTER TWENTY-THREE

Our assignment was in Ozernaya, part of the Chukot National Area. The majority of the people are Chukchis, about two thousand Eskimos in the coastal settlements who live by reindeer-breeding and hunting fur-bearing animals, especially ermine and squirrel. They also hunt walrus and seal, and in the summer wild geese are caught for food. Dogs and reindeer are used for drawing sledges and are important domestic animals. The Chukchis came under the control of Russia in the eighteenth century. The lure of furs, to which was added the lure of gold, continued as strong as ever into the present century. In 1904 as much as £200 was paid by London furriers for a perfect black fox pelt. In 1898 traders in north-eastern Siberia paid trappers the equivalent of £8 for a silver fox, fifteen shillings for a polar bear and a penny for a pure white ermine.

At last we were airborne from Nicholaeyvsk to Anadyr Airport, two to three hours' flying. Tired and hungry, after waiting in a cold shed with freezing water covering our ankles as the great thaw had begun and the whole area of the airfield was awash with water, with wet feet, miserable, we took our last flight that day to the Gulf of Kresta.

Kresta was a tiny town with a small landing-field. We were now in Soviet 'Alaska'. There were three of us now: a doctor, Catharina and me. Using the telephone from the airport control centre, the officer telephoned to the Ozernaya tuberculosis sanatorium to inform them that we had arrived. The head of the sanatorium was rather surprised but after some time she sent a truck to fetch us. It took about two hours, sitting in the back of an open lorry on a wooden plank. We were surrounded by mountains covered with snow from which streams of gushing water pounded down the mountainside covering the road with a river of water. It was a new and exciting experience. We were frightened that the force of the streams would overturn the lorry. We made many stops until we reached the Medical Centre, where we drove up to the entrance of the main office and were met by the director. She was a typical Russian woman, a strong bully who had climbed the ladder through her ability for organization rather than through intelligence. She was abrupt, strict and to the point. 'I am sorry, there is no vacancy for nurses. For the doctor we have a place, and we have a place for a cleaner.' This Catharina immediately decided to accept. She offered me the post of a teacher with pre-school-aged children. She told me that I would get less pay in this job than as a trained nurse, but there was no option.

And so I became nursery-school teacher to a group of thirty children, Chukchis and Eskimos who all spoke Russian but also their own national tongue. Their ages ranged from three to seven years, and they all came from families with a history of tuberculosis. These children had been taken from their mothers when they were born and kept under the control of the sanatorium. It was a big medical programme to save this Chukchis and Eskimo generation there from extinction, as 100 per cent of the population in that national area were infected with tuberculosis and the eye disease trachoma.

Apart from my duties as a teacher I was part of a team of medical staff who went out in the summer into the tundra where the reindeer were pasturing on the mossy undergrowth which provided them with valuable food. The Chukchis lived in *yurtas* (reindeer-skin tents like Indian wigwams). There we examined the families, especially pregnant mothers. If there were newborn

197

children, we would take them away. This was sometimes difficult as the mothers naturally resented giving up their children and would hide the babies under piles of reindeer skins. The main mission of our team was to separate the newborn baby from the mother as soon as possible.

The tragedy was that most of the mothers were alcoholic like the men. From childhood to old age (forty-five) they were saturated with alcohol and they all died young. Because of alcoholism, syphilis, tuberculosis, the babies were born contaminated with all these diseases, and only 50 per cent of the babies we took back to the sanatorium survived.

The children were under medical control from birth until they were sixteen years of age, and there were about two hundred in our Medical Centre of different ages. For the older children there were schools where they studied Russian and their own language. They were well provided for, and besides food and medical care received from the Mainland fine clothes, boxes of toys. They had everything, even oranges which they threw away and did not eat. It was not their food. Feeding them was complicated as they preferred salted raw fish and reindeer meat.

Observing the children during my work, putting them to bed, dressing them, occupying their minds, supervising their mealtimes, I noticed that toys did not interest them. When we opened a new box of toys there would be great excitement, but within half an hour the toys were lying about without arms and legs or wheels. They did not like to paint, write or read. They had no talent or interest in anything. They were the dullest children I had ever met, in total contrast to the children of Karaganda. I could not do anything with them, only be patient, kind and love them. We tutors had great difficulties, but I would never insult the children and they understood and respected me. When we played in the tundra in the summer all the children would escape from the other

198

tutors but mine always stayed with me. We gathered the tiny wild flowers and made them into posies and gathered the golden *moroshka* berries and made wreaths for our heads. They felt a warmth in me like a mother, but they were difficult, always quarrelling among themselves, and they would not stop at drawing a knife if they became angry. The violence in these children was awful.

Each child had a plain iron bed, but as they were not used to sleeping in beds – only the ones who had grown up in the sanatorium – they all slept huddled together on one because this meant that they did not have to make the others in the morning. In their family life they had slept in the *yurtas* all together on mounds of reindeer skins.

I worked from 9 am until 5 pm, and my evenings were free. Our only recreation was taking the bus to Kresty, which came out once a day, and doing a little shopping. The shops were filled with souvenirs and furs. In the evenings we went to the cinema, which was also used as a meeting-place and for dancing. Our community of five hundred was mostly women who worked in the various departments of the Medical Centre. The doctors lived their own lives and the nurses theirs.

The men who came in from the surrounding district for the dancing in the evening were miners, prospectors, manual labourers – rough coarse men who only came to the dances to pick up women. Even walking long distances, because they had no transport, did not deter them. I got used to the fact that on Saturday and Sunday nights the women in my dormitory shared their beds with men. These were not permanent liaisons but usually one-night affairs – a matter of convenience on either side. The director of the sanatorium did her best to control the morality of her staff, but it was hopeless. We had to live with it and, thank God, I was a good sleeper.

I sent sixty roubles every month to Mother, but the letters took a long time arriving in Leningrad. As a tutor I could eat with the children and so save money. We

199

mostly ate reindeer meat, which was sweet and I liked it. To occupy myself I had taken with me some drawing-paper and a set of watercolour paints. Someone lent me an old bicycle, and I had my own camera. I used to leave the sanatorium and ride out into the tundra along the rutted roads. I found places where there were still remnants of barracks dug out under the earth which were the remains of the old labour camps. It was very sad to look at these relics, and I always thought of poor Sammy. Maybe he had died here. I would pick small flowers from the tundra and place them on this grave-yard.

When the weather was good I went far away on my bicycle to take photographs and to paint the volcanic mountains and those extraordinary skies. I had met some of the Eskimo parents, who used to come to see their children, and in talking to the fathers I asked them lots of questions: 'How can you live in the cold all the time?' 'Is the American Alaska far away from here?'

They explained to me how some of the Eskimo families had relatives in America and when the Bering Strait was frozen in winter they travelled to see them on their sledges in a few hours, but they were always afraid the Russian border guards would shoot them.

'Very bad Russian man shoot Eskimo . . . *poof, poof.*'

The Eskimo parents admired me for what I was doing for their children and were my friends. They warned me to be very careful when I went far away because of the 'bad winds' – blizzards that carried people away.

'Bad wind . . . man standing . . . no man.'

I really believed them because I had heard a lot of stories of men being lost in the Arctic.

It was becoming colder, and the winter winds were blowing. One day we were told that we were all to go to the director's office for a check-up by the Militia Boarder Guard. At first I was not worried, but waiting for my turn I heard the girls say that this had never happened before; usually they did not come to the sanatorium but everyone was ordered into Kresta. This put me on my guard because I had had no encounter with the Secret Police since my American incident in 1957 in Kiev.

I entered the room and sat down. There were two young men in military uniforms, and the senior began to interrogate me. 'Why did you come to the north? We have been watching your steps since you left Leningrad.'

'As everybody else, I came for higher wages. I want to buy a flat for my mother and this was the only chance to save enough money.'

'What were you doing three days ago out beside the old camps? Why are you always walking or cycling in the direction of the border?'

'I was not looking for the border. I was just searching for beautiful scenery to paint.'

'Yes, but you were photographing the electric power station, and we would like you to give us your camera. We have been watching you and we want you to tell us the truth. You have been speaking to the Eskimos. Thinking of going over the border?'

'What nonsense. I went there to paint.'

'But we don't believe you. There was another reason, and you are going to tell us.'

Though he was firm in his questioning, he was not frightening, and for once I felt quite at ease in front of the KGB. The second man went with me to get the camera and took out the film. Now I realized that from the moment I had left Leningrad all my movements had been under the surveillance of the KGB. The officer had made a slip when he said: 'We have been watching your steps since you left Leningrad.'

This is how the KGB works. When I gave in my papers to the Special Department for Voluntary Work in the North I had forgotten that this all went through the Special Department of the KGB. I suppose everything about me was known to them including my association with the Americans in Kiev. Again the syndrome of fear

201

crept under my skin. I made up my mind to be as polite as possible and remember what I had been taught in the camps – that it was better to say nothing until you had been asked.

'We will continue this conversation in my office in Kresta tomorrow morning at 10.30 am,' he told me. 'If there is no bus, come the following day but come quickly.'

Our little sanatorium was situated about fourteen kilometres from Kresta, and I was lucky that the bus came in time that day so that I arrived in time to keep my appointment. We exchanged greetings, which was unusual. He asked me to sit down and – what was really unexpected – he smiled at me and I returned the smile.

'Flora Alexandrovna, you are a clever woman and you know perfectly well that the check on passports was the reason for our seeing you.'

He was from the second generation of KGB. More intelligent, better read and more subtle than I had previously encountered.

'Why should a woman like you come to such a place? I don't believe that you came here for an extra fifty roubles. I know the terrible conditions you live under with these women and their men. I also know that you did work for the KGB in Kiev. Have you noticed anything unusual among your companions? Did anybody confide in you that they wish to go over the border?'

His attitude and his repeated questioning made me very angry. Why? Why? Why? He made me so furious that I lost my temper and I shouted back at him: 'Why can't I go where I want to and do what I want? You invite us here to work. I am a qualified nurse with more than twenty years' experience and they don't even use me as a nurse and, excuse me, I am living in a brothel.'

Suddenly I looked at him and thought: My God, what are you doing, Flora? If they have nothing against you now, you are shouting at a KGB man only doing his

202

duty; this could be labelled 'hooliganism'. I shut up and we looked into each other's eyes.

He calmly said to me: 'I know that the position of working here is very difficult because a lot of people come without a contract and take up the jobs. I will see you in two days' time at eleven o'clock as you are too upset for any further conversation now.'

At this time Catharina was having so many love-affairs, with breaking windows and jealous quarrels between the men – she would be sleeping with one man when another pushed down the door to get in. The director wanted to dismiss her, but I pleaded for her as she really was a good soul and a very good worker. She was allowed to remain under certain conditions. How and where she found her miner I cannot imagine, but before I could count one, two, three, she was off with him and I never saw her again.

At my next interview with the KGB man he told me that I was very lucky as there was a vacancy for me as a nurse in the children's nursery where I would have a little room to myself. I thanked him and I could not believe my luck. He told me to return to my director, who knew all about the arrangements. Though I knew I could never settle in the north, at least my living conditions were much better. The nursery was warm with central heating, like all the houses, and was not far from a settlement where the administrative staff lived. They were normal houses with comfortable well-furnished flats and every convenience.

During our recreation period I went to a fishing party on the Gulf. Ten of us from the sanatorium set out early in the morning in a land-rover. The noise of the land-rover driving over the rough stony ground was so deafening that we could not hear one another, but one thing I did realise was that our fishing expedition was illegal as it was the season when the *keta*, Siberian salmon, were spawning.

When we arrived at the beach in the dreadful biting

cold we built a fire from driftwood. Meanwhile the men were putting out the nets into the sea, and when the time came we saw shoals of salmon passing by and all quickly helped to pull in the nets. We caught about twenty to thirty fat salmon half a metre long. The Chukchis guide cut the bellies open and squeezed the sack of eggs out into a jar and we began salting them to make our own red caviare. The rest of the fish we took home and some we used to make a fish soup which is a delicacy of that area. We sat around the fire with our soup and drinking vodka. This was all highly illegal, but it was fascinating.

Winter with its ghastly blizzard winds had arrived. The cold was terrific, and into my little room through the small joints between the window-frames the snow piled on the floor. The wind was so penetrating that there was no protection from it. The room became so cold that I had to sleep in my warm coat and *valenkis* with two warm blankets piled on top of me. To read in bed I wore gloves and wrapped up my face so that only my eyes were visible.

We tried our best to keep the nursery warm but we had to take the children out for some fresh air. We dressed them in so many layers of clothes that they could not stand on their feet, and taking them out into the playground in our arms one by one they looked like little bundles as we placed them there. One frosty day when everything appeared to be quite calm, although −30°C, a sudden fierce gust of wind from nowhere swept the children off their feet and some of them went flying in the air as if in a whirlpool. We were so frightened that we would lose them but thanks to God, the wind passed and they all fell to the ground about four metres outside the playground. It was the fright of my life, but owing to their clothing they were unhurt.

Snow drifts closed the bus route to Kresta, which meant that we were closed in at our sanatorium. The KGB man did not bother me any more. I suppose he lost interest in me because what information could I give about whom? The babies? The cook and staff whose families were feeding off the nursery rations?

In the Polar Circle the transitional seasons of spring and autumn are almost nonexistent; in some parts the winter lasts eight months and the sun does not rise above the horizon for about three months and does not descend for the same time in the summer. The long dispiriting winter days, punctuated by only a few hours of light before dark gloom descends, envelop man and beast alike. That man survives at all in these conditions is a triumph of the human spirit.

The colder it became the more miserable I felt, and I was lonely as I had no friends. I stuck on until early spring, then cancelled my contract, refunded the Volunteer Centre who had employed me 500 roubles, telegraphed Mother that I would soon be home. My return flight was through Kresta, Pevek, Moscow to Leningrad. It took me about twenty days to get home owing to meteorological conditions, staying in the most horrible transit barracks of the Soviet Polar Circle.

Mother and the girls met me at the airport. I felt foolish, that I was a failure and had run away from difficulties. The girls laughed and teased me, asking if I had met my millionaire, but Mother's attitude towards me had changed. I know that I am a very dominating person, and by nature Mother was independent. My North Pole odyssey had been necessary and beneficial for us both.

CHAPTER TWENTY-FOUR

All my colleagues at the Institute were pleased to see me again and tried not to hurt my feelings by telling me to my face that I was a fool to have gone to the Far East with my illusions of Big Money. I had made a blunder and I knew it, but I had good friends in Leningrad and I was glad to be back.

In September 1964, I was summoned to the office of the director of our Institute. Would I, he asked, be so kind as to act as interpreter for medical visitors from England? I should be given four days' leave from my laboratory duties and I was to go to the stockroom and choose a brand-new white coat and starched hat.

Next morning the staff was also all starched up in clean uniforms and the Institute was polished from top to bottom and in every corner – *pakazukha* (showing off) at its highest level. I approached the motorcar as it pulled up outside the main entrance and welcomed our guests, Dr John Edge and his wife, Mrs Brigid Edge, introducing myself as their interpreter and telling them that my name was Flora. I ushered them upstairs, smiling and talking, and immediately I felt there was a friendly rapport. The director and the secretary were standing stiffly outside the office waiting to receive them. Then in the director's office we began with the usual social smalltalk, which then flowed into the subject of gerontology.

Dr Edge had gained a three-month travelling fellowship from the World Health Organisation to study the needs of the elderly in Scandinavia. As he felt that his study would not be complete unless he compared the facilities there with those provided in the Soviet Union he had come on to Leningrad. Mrs Edge helped her husband with the secretarial work. It was very complicated for me to translate from one language to another on a medical subject with which I was not conversant but, with the director helping in his bad English, it made us all laugh and relaxed the tension. In this friendly atmosphere tea and cakes were served on beautiful bone china from the sideboard of the secretary's house. Showing off is showing off!

I was to accompany Dr and Mrs Edge and a professor from our Institute in visits to two homes for the elderly. One was called 'The House for Veterans of Art' (ballerinas, actors and opera singers) and the second 'The House for Veterans of the Revolution', and Dr Edge admired them as they were exceptionally well run by Russian standards. After our official visiting I took them to the Hermitage to see the superb collection of European painting and modern works, as Mrs Edge herself was a painter.

As usual when speaking about myself to people, I never told them that I had been in a labour camp but merely that my family had suffered during the Leningrad siege. There was such a social gulf between us that I could not bring myself to tell them about the camps that I had seen. These horrors were my own, and I could not share them with anyone. I had been brainwashed with fear that to expose the camps was a crime.

The Edges wanted to go shopping, so I took them to Gum, the largest department store, where the doctor wanted to buy a typical Russian fur hat, but when I asked the salesman for his size he told me that they did not have it. I felt embarrassed that I could not please my countrymen. Dr Edge is a tall, well-built, fine Englishman, and in size the Russians cannot compete with him. I braced myself and firmly told the salesman: 'These are foreigners. He is an English professor, and you *must* get him his size.' The word 'English' worked like magic, and after a short time a hat was produced from nowhere. The salesman was impressed to hear the English language, and we left all smiles. To this day Dr Edge still has that fur hat.

When I parted from my new friends it took time for me to overcome my nostalgia for England. Dr and Mrs Edge were the most wonderful people in the world for me, and who knows for what spiritual reason they had been brought into my life?

Times had changed with the 'Swinging Sixties', and people brushed aside politics to dive head over heels into Western music, the Beatles and Elvis Presley. French films with stars like Yves Montand, Jeanne Moreau and Gérard Philippe were blazoned across the screens of our cinemas and their performers the Soviet Union's honoured guests. Marilyn Monroe, Brigitte Bardot and Sophia Loren were the pin-ups for women of all ages. Russia in those years was like a rich Christmas pudding filled with capitalistic 'goodies'. Queues stood day and night along Nevsky Prospekt to see films such as *Some Like It Hot* and the Norman Wisdom comedies. Lovers of classical music – including myself, Nina and Dasha – stormed the Tchaikovsky Conservatory to listen to the handsome young American pianist, Van Cliburn, who captured our hearts playing Tchaikovsky's First Piano Concerto, my favourite piece. After his interpretation I had a new understanding of this great work.

I was never interested in modern Soviet literature as I am an admirer of Russian and European classics. I am rather old-fashioned in my views, especially in art, preferring the seventeenth and eighteenth centuries. Rubens is one of my favourite painters. Thank the Lord that not all Russia was red banners and slogans! There was the Hermitage, built in the eighteenth century and with its magnificent art collection of the late eighteenth and nineteenth centuries. My happiest times were spent there all alone looking at these beautiful pictures.

The annual conference for occupational therapy for the disabled, and other medical research work, which was held every December at the Institute, brought doctors from all over the Soviet Union. There I met again my friend Dr Petrauskas from Lithuania, who said that he would like me to join the staff of his Institute in Vilnius.

'Flora,' he said, 'we need specialists like you with your knowledge of functional diagnostics. You would be very helpful in training nurses in this special field, for which, if you come, I will pay you extra. I remember your communal-flat problems, so I am offering you accommodation. My brother has a small one-roomed flat, and it is empty as he is working in the north and he will not be back for five years or more. The flat is there for you to take.'

I thanked Dr Petrauskas and told him that I would talk it over with Mamma. The family conference consisted of Mamma, Nina and Dasha, and after listening to my proposal for leaving Leningrad the only one who raised her hand in voting 'for' was Mamma. My friends only raised their eyebrows and shoulders 'against'.

'You Leipmans are like that. You cannot stop anywhere for more than five years. You are rolling stones. Something always pushes you on,' Dasha laughed. Other friends and colleagues felt the same. 'Flora,' they said, 'can't you and your mother be happy here in beautiful Leningrad? Here you have all the culture that a big city can provide as well as all the entertainment that you could wish for. How can you leave your beloved Hermitage? You made one colossal blunder going to the north, so don't make another. You will not even be able to speak the language.'

But the temptation of a flat of our own was too strong to resist, and I was adamant: '*You* can live in communal flats, *we* can't. How can I leave my deaf mother the whole day by herself in a house full of people who cannot understand her? And Mamma is always finding fault that

209

there is no hot water when it is our turn for the bathroom. The others are impatient when she complains to them that the lavatory is engaged for hours, and often blue with smoke from the previous occupant, and that she is frightened bv the rats and why don't they telephone for the pest ˄'ficer? And why don't they do this and why don't they do that? You know Mamma. These women are tired when they come back from a day's work, and are hurrying to finish their cooking for their families, and suddenly Mamma begins to tell them that she could not find a little white cotton sunhat in the whole of Leningrad and that for weeks she has been looking for a pair of gloves to match her handbag and shoes. You know how she likes to boast about her life in Paris when she was young and where she could buy everything. Can't you understand that I cannot allow Mother to spend her last days among people who have no consideration for her age, her deafness, her life and her tragedy? We must have our own private flat.'

Vilnius has a mixed population of Poles, Germans, Estonians, Latvians and Jews. It is the capital of Lithuania and is situated among forested hills. It was small in comparison with Leningrad and had one operahouse, a conservatoire and a Philharmonic Orchestra. There was a large monastery and a convent for nuns as well as a fine old cathedral and many churches, some of which had been converted into museums.

Our little flat was situated in a massive housing estate not far from the Neris river. The name of the street was Putna after the famous general who, with Marshal Tukhachevsky and six other high officers, was executed for betraying military secrets to certain hostile powers and for working as a spy to overthrow the Soviet system and restore capitalism. He was posthumously rehabilitated, and the Lithuanians, out of respect, named a street after him.

Since 1933, when we first arrived from England, this was the very first flat of our own. It consisted of one room, about thirteen square metres, with a small kitchen, a lavatory and a shower, and was on the second floor with a small balcony looking out upon a garden where were a children's playground and benches. Mamma took over the housekeeping, and I began my job in the Institute where I had been invited to work by Dr Petrauskas. It was about twenty minutes' journey in the bus, which was always overcrowded.

The director came from a German background, and many others holding top positions were of foreign descent, which made it easier for me to work with them as we shared the same mentality. Their outlook was more European than Russian, and I was looked upon as one of them. Even the 'Special Department' (KGB) put no objects in my way. But Lithuanian was the language spoken throughout the Institute and in the city, and it was as though I were in a foreign country. This language barrier was a hindrance, but thankfully there were a few Russians on the staff with whom I could speak.

In this relaxed situation I applied to the Social Security Department to get my mother an old-age pension, and to my satisfaction she was acknowledged as an invalid (first category) and her fifteen years of hard labour in prison plus her five years of working in Yalta made up the twenty years necessary. As an invalid she received fifty-two roubles a month, and my salary was ninety roubles, not counting the money I received from giving lessons to Jewish families who were preparing to emigrate to Israel.

During those three or four years of my life in Vilnius many of my Jewish friends emigrated to Israel. I was sorry when my hairdresser, my shoemaker and other friendly tradesmen and craftsmen left. Many doctors were also leaving Vilnius, and one of them, Dr Levanauskas, told me of his troubles. The Soviet Union insisted that professionals such as he should repay the money invested in them during their university education and postgraduate work, which amounted to about

25,000 roubles. If they had a family of scientific research workers, every one had to repay this sum. In his case his wife, son and daughter-in-law were all research workers, and he must pay more than 100,000 roubles for them as well as the price of four visas, which cost 900 roubles for one person. Paradoxically they were allowed to take all their furniture and personal belongings with them.

This was a tremendous sum of money he had to find, but nothing kept him back, and others like him, for the sake of emigrating to a free country such as Israel. When the Levanauskas family were leaving I went to see them off, and the scene that I witnessed at the railway station was astonishing. The noise of hundreds of people speaking together – the ones who were departing and the ones who were staying – rejoicing in their freedom, brandishing aloft their Israeli passports as a shield against the System which had actually robbed them of their religion. Some used foul language to the militia standing looking on, abusing the Soviet Union which had destroyed their synagogues, Yiddish language, newspapers, theatres and schools. Their entire Yiddish culture had been erased.

Others were sobbing their hearts out at leaving behind relatives and roots sunk deep into the soil of Mother Russia, which had suckled them for generations. To break the traditions of a lifetime was like cutting away part of their bodies. To cross that Rubicon was an emotional and heartbreaking ordeal.

The young were the revellers – dancing, jumping to the music of the fiddle, singing Yiddish folk-songs and yelling loudly to the explosions of popping champagne-corks. These children had been taught from their cradle that the Russians hated the Jews, that Soviet discrimination against Jews was the reason that their applications for higher studies had been rejected.

Dancing with glee, their dark eyes sparkling like precious gems, they threw to the devil boring compulsory Pioneer and Komsomol duties, meetings, slogans and dull textbooks overcrammed with communist propaganda

212

from mathematics to music. For them it was at last 'Down with Soviet Power'.

At Vilnius I not only buried myself in my new work but also became involved with all facets of life within the Institute. Every year my photograph hung in a frame in 'the Red Corner' along with the other best workers. My workbook contained more than twenty stamps just like English children get at Sunday school for good work. It was typical of the Soviet Union that on 1 May and 7 November the director and a special committee should select the best workers and reward them with money and presents.

The staff of our Institute was 97 per cent women. In the Soviet Union there are twenty million more women than men, and wherever I lived in Russia or wherever I went – place of work, theatres, concerts, meetings – the predominance of women struck me immediately. After a revolution, labour camps, the First World War and the Second World War – in which it is claimed that twenty million died, two-thirds of whom were men – this is not surprising.

What did confuse me with my Western mind, and still does, was the little regard that the Soviet system has for the welfare of its powerful workforce of women. They are neither given nor expect any kind of special consideration or comforts, and this reflects even down to family life where the wives are expected to take care of the family in addition to doing a full-time job and queueing for the barest necessities of life. So strongly ingrained in them is the need to work that to be an ordinary housewife carries its own stigma.

This disregard for women reflects itself in many ways. To take, for example, such a personal item as sanitary pads. Though Russian sputniks were rushing round the heavens in the Sixties, in Vilnius such a simple consumer item as sanitary pads simply did not exist in the shops, and women had to make their own. I used to receive 400 grams of cottonwool a month for use in the department

213

of the Institute, but I could never refuse a colleague who poked her head round the door of my office and asked me to give her some. Even the director – embarrassed or not – collected his quota every month to take home to his wife. The result was that the patients suffered. The whole system was corrupt. The butcher, the baker and the candlestick-maker all pinched from their own shops because of the *defitsitny* (deficit goods), and things became even worse when in 1968 Russia invaded Czechoslovakia.

As the head nurse of my department I was called urgently to the sister's office where there was a squabble. Two Russian and Lithuanian nurses were brawling and fighting, screaming and tearing each other's hair out. After a great deal of persuasion we managed to separate them. The reason for the conflict was that the Lithuanians would not speak Russian with their fellow-nurses.

The tension in Lithuania was particularly acute at that time, as was witnessed when a young student poured petrol over himself and cremated himself in front of many people in a public park. Mobs of students rioted, smashing up shops until the Militia had to be called out. The papers were filled with this incident, and the Lithuanian Politburo tried to cover it up by saying that he was not a martyr but merely a poor young boy with a deranged mind. This was not true. It leaked out that several boys had been involved and drawn lots to see who would make the sacrifice. It was a protest against the Russians and at how the Lithuanians hated the occupation of their country and the way the Lithuanian officers in the Army had been replaced by Russian ones. There were many films also at that time which concentrated on the nationalistic hatred between Lithuanian and Russian communists. Since 1926, Lithuania had been ruled by a benevolent dictator, President Antanas Smetona, who left the country for America at the time of the Polish partition and died there in 1944. The Soviet authorities had purged the country in 1940; some 5000 persons were shot and from 20,000 to 40,000 deported, most of them to die in exile.

I was elected chairman of the cultural section of the Institute, and my function was to produce concerts and plays for the various celebrations and important historic Soviet dates. One of the plays I produced was called *From the Storm of the Winter Palace to Cosmos*. At the climax all the performers had to sing the 'Internationale', waving small flags, banners held high; and the audience had to stand up and join in with the song: 'Arise, ye toilers of all nations, Condemned to misery and woe.'

When I looked down at the first row I noticed that the head surgeon and two other professors were sitting with their hands folded while all the rest of the staff and patients stood. This was an important celebration for the Fiftieth Anniversary of the Great October Socialist Revolution and was controlled by the KGB. Seeing those doctors sitting there like fools making their own protest, I walked forward to the front of the stage singing with the rest of the cast and, conducting with my hands, looked straight into the eyes of the surgeon and waved him to stand up. He caught my message, nudged his neighbours, and they all stood up. Afterwards I asked him, 'What the hell were you doing?' and he said: 'Thank you. You were right, Flora.'

It is not surprising that in my free time I tried to escape as far from my work as possible. I went sightseeing and travelling to the magnificent lakes of Lithuania, swimming all summer in the Neris river, while in winter, when the trees were covered with sparkling white snow, I used to take to the ski tracks through the forests. I am not a competent skier racing down hills, but I could slowly travel on the level kilometre after kilometre. The woods echoed from the shouts of families skiing with their children. I had more pleasure in Vilnius than in the north.

One day I had a very interesting and strange experience when with a group of sightseers we made an excursion to one of the oldest Catholic churches and visited the underground vaults of the chapel. The guide explained that ten years before when medical students and archaeologists were exploring some vaults they came across a stone slab on the floor. When they removed it they found a staircase leading to another vault at a deeper level. To their amazement, in this deep vault they discovered hundreds of corpses – men, women and children – lying in open decaying coffins. The corpses were in good condition, some still had parts of their clothes clinging to their bodies and wore shoes. By some unexplained phenomenon the vaults had become a natural air-conditioned chamber which had preserved them. Medical research proved that the poor people had died from cholera during Napoleon's retreat from Moscow in 1812.

One of the archaeologists involved was inspired to make an exhibition of these mummified corpses. Looking through glass windows into the various vaults in the dim blue light we saw what looked like a stage with naked corpses arranged in various groups. The women with flat dried breasts were holding babies in their arms, and the men held their arms outstretched as if appealing for help. Their faces were unforgettable. They were a brown-bluish colour with the corners of the lips dropping downwards and the eyelids closed on empty sockets. To me they seemed to have expressions of despair and pain, and a vision came back to me from many years before of that vast cell in the prison in Leningrad with the women in the early dawn leaning their heads on their neighbours' shoulders. They were the same bluish colour, and their faces had the same expression of darkest despair. It was a horrible scene that would always haunt me.

CHAPTER TWENTY-FIVE

By 1973 we had lived nearly eight years in Vilnius, and Comrade Petrauskas had been so good to us that he had managed to transfer the lease of his brother's flat to our name. This was not easy to arrange, but his influence in the Politburo was strong. *Blat* was everywhere – in commerce, at work and in all walks of life.

I sent in an application to the Housing Changing Bureau for any flat or room on the coast of the Black Sea because Mother wanted to go back to Yalta where she had been so happy. Over the years we received many offers, but they were not suitable for us and the only one worth considering was in Batumi in the Adjarian Autonomous Soviet Socialist Republic, which is in Georgia. A Lithuanian woman wanted to return to her family in Vilnius. She had a large room, about twenty-feet square, a separate kitchen, and what really tempted us was the small garden with a cherry-tree and a peach-tree, figs and a grapevine. In the balmy sub-tropical climate I could see Mamma spending many pleasant hours in that garden.

Mamma was very excited with the move to the south, and her spirits were high during our three-day journey to Batumi. The nearer we came to the Black Sea so the vegetation changed and the scenery became lush with mimosa, oleanders, palms, eucalyptus and camphor-trees, huge magnolias, with their shiny dark-green leathery leaves, and other exotic and colourful flowers. Batumi is both a holiday resort and an important port and oil refinery of the eastern Black Sea coast, as the oil comes by pipeline from Baku. It is the only part of the Soviet Union where citrus fruits and the growing of tea are a major part of the agriculture and economy. It was a fascinating place with a mixed population of 96,000 people, mostly Adjarians, Georgians, Migrales and Armenians, and the children, who lived their lives in the streets, were fluent in several languages apart from Russian.

The dwelling where we had our room was situated outside Batumi and was not far from the sea coast with a background of impressive mountains towering behind. The building was a long one-storey barrack, and the occupants each had a small garden patch in front. However, there were drawbacks, and one of them was that the only lavatory was a public one in the street and the water supply came from a tap in the garden. I accepted these discomforts, which I knew that I could rectify given time as I planned to pipe water into the house and make a few more arrangements for Mother's comfort.

The Ministry of Medical Health Service of Batumi offered me a job in one of the hospitals for tuberculosis as an electrocardiographer for three days a week. I was appalled at the insanitary conditions of this hospital. There was a ward of elderly patients mostly with paralysis, and they were the most neglected patients that I had ever encountered. They would lie for days in their excrement and urine, the stench was nauseating and the room was always filled with flies. I saw old women dying with their open mouths filled with flies. It was horrible. Nobody cared. Those patients who had money could allow themselves proper care, but lonely old women without any relatives met a fate – and death – which was a disgrace to a nation boasting of medical achievements. I spoke out many times at meetings protesting against the atrocious conditions, and the officials listened but everything remained the same. After a while I could not cope with this indifference to fellow human beings and I left. As the Russian saying goes: 'One man in a field of battle is not a warrior.'

After I gave up nursing we were more or less content in our new life. Now I could devote more time to Mamma, and she was not left alone with her thoughts for hours on end. We had plain sensible food and enjoyed the harvest from our little garden. I made cherry jam from our own tree, and in the autumn pressed the bunches of luscious black grapes from our vine and made our own wine. Every day during summer until late October I went swimming at the beach while Mother sat in a deck-chair on the seashore under a large straw hat enjoying the life around her and basking in the golden sunshine. She looked so happy and my conscience was cleared, even if there was no hint of luxury and none of the ordinary domestic amenities that we had enjoyed in Vilnius. The sunshine and flowers filled her heart with joy, and the days of depression were fewer than before.

Mamma loved fruit and, though apples and other fruits were very expensive and money was short, the winter tangerines that grew on the large plantations lasted until March. As I was no longer working, one of my Russian neighbours, called Assia, asked if I would like to go with her to the hillside, about two hours' journey in a bus, to pick the wild violets which grew there in profusion and make posies to sell on 8 March, the International Women's Day, which was a gala holiday for everyone. For weeks beforehand the newspapers, radio and television had been reminding every man and every child that on this day they should present their women with gifts, attention and respect. Otherwise, I suppose, the males would have forgotten the event in their eagerness to drink a bottle of vodka with their friends on this free day. It was a mock respect for these hard-working women who even on their own special day had to shop, queue and cook, from morning until night, as well as sitting for hours at special meetings arranged in their honour which took up precious time

219

which they should have spent relaxing in armchairs at home. It is not surprising that one in every three marriages in Russia fails and, owing to the shortage of men, many husbands have two or three mistresses.

In the early morning the rising sun bathed the hillsides in a yellow glow, and through the carpet of green foliage, I saw tiny purple flowers gleaming like jewels. Picking the delicate stems of the violets we gathered them into bunches. It was not an easy job as we slipped and slid on the dew-drenched earth which smelt of mushrooms. My back ached unmercifully, but by five o'clock in the evening we had made more than five hundred little posies. We placed them gently into baskets between layers of fresh moist leaves and we arrived at the station just in time to catch a train to Sochi, a famous resort for foreigners and the Russian élite. All the top men from the Kremlin have their dachas there, and the hillsides are dotted with enormous sanatoriums for the privileged.

We arrived at Sochi at 3 a.m. and we waited at the small station until morning, taking it in turns to sprinkle the delicate violets with water so that they should not wither. With the first rays of sunlight, still shivering from cold, we took our precious baskets and began walking on the streets, promenades and beach offering our fragrant posies of violets to the men holidaymakers for fifty copecks each. We had to be wary of the Militia because selling flowers was a breach of the law and we could have been arrested for 'speculating'. Private enterprise, even the most innocent such as selling wild violets, was forbidden. Late in the evening, when we had sold all our merchandise, we had difficulty in getting on to the overcrowded train. My Assia was a very efficient woman and knew her business well. She bribed the train attendant, and he allowed us to stand in the passage, but we had to pay the same amount as if we had a seat. Returning home after the two days we had each earned 120 roubles. This was a lot of money for me.

Good news. Vera, my little Vera, was coming from

Kiev to stay with us for a few days. Her father wrote to me that she was on a conducted tour of the Georgian Military Route, which ran across the Caucasian Mountains and finished in Batumi. 'Would I be so kind as to look after her?'

Not since I had received a letter from Berthe that Dimitri had married did I ever mention this event in my letters to him. It was too deep a wound to be touched. The day Vera was coming Mamma and I were waiting in the garden when suddenly a noisy grumbling motorbike came in sight with a young girl astride clutching a curly black-haired Georgian. She jumped off, her long shapely legs bared by a tiny miniskirt that hardly covered her thighs. 'Fofa,' she cried, using the pet name she had given me. My baby Vera. The last time I had seen her she was twelve years old, and now this tall nineteen-year-old goddess with shining black eyes and long black hair rushed into my arms. Mamma, Vera and I cuddled together.

It was a late warm autumn day and the table was laden with a boulder-sized water melon, grapes, figs and a roasted chicken from the black market. We celebrated far into the night, and when Mamma was asleep Vera told me, smoking a cigarette, how she disliked her father's marriage and how she had conflicts with her stepmother every hour. She had loved only me since her cradle, and Zoë was an intruder who had only wanted to marry a professor. When Vera's grandmother and grandfather had died she had seen her chance. She was the right woman at the right time!

Vera continued talking, chain smoking all the time, which shocked me. She was a spoiled clever child and knew six languages and was getting on well with her studies in the University of Foreign Languages but she was quick-tempered, impulsive and strong. She had been motherless since birth and was different from other children. I knew how she had suffered when all around her the other children talked about their mammas. This

221

motherlessness had changed her character completely, and now she was shrewd and ruthless.

She also confided in me her own worries. She was in love with a boy she had met in her ninth form at school, but he was from an alcoholic family and had taken to drink himself. Once at a riotous party he had tried to hang himself when he was drunk. 'Don't begin your life with a mistake that you realise yourself,' I cautioned her, but throwing everything to the wind when she returned she did marry him, against the wish of her father, her stepmother and me.

Mother was the one to make friends wherever we lived. Now she passed the time sitting on benches and talking to the people in the parks. In spite of her eighty-nine years she read newspapers, journals and magazines and enjoyed television. By this time she had a more modern and efficient hearing aid, which enabled us to talk and to argue about political events and achievements which I would criticize as bunkum, but Mamma had a quite different angle on Soviet life. She took all that she saw on the television for granted, and it hurt me to see how she swallowed the propaganda preaching the greatness of the Soviet Union and had drawn a veil over the past, even hiding all the photographs of her children. Every day I had to tread on thin ice to protect her from memories of the past.

My new acquaintances in Batumi were a family consisting of Paulina, a teacher of French and English, and her husband Boris, a turner, and their two children, a boy and a girl. They were to remain my only friends during all my eleven years in Batumi. In his younger years Boris had been a sailor and travelled to Liverpool and London. He was worldly wise as his father and many relatives were of Greek descent, and he liked to boast of his ancestors. With him I could talk freely about my experience in camps because during the Stalin purges in the Thirties all Greeks had been repressed, some imprisoned and the rest sent out of the country into exile in

222

Uzbekistan. There he had met his Russian wife, Paulina, whom he took back to Batumi, the land of his fathers and where there was a large Greek community. Boris and I would talk about anything and everything concerning the system, but there were two topics that I was not allowed to mention in front of his wife, who was pro-Soviet, and they were my experiences in camp and my criticism of the Soviet state. They had a two-roomed flat on the fifth floor with no lift. It was well furnished because in Boris's sailing days he had bought *defisit* goods such as mohair, porcelain and jeans, which sold well on the black market, and with the profit he was able to buy furniture for their flat.

They had all the conveniences of modern life, including a Soviet washing machine that was always breaking down and was impossible to repair because of the shortage of spare parts, a television set and a transistor radio – everything to make life comfortable and enjoyable. But everything was ruined because either there was no gas or water in the block, and Boris had to carry pails of water up to the fifth floor, or during the night when there was water they had to get up and fill the bath and every available vessel. On the days when there was no gas Paulina would come to me and cook on my stove as I had one which ran on cylinder gas. I was very sorry for Boris as to eke out the family budget and to increase their combined income of 300 roubles a month he had to 'moonlight' in his spare time, which was illegal. Because Boris, and husbands like him, could not buy spare parts they used to make them at their work using the factory materials. This resulted in the creation of a special office which was called the Department for the Struggle against Plundering of Socialist Property (OBKHSS) and had the special function of punishing offenders by fining them or even sending them to gaol.

In Batumi it was quite normal for the people to say to each other: 'You know, Zhia, my husband has paid five thousand roubles to the big man at the top university to enter our scamp.'

'That is nothing. We had to give an extra two thousand not to get our darling Revas kicked out from the third term, not to mention the tangerines and wine we sent the tutor.'

To occupy myself, at the Palace of Culture I organized English and handicraft lessons. We made puppets and I arranged a little show of *The Three Little Pigs* spoken in English. There I met an artist, and to my astonishment she was related to the famous Dostoevsky and she bore the same facial characteristics with hooded eyelids. She reminded me of one of the characters in Dostoevsky's book, *Poor People*, as she was living in appalling conditions. Her one room was filthy with the smell of paints, numerous cats and dogs and a bedridden mother. The place gave a feeling of depression, poverty and an inability to struggle to make her life better. She had approached the officials in Moscow and Batumi many times to improve her living conditions, but there was no reply and she had lost heart and accepted her fate. She loved every living creature and scolded me if I wanted to kill a fly. 'Flora, it has every right to live, as much as you.'

It was the coming of the New Year, and Mamma said to me: 'Why don't you send a postcard to your friends in England, Brigid and John Edge?' This I did, and we were so delighted to get a card back from them giving news of their life, about the house they had bought and a drawing of their new lurcher dogs. They also invited me to come and stay with them. This natural kindness of the English, in contrast with the abnormalities of Soviet life, was embarrassing as there was no possibility that I could accept their warm invitation.

Something strange was happening in Batumi. Because of the shortage of food people queued for hours in the hope that some kind of supplies would be 'thrown out' – chicken, meat or butter. They bought not only for their immediate use but also for hoarding against the barren months ahead, and this caused the total disappearance of all the main products.

For years we had not seen toilet paper, and if it did appear in the universal department stores it was sold only through the 'back door'. There was no chance of people like me to get one single roll as the limousines of the élite would arrive and buy up boxes containing hundreds of rolls. In thirty minutes there was not one left.

One day, returning from the shops after a fruitless search for food, I saw a car standing outside a 'closed shop' for the élite. The boot of the car was open and it was filled with plump Bulgarian chickens wrapped in red cellophane. I shyly asked the owner of the car: 'Can you spare me one chicken for my old mother?'

He curtly answered: 'No. This is for a funeral wake.'

It seemed sad that they could get food for the dead but not for the living. I cried all the way back home.

Waiting in a queue in the market one day for a chicken there was complete disorder because, if a Georgian woman was standing in the queue, in fifteen minutes she would organize the whole family ahead of her because only one chicken was allowed per person. If she put six of her family in front of me, there were then six chickens less between me and my chicken. I was furious and disgusted as I realized that soon there would be no chickens left. Suddenly there were rumours in the queue that they were finishing, which aroused a panic, and the line became a screaming mass of desperate people.

I had already been standing for more than three hours, and if I did not get a chicken for Mamma that day I would have to wait another month or so. Infuriated I rushed to the Militia station in the market where the policemen were sitting playing dominoes. Controlling my rage, and my language, I excused myself for interrupting their game and said: 'Would you kindly come and organize some order in the queue where people are killing each other for a chicken?'

An officer came with me but he did not return to the front of the chicken-stall but went to the back door. He knocked on the door, it opened, and before entering he said to me: 'Give me ten roubles.' Grabbing my shopping-bag he disappeared inside and the door closed. In a few minutes he came out and pushed the bag, filled with chickens, into my hand, saying: 'Take it and leave quickly.'

Amazed, I asked: 'Why are you doing this for me?'

'Because I like beautiful women,' he replied in his rich gurgling Georgian accent.

I sneaked away like a puppy with her tail behind her. This was the easy way for him to cope with the situation because all the king's horses and all the king's men could never have got that mob of angry, aggressive, hungry people into order.

In late 1978 there was no point in queueing. For months there had been nothing in the shops. Macaroni, sugar, flour, butter, margarine, meat and cigarettes had simply vanished, and only vodka, wines and inferior tinned fish, which nobody bought, were left on the shelves. Food was available only at restaurants and sanatoriums, but even that only consisted of macaroni and rissoles containing more bread than meat. Though one had to queue for bread, there was always plenty of that, and I used to go to the market to buy potatoes, carrots and other vegetables which we made into a soup.

In those bad days I sometimes went to the restaurants and pleaded for a piece of butter because the only thing that Mamma liked to eat in the morning was bread and butter with her tea. Sometimes I got a little butter, although I had to pay five times the normal price; but mostly they refused to sell. If the cooks could economize in any way in the process of preparing the food, they would take what they had saved home to their own families.

Sitting down one evening in desperation I took my pen and paper and wrote to Leonid Brezhnev, leader of the Communist Party of the Soviet Union:

My mother is ninety years of age. She had fifteen years in prison, her two daughters and her only son have also perished in camps. She is rehabilitated and receives an invalid pension of seventy roubles a month. I receive a pension of fifty roubles a month. I have put my name on several collective letters that have been sent to Eduard Shevardnadze, the First Secretary of the Communist Party of Georgia, in protest that Batumi has had no food for the last two years. I appeal to you to help me to obtain in some way the necessary nourishment required for my old mother. I cannot stand in queues as I cannot leave my invalid mother for three hours in such a useless waste of time, and even if I have the money I cannot buy a piece of butter. For months there has been no meat. Nothing. I am sending one copy of this letter to the Georgian Communist Party and one to you, Comrade Leonid Brezhnev.

Signed: FLORA LEIPMAN

CHAPTER TWENTY-SIX

With all these food problems and scarcities there were different interpretations as to what was happening in the Soviet Union. Some said that it was due to the fact that we were saving the food for the coming war, others that it was because of the billions of roubles spent on space research, and the intellectuals spoke of the inherent inefficiency of the whole agricultural system and the increasing needs for an expanding population. The demand for meat necessitated the need for grain to feed cattle to produce meat.

Batumi was not the only city where there were shortages, as holidaymakers coming from all over the country brought news of places in the Soviet Union where there was not even bread. Not only food and toilet paper disappeared, but also it was utterly impossible to buy a sheet, a pillow-case, linen and cotton materials, cosmetics, nails, pots and pans, potties for babies and even dummies. If the shops did 'throw out' these articles, only the black-marketeers could reach them. People changed and pleasure vanished as the only aim in life for the ordinary person was the search for food.

Moscow, Leningrad and Kiev were the centres where there was still a great supply of food, which made people from all over the Soviet Union flood these cities. They descended on the shops like locusts, creating queues and devouring the supplies. These intruders were looked upon by the big-city dwellers with disgust and anger. Because of this constant travelling the air services were overbooked and in the Eighties the Soviet government put up the prices of the air flights by 200 per cent.

My mother was deeply disturbed because of the coming fiftieth anniversary of Papa's death in January 1979. 'He is lonely. Why don't you go to Glasgow to the cemetery where your father lies? You can also visit your friends John and Brigid Edge. In their last letter they invited you, remember? Why don't you write to Gromyko and tell him your story and that you were born in Scotland and that you want to visit Papa's grave? I am sure that he will allow you to go.'

I was dumbfounded, but I did write to Andrei Gromyko, the Minister of Foreign Affairs. I had forgotten all about my letter to Leonid Brezhnev, which I had written several months before, when one day I was looking out of our window and saw two large chauffeur-driven Volga limousines, one black and one red, driving slowly down our road. As no one ever came there I was fascinated. Who were these VIPs and whom were they visiting? The cars drew up not far from our gate and, mesmerized, I watched as four immaculately dressed men in dark suits and white shirts and ties, carrying briefcases, picked their way gingerly across the dusty verge and entered our garden. They knocked at the door, and I opened it.

'Do the Leipmans live here?'

'Who are you?' I asked, inviting them into the room. They introduced themselves – one came from the Batumi Social Security, one from the Communist Party of Georgia, and two men from the Party Committee of the Oil Refinery which sponsored our district.

'Did you write to the Central Committee of the Communist Party?'

'Yes, I did.'

'Please be so kind as to show us your rehabilitation papers and internal passport.'

When this official part was completed he asked me:

'What can we do for you?' The young man, Giva, the secretary of the Party Committee, was extremely friendly and he approached and sat down on the sofa next to Mamma and took her little hand into his and patted it. There was silence in the room.

They listened quietly and attentively as I unfolded the whole of the Leipman saga from the day we had arrived in Leningrad in 1933 up to our present plight, when I could not get sufficient nourishing food for my mother because we did not have the money to buy on the black market.

Clearly they were deeply impressed by my story, and the Georgian said: 'We want to help. What can we do for you?'

The consequence of all this was that I received an official word from the Communist Party of Adjaria that Mamma was going to receive every month rations of two packets of butter (400 grams), two chickens, three kilos of buckwheat and twenty eggs from the shop on the premises of the oil plant. Passing through the village a Georgian woman brought us our food, clasping under her left arm two chickens and in her hand held aloft a tray of eggs; she carried the rest in a brown paper packet under her other arm.

'Where are you taking all this food?' all the people living in the village asked.

'To the *Inglisi*,' she replied, 'to the *Inglisi*' (Georgian for 'English'). There were no more comments. The Batumsy were in awe of foreigners. In the region where I lived everybody knew everyone else and, if a letter with a strange postmark arrived in the post office, within an hour everybody had heard about it.

It was now the summer of 1978 and through the years I had not lost touch with Berthe, who was a widow and lived in Sweden. She informed me that she would be in Leningrad on a package tour and if I could come there we could meet. Mother agreed that I should go as she was anxious that I should meet our old friend who would bring us news of her new life abroad. Paulina and Boris gladly volunteered to look after Mother, and I decided to go. With difficulty I received my tickets and by train I journeyed to Leningrad, where I stayed with Nina, who was still a spinster, in her three-roomed flat. Sitting over coffee we discussed our lives as we had not seen each other for more than ten years. I confided to her that Mother had a desire that I should go back to England for two weeks to visit Father's grave.

'I don't want you to speak about going to England in this house or anything to do with foreign connections.'

'For God's sake, what are you talking about? We have been such friends and have criticized many aspects of the Soviet system.'

'Don't forget I am a Party Member and have been so for a long time. Only a week ago, during a Party committee meeting we were told that any connections or thoughts about foreigners should be reported immediately.'

I was astonished that my friend of twenty years should tell me such appalling nonsense.

'Why should you report me?'

'Because you are talking about your intentions to go to England and that means you are a traitor to your country. My niece, who lives in this flat, is a Komsomol (member of the Young Communist League), and they have been given orders to heighten their vigilance. If I do not inform on you, she will and, Flora, I don't want any trouble. You have lived far away in Batumi these last years and you are so occupied with your mother that you really don't know what is happening here. Things have changed for the worse. Before, in the Sixties, we could talk freely and meet foreigners, but now with the Dissident Movement and the Jews going to Israel, all this disturbance has made our lives unstable. The conflicts between those going, wishing to go, and those who don't want to leave the USSR divide us Jews into several political categories. For instance, I have lived all my life here. My parents and their parents are part of my roots, my very soul; even if I have my doubts and my criticisms of Soviet life, we know that every country has its good and bad. While I play the game of being a loyal Soviet citizen and stick to the rules I am all right and I love Leningrad. It is my inheritance.'

I wished her no harm, though her attitude to me had now changed. We were still the best of friends, and I was welcome to the house. We did not speak again about foreign affairs, and I knew that I would never be able in the future to confide in her freely about my plans.

Berthe telephoned me at Nina's house from the Astoria Hotel and we arranged to meet. I was happy to meet her, and in spite of her limp she looked very well. She was dressed in a Persian lamb coat and a beautiful white fox-fur hat. There was an aroma of Europeanism about her. She lived in another world – a free world.

I told her that I had written to the Ministry of Foreign Affairs for a temporary exit visa. I explained that Mother was getting old and very weak and anything could happen, and as Berthe knew our story I asked her could she possibly contact the British embassy now that she had a foreign passport and find out the procedure for an exit visa. Parting she promised to do so and handed me a few presents for myself and Mamma.

Six years had passed since we first lived in Batumi. The new surroundings, perfect warm weather, picturesque scenery and the fact that Mamma just had to open the door and there she was in our little Garden of Eden made her happy. She enjoyed her new life, and the Georgian and Adjarian neighbours were kind to her as they sincerely respected the old.

But that autumn of 1978 Mamma's personality changed and she began crying a lot. Taking out our precious album, tears of distress and anguish would suffocate her. 'Flora,' she would say to me, 'I am dying. I feel strange, and visions of my poor children haunt me. Oh, what have I done? I am responsible for their early

232

horrible deaths, and you also have suffered, Flora. I know you sometimes hate me; your longing for your Britain is in your bones. Oh, God forgive me. Flora darling, when I die what is to become of you, all alone in this dreadful country?' Day and night she repeated: 'Oh, Flora, what will become of you all alone? No friends. Nobody.'

It was impossible to comfort her. All my efforts were broken down by her decision that she was to blame for everything. It was impossible to bear. I tried to make her put on her hearing aid so that I could speak to her, explain and tell her that I did love her, that she should not take the responsibility for the death in camp of my sisters and brother. 'Don't you see, Mamma,' I said, 'it was this dreadful Soviet system that had made all our lives so completely miserable.'

These days were so difficult. She was so distraught. She would stand in front of the window, her hands clasped together in prayer: 'Oh God, oh God. Take me away. I am so tired waiting for my beloved son Samuel.' I would take her into my arms, put her hearing aid on and softly speak to her. To my surprise she was not aggressive. Her face lit up with a strange expression when she heard me say: 'Mamma, don't be afraid to die and don't worry about me. You will go to another peaceful world where you will be reunited with the children. They are waiting for you. I will come later. You know that I cannot live without you.'

Day after day I steadily, with great caution, forced her to believe that soon we would all be together. She became more placid and peaceful, but the same strange expression came over her face as if she was hearing, feeling, something that only she could understand.

Her illness assumed a grave aspect. She had developed a high sensitivity of the skin. The doctors prescribed various drugs, but they did not help her skin disorder. They told me that I must be ready for the end. These symptoms were serious, and all her reflexes were very low. Mamma could not bear any clothes on her body, especially synthetics. I could not find any cotton material to make her a nightdress, but through a friend I met someone who sold me a few metres of white cotton printed with blue flowers. I gathered the neck up with a blue ribbon, and she was very pleased and she looked much better that night. Her itchiness had disappeared, and standing in front of the mirror, taking the folds of the nightie in her fingers, she curtsied several times to herself, saying, 'I am a bride . . . I am a bride,' and then burst out laughing. I looked at her. Her eyes were gleaming. She looked so young and was in another world of her own. I was frightened.

During the night I woke up as she was calling me. 'Flora, Flora, I feel bad.' I quickly approached her and gave her medicine, but she soon lost consciousness. She had a stroke and her left side, face, arm and leg were paralysed. Seven days she was fighting for her life, and on the morning of 19 August 1979, at the age of ninety, my mother was no more. She died peacefully with a smile on her lips. Mamma had outlived my father by fifty years. Her life was finished, but her pain and loss are always with me.

I appreciated my friends Boris and Paulina and all my neighbours, those plain hard-working people who came to my help, also a young man from the Party Committee of the Refinery who made arrangements for the funeral. I buried Mamma in a Muslim cemetery amid an arbour of beautiful sub-tropical trees. It was a lovely resting-place.

Mamma's death was the fulfilment of the law of nature. This I realized, but it did not ease the agony that flooded through my mind. For forty-four years I had struggled to protect her and now I was in a state of deep depression. The utter uselessness of my life now faced me. What was I going to do with myself? No more petitions, no more struggle to get food for her and to protect her from the harsh outside world. Now there was only a vacuum.

The pain I suffered looking every day at Mamma's

empty bed was too much for me, and I missed her presence every minute of the day, so I wrote to Vera in Kiev telling her that Mamma had passed away. I received a telegram of condolence and she invited me: 'Just close the door and come to me.'

I took some money for the trip out of the small savings that Mamma and I had accumulated over the years. Going through the frustration of standing from early morning to buy an air ticket distracted and helped me in my grief. During the three-hour flight I realized the problem I was facing. My pension of fifty-seven roubles a month, without Mamma's income of seventy roubles, would not be sufficient for me to live on. From this amount I had to pay six roubles for electricity and gas, seven roubles for rent, and this would leave me only forty-four roubles on which to live. The market price for carrots and potatoes was two roubles a kilo, a pair of shoes cost about forty roubles, and clothes and other things were out of the question. The only advantage of living in Batumi was the warm climate where sandals and a light dress were sufficient almost all the year round.

Kiev was overcrowded at that time of the year with holidaymakers, tourists, delegations from all over the Soviet Union and masses of foreigners from everywhere in Europe. It was amazing to see the food in the shops, but the queues were as usual in the Soviet Union. The quota per person for butter was 400 grams, *kolbasa* (sausage) one kilo, and two kilograms of meat. To provide for the household the whole family, including the grandparents, had to stand in the queues. The shops were filled with Russian-made merchandise which did not attract the attention of the intellectuals, who preferred foreign-made goods which they bought on the black market. Youngsters like Vera, who bought all their clothes this way, economized on food to possess a pair of imported frayed jeans that might have been worn by some cowboy at the rodeo. It did not matter how worn out they were as long as they had a well-known brand-label: Wrangler, Rifle, Levi and Lee.

The evenings were occupied visiting Vera's friends, listening to pop music, drinking coffee in the cafés and speaking with foreigners whom we met there in the most natural way.

It was more than seven years since Dimitri and I had last met. Waiting and listening for his footsteps I stood in front of the mirror looking into my own face. Seeing the wrinkles that age had printed on it, despite my make-up, my coiffure and dress – they could not hide the truth. I was sixty-one years of age and I was tired of life. Seeing him again, what would it mean to me? I was hurt that he had not proposed marriage to me. I suffered during our separations, but did I really want to marry him? No, I contemplated; it was an illusion. I could never have been happy with him because in my subconscious I always had this resolution to return to my homeland which was much stronger than my love for him.

Looking back, Dimitri and I had a most strange relationship. At the beginning, though he was married then, there was a feeling of gravitation, and the yearning to see each other was powerful. After he became a widower, baby Vera became a link between us. Later when we became lovers, just as all women wish to have a family I had a belief that we would marry and that the three of us would be happy. Years passed and he never spoke of marriage. We were more intellectually suited than sexually and, as we saw each other rarely, when we did meet we talked the whole night through. Now I realised that my love for him was more in my imagination.

Dimitri was a man with a discreet nature as far as his inner feelings were concerned. Our reunions were full of joy, and when baby Vera was three years old he would sit me on a small sledge with her on my knee and race around the park in the cold evenings when the trees were dressed in their winter white clothes. These were happy

236

days. Or we would meet in the park in the drizzling rain, getting wet through, but hugging each other we were content and happy. It was a union of immense understanding.

The door gently opened and turning around I encountered Dimitri eye to eye. There he was, an elderly man with grey hair, sheepishly holding a bouquet of red roses. His short-sighted eyes blinked with tears behind his glasses. We embraced, cried and laughed through sheer joy of being together again. Interrupting each other in our haste to relate our life-stories, we remembered with compassion our parents who were no longer with us. He was now a professor and the secretary of the Politburo of his Institute. During my visit we went to the Kiev Art Gallery, a small building with a beautiful collection of the great masters. We were both amateur painters, and the pleasure of being together to share our impressions was comforting.

This was our last day. Dimitri confessed to me that he had always loved me and that even at the age of sixty his love was as strong as twenty-five years ago. 'I know that I have hurt you,' he said, 'and you know why; because of my career, my Party membership, and the influence of my friends, who said: "How can you possibly marry a woman with such a background, a convict family, Jewish nationality and foreign birth?" Flora, I was a downright imbecile, but I believed that I was doing right. I am sorry that I sacrificed the happiness of my child, who loved you as a mother, and my own, too.'

Parting from him I had a sense of relief that our long relationship was over. I knew that he was too Soviet-educated to appreciate and understand my struggle for freedom of speech and thought and expansion through the environment of the outside world. But in spite of all the turmoil that I had suffered my love for him gave me something to live for.

CHAPTER TWENTY-SEVEN

In 1980 I received from the consulate section of the British embassy in Moscow a statutory declaration allowing me permanent residence in England and other formal papers necessary for the procedure to obtain an exit visa. These had been sent by Dr and Mrs John Edge, who had undertaken to act as my sponsors in England. I hugged Brigid's letter to my heart and danced round the room from sheer appreciation, but deep inside I had a premonition that this was only the beginning of my fight to get out of Russia.

Batumi has a small KGB centre and MVD (Ministry of Internal Affairs) where the OVIR (Department of Visas) is centralized. Waiting my turn, standing in a small office, I handed over my papers to the woman in charge. Glancing at my British documents with their impressive official stamps, she returned them to me, saying with disdain: 'We do not accept papers from or allow exits to capitalist countries.' That was all. I was so upset and disappointed that the British embassy and my friends in England had taken all that trouble and now the documents were not accepted. It was appalling and illegal, and at the same time I had also received from the Foreign Ministry an answer to my letter written before Mamma died with a refusal for a temporary visa. So I was not allowed to visit my friends in England, and I was not allowed to live where I wanted. In a terrible state of excitement I flew to Moscow where I stayed with some friends. Bella was a divorcee with a teenage son and they were also waiting for exit visas to Israel, but in their case their papers had been accepted. Bella still had her three-roomed flat, though most of the furniture had already been sold.

Bella and her son were studying English and, though I was a slight acquaintance, they were pleased to have me. Listening to my story with sympathy, she told me that she knew a good Jewish lawyer whom we could only see in the evening. At 6 pm we arrived at one of the synagogues in Moscow, and walking towards it she said in a hushed voice: 'Be very careful, and the minute you see the Militia run for your life.' In spite of the frost, which was more than −25°C, in the dim light of a side-street beside the synagogue I saw a crowd of Jews, all of whom had applied for exit visas to Israel and been refused. The English-speaking countries called them *refusniks* but there is no such word in the Russian language. They were all interested in one another's case and I really did not understand why they were gathering there except that being together and sharing their fate gave them some kind of consolation and was a small show of protest against the system.

Finding my lawyer amidst them, he told me: 'Russia has no lawful right to detain you here nor to refuse your British credentials as you were not born in the Soviet Union.' He advised me to go to the head of the Moscow OVIR and state my case. I thanked him and expressed my admiration for the *refusniks'* courage in daring to defy the system. The next morning I found the building and made an appointment. Here to my surprise the proceedings were not so complicated as they had been in the Leningrad OVIR, where I had been the previous year to get advice. Even so, sitting in the waiting-room with the others in great silence you sensed a feeling of guilt. *They* (the KGB) had made it a most humiliating atmosphere for those who intended to leave the country. In their understanding that was treason.

When it came to my turn the middle-aged woman receptionist said: 'We do not grant visas to capitalist countries. And if you are going to persist in your British rights,' she added, 'with your Russian citizenship you will be in deep trouble. Next.'

The office I was ushered into was a large one, like all other KGB offices I had been in, with its usual aura of power and Lenin on the wall: and there *he* sat with a woman KGB officer. Looking through my beautiful English papers, and after listening to my outpourings, he answered in a casual way: 'All that you have told me happened many years ago and you are now a Soviet citizen, so we cannot allow you a visa. We do not permit visas to capitalist countries to visit friends. The law is that exit visas are allowed only to see near relatives.'

In a state of absolute hysterics and losing complete control of myself, I shouted at him: 'For you, Stalin's purges are history. You know nothing about the innocent people who suffered and died in camps. For me, it is not only yesterday, it is today. Now I am a lonely old woman. I have lost my family. I have nobody. My mother's dying wish was that I should return to my native land.' Between my sobs I pleaded: 'Why do you need to detain me? Why do you make a problem just because one woman wants to return to her homeland when instead you should be showing me the humanity that the Soviet Union boasts about?'

My hysterics made him get up from his chair, and he began walking up and down. He asked his assistant to pour me a glass of water. Pacing to and fro he clasped his forehead with his hand as if deep in concentration. Looking at him I decided that he was a Brezhnev type, with the same bushy eyebrows, but this man had a jovial expression on his face. Suddenly he turned to me and said: 'I am going to try to push forward your application.'

I was not to be taken in by that. I replied: 'What guarantee can you give me that my application will be accepted and the result will be positive? What is the use of my appealing to you again if you are going to refuse me?'

'Leave me a written statement that you want to leave

the Soviet Union and just go home and wait hoping for the best,' he assured me in an authoritative voice. *'Budem probivat . . . budem probivat'* ('We'll break through').

Leaving his office I wanted to believe him as during my negotiations there was something in his eyes, in his expression, in his whole being that convinced me that he really was touched by my sad story at that moment and I thought he wanted to help me. Full of excitement and anticipation I returned to Batumi.

Two weeks later I received an order to appear at the OVIR. To my surprise the Georgian woman in charge had adopted a new attitude to me. Smiling, she said: 'We have orders from Moscow to accept your papers for an exit visa.' I was on top of the world and immediately informed the British embassy that at last my papers had been accepted. Her Majesty's consul, Mr S. Bonde, answered in his letter: 'God forbid that they refuse you.'

After waiting two months I was officially informed by the OVIR in Batumi that my application for an exit visa had been refused. It was no use crying. Flora, you felt it, I told myself. That KGB man in Moscow must have been laughing up his sleeve. He had just been pacifying me, treating me like an aggressive psycho, but his main object had been to get me out of Moscow as it was preparing for the great event of the anniversary of the Great October Socialist Revolution. He was taking no risks that I might create a scene.

In 1982, after the death of Leonid Brezhnev his successor was Yuri Andropov, the former boss of the KGB, and I felt that with this man I would never be allowed out of the Soviet Union.

Neverthless, throughout the year 1983 I was in active correspondence with Mr Bonde of the British embassy, who sent me an application form for a British passport which was issued to me that October. The dark blue passport was so handsome, embossed in gold with the royal coat of arms and those inspiring words 'dieu et mon droit', and at the top in a little window in strong black letters was my name. I was thrilled and thanked God that I should have been endowed with this honour. The whole pity was that it could not be used without a Soviet visa to leave the Soviet Union. I had waited so long. I must be patient.

Mamma's portrait was my altar. To her I spoke and to her I prayed. She seemed to smile at me, and I knew that she was always beside me, looking after me, happy when I was happy. When one lives entirely alone one has to have a belief or do something practical, otherwise you can go mad. I began to paint, copying from postcards, reproductions of famous masters of the seventeenth and eighteenth centuries and Byzantine icons from the Middle Ages. Month after month I worked from morning until night painting every detail, and this took me away from reality into my own world and saved me from insanity. The walls of my room were hung with copies of paintings by Leonardo da Vinci, and the Russian painters Brullov and Aivosovski, and Tropinin and others. I would lie on my bed waking up in the morning and these portraits were my friends. Because of the difficulty in finding suitable canvas I painted on cardboard, plywood and wood, tin, anything that I could lay hands on. From one of the attics in a school a friend brought me a large worn and torn portrait of Brezhnev which I patched and covered with white paint. Over it I copied a Brullov painting of Italian peasant girls gathering grapes.

I had an appointment to keep in Moscow in the Burdenko Institute of Neurosurgery because I had a suspected aneurism in my brain. I managed to get an address where I could stay as a paying guest in the house of a woman professor of gynaecology. Her son and daughter were living in Israel. She was a *refusnik* and was also waiting for an exit visa to join them.

When I telephoned Mr Bonde he was pleased that I was in Moscow and invited me to the British embassy.

242

He was waiting outside the gates of the embassy when I arrived and, greeting me with a smile and shaking my hand warmly, he gave me confidence. Taking me by the arm he asked if I had my British passport with me. I showed it to the Russian guards, who inspected it and then saluted me. As we passed through the gate Mr Bonde asked me: 'Frightened?'

'Yes,' I replied, 'I am green with fear.' Laughing and talking, we reached the consulate section. Sitting in the warm office I felt relaxed as he inquired about my health, and our conversation led us into my present situation. A tall man entered the room, to whom Mr Bonde introduced me, saying: 'This is Mr William Somerset, who is taking over my post and will take care of your case.' We agreed my case was especially complicated, and they were distressed because I had been twice refused.

I was touched by their concern about my state of health, and leaving the consulate I thanked them warmly for all their efforts to get me home. Before I went Mr Somerset presented me with an invitation from the ambassador, Sir Iain Sutherland, and Lady Sutherland for the coming 'Christmas drinks'. I was sad to say goodbye to Mr Bonde, who was leaving, but Mr Somerset asked me to keep in contact with him.

Returning to Batumi I hid in my wardrobe the posters I was given in the embassy. One was of the Queen and the Duke of Edinburgh in the Long Gallery, the other of Prince Charles and Princess Diana on their wedding day in the royal carriage; also the booklet *The Monarchy of Britain*. They were so precious to me and, as a miser counts his treasures in the dark of the night, I would unroll my precious posters and indulge in the pleasure of looking at the Royal Family. It took me back to my youth during the reign of King George V when we sang 'God Save the King'.

I could not share my gifts with anybody. I wished I could hang the posters in my room, but to do this would be an act of protest and defiance against the Soviet state. It was too dangerous to show my contempt of it. It could not be done.

I hurriedly began making a dress for the 'special occasion' at the embassy; as I had not worn high-heeled shoes for a long time I put them on and practised walking round the room every day. In a funny way it reminded me of Cinderella getting ready for the ball, but this Cinderella was over sixty. Doubts invaded me. Should I go or not?

It was a very cold winter, and staying in a hotel in Moscow was out of the question for a plain ordinary person. Only the privileged, tourists and foreigners, could have the convenience of a hotel, so I had to look for private accommodation. Everything was complicated, but the will to go overcame all these difficulties. It was a chance of a lifetime, and no wild horses would keep me away from my decision.

Climbing the Gothic staircase I reached the landing where Her Majesty's ambassador, Sir Iain Sutherland, and Lady Sutherland were standing welcoming the guests. Pamela, a member of staff, introduced me to them, and the ambassador said: 'It is admirable of you to take all that trouble and travel for three days to be with us here tonight.' The drawing-room had a large portrait of the Queen on the wall, and on the white grand piano stood a photograph of Mrs Margaret Thatcher. It was crowded with people talking, smiling, and with waiters circulating round offering drinks and canapés. It was so English that I could not believe that behind the brocade curtains was the grim world of the Kremlin and the onion domes of St Basil. Another world.

The whole scene had a dreamlike quality as I was introduced to various members of the embassy staff. Lady Sutherland, Peter Ruff, the Moscow correspondent of the BBC, and I spoke of the way the Russians jammed the World Service, and they were very surprised to learn that in Batumi I heard the BBC more distinctly on my little radio than in Moscow. I told Peter Ruff how I used to wait until midnight in my little room and how I tuned in to the World News, the Promenade Concerts in the Albert Hall, 'Brain of Britain' and plays till five o'clock in the morning because of the five-hour difference in time. I learned all about Britain and I heard the voice of the Prime Minister, which thrilled me, and even Arthur Scargill.

Though my ludicrous journey was difficult, once inside the embassy I was back on British territory again. It was a brief moment of ecstasy. Two hours on a piece of British soil helped me to gather up my courage and think that things were not so bad after all.

Back in Batumi I was called to the OVIR, and there in the presence of the clerk and another person in plain clothes the KGB officer said to me in a sweet voice: 'We know that you have received a British passport, and it is not lawful to have both British and Soviet citizenship. Will you please give us your British passport?' I felt sick. It was such a smack in the face after all my dreams and hopes.

'I haven't got it with me,' I answered: and, feeling that I was going to lose my temper, I ran out of the office. In desperation I immediately telephoned to complain to Mr Somerset in Moscow. It was as if something was protecting me as to my utter surprise I got straight through to him – a miracle for the Moscow-Batumi telephone service.

'Tell them that the British passport is the property of the British government,' he answered, 'and that you can only surrender it to Britain,' and he said that he would be in contact with the Foreign Ministry. After our conversation everything seemed more or less quiet and nobody molested me, but all the same I lived in fear of the KGB and sometimes I did not sleep at my place because I felt that I was being shadowed.

On the 26 August 1984 came the wonderful telegram from William Somerset that I should urgently telephone to the consulate. Holding the telegram in my hand I suddenly realized that all my scores with the Soviet Union were over. Standing in the dirty fly-filled telephone-booth I heard the most beautiful words in the world: 'Exit visa was issued' and 'Foreign Ministry'. The rest I could not grasp as there was so much interference.

This came about because, in July 1984, Sir Geoffrey Howe, the British Foreign Minister, visited Moscow. Sitting in the Kremlin with his Soviet opposite number, Andrei Gromyko, he referred to the list of personal cases of British subjects wishing to return to Britain and singled out a number, including my case, with a special plea for their early resolution. These lists had been periodically submitted to the Soviet Ministry of Foreign Affairs by the embassy and supported first by Mr Bonde and then by Mr Somerset.

I felt a colossal relief as if heavy chains had fallen from my hands and feet. At last I was free. It was unbelievable. It took many days in Batumi to complete all the official rigmarole before I could leave for Moscow. I was given a month's notice to leave the Soviet Union, and to hasten the procedure of getting my documents and cutting through the red tape I had to bribe the inspector at the OVIR with a bottle of expensive French perfume.

My friends who knew that I was leaving implored me not to write to them. Any link with those who leave the Soviet Union is against the Soviet way of living. How dare I leave the Soviet Union which had become for more than fifty years my second Motherland? They were worried about how I would cope in my new surroundings because the only television programmes they saw of capitalist Britain showed the worst side – drugs, and pensioners on the poverty line, and unemployment.

Preparing for my journey I bought myself a few new clothes and gave away my furniture and belongings. I was only allowed to exchange a hundred roubles (£80) to take with me. I said goodbye to my Adjarian, Georgian and Armenian neighbours, who, poor souls in their ignorance, wished me 'bon voyage' to Israel. At the railway station the only person to see me off was Boris; the rest of the friends with whom I had lived for ten years side by side were hovering in their huts in fear that their friendship with me would bring them into trouble. Poor devils, I don't blame them; as you make your bed, so you lie.

At the British embassy in Moscow I received my last visa and, thanking everyone for all their work, trouble and kindness during the five years' struggle to get me home, I said goodbye and caught the train to the West. The train was full of Westerners, and I made acquaintance with my neighbours in the next compartment. They were an elderly couple, and she told me that she was born in Russia and during the Second World War was living in Litva where she was taken as a prisoner to Germany. She managed to escape from the camps with a Frenchman, whom she married, and now lives in France with her daughters and grandchildren. Everyone has their own life-story, I reflected.

Early in the morning we stopped at Brest on the border and the Customs men came straight for me. 'Take out all your things,' one of them said, 'and get out, get out, and go to the Customs House.' Only after four hours' waiting in the cold building did they begin to search my two suitcases. After this I was personally searched and X-rayed; even my shoes were X-rayed, presumably for gold. Then the officer who had spoken rudely to me in the train asked me to sit down. 'If you will tell me where you have hidden your gold, we'll stop the search,' he said.

'I have no gold, and why are you treating me in this way?'

Then he grabbed my handbag, throwing out the contents on to the bench, and, seeing my British passport, he examined it. 'Why do you have a Russian travelling passport and a foreign one?' he sneered with an expression on his face as if to say: 'See – I have caught you.'

I felt as if my heart would stop, and then my pulse

suddenly began beating so fast that my whole body was one great throb and I was on the verge of unconsciousness and, by some spiritual force, I clutched my British passport out of his hands shrieking, 'It's mine . . . it's mine!' There was a dreadful silence, then with supernatural energy I began thrusting all my scattered belongings, my precious photographs, into my suitcases. Some kind soul saw my dilemma and began to help me pack. The KGB let me go. A porter from nowhere took my luggage. I ran after him; the train was already moving when I actually jumped in, and somebody kept me from falling. My suitcases were thrown in after me. All the passengers had been looking out of the windows of the train bewildered by the ugly scene and wondering who I was and what I had done.

I was half-dead when some Americans brought me coffee and gin to revive me. Why did the KGB do it? Maybe they wanted to catch me, make a career for themselves; or was it spite, sadism, because I was leaving the Soviet Union?

I lay on my bunk unable to speak or move, but as the train went westwards I looked out of the window at the passing scenery thinking of this wild Russian country with its wild habits. During my lifetime of fifty years in the Soviet Union I had outlived Stalin, whose era of monstrous crimes represents half the history of the Soviet Union; Khrushchev with his exposé of Stalin's crimes bringing rehabilitation to millions of prisoners; President Brezhnev's leadership with all its forms of corruption – chronic alcoholism, bribery and speculation, black market, and counter-economy, and the chronic shortage of food; Andropov with his struggle against corruption which continues to this day under Mikhail Gorbachev; and then Chernenko under whose leadership I left the Soviet Union.

I left behind the graves of my tragic family, and took with me the saddest of memories. The painfulness of my experiences in prisons and camps and in everyday life will shock and disgust me to the end of my days. I had seen the worst side of life and also a few of the good things.

My only relative, my sister Cecile's daughter, Marina, had spurned us. She was ashamed of her British relatives and wished no contact, frightened that it would sully her Soviet reputation, and like all Soviets she did not believe in our innocence. Friends whom I knew for many years had discarded me, and pleaded that I should not write to them. My leaving the Soviet Union was in their Soviet psychology an act of betrayal, treason!

My dear mother, after fifteen years' hard labour in the Gulag, was released only to learn that in her case there was no *corpus delicti*, no substance to the crime. She received no proper compensation from the Soviets, not even compassion, no regret.

My memories drifted back to the Thirties, when I first heard of Lady Astor and George Bernard Shaw, whose visit to Soviet Russia must have influenced my mother's intention to return to her homeland. Was this the nucleus that turned over my whole life or was it a predestination so powerful, so strong, that it forced my mother to her fate?

But as the train lulled me to sleep a feeling of great happiness embraced me and I whispered gently to myself: 'Flora, you are free. You are free and you are going home.'

EPILOGUE

Flora Leipman's dream of returning to her homeland did come true, though it took fifty years of hardship, struggle and frustration. She told me, as we worked together on the book, that even during the darkest despairing years spent in Stalin's labour camps, and working in bitter conditions in the coalmines of Kazakhstan, she never gave up hope or lost her spirit.

Britain was her homeland, and she did not doubt that somehow, some day, she would return. From the hour she set foot on Russian soil in Leningrad in 1933 she vowed to herself that she would return to Britain and that she could never assimilate into the harsh greyness of the Soviet Union.

In the days of her solitary confinement in a Leningrad prison, and throughout all the hideous years that followed, she nourished her soul with the memories of her childhood in Glasgow – playing with her sisters Cecile and Mathilde and her brother Sammy in Kelvingrove Park, walking down Sauchiehall Street, gazing into the shop windows laden with enticing goods, and Papa bringing home boxes of bright red apples. And always in front of her, like a recurring dream, was the face of Jenny Barrie, her friend from Garnetbank School. When she was at her lowest ebb she had only to conjure up Jenny's face and she was right back in Glasgow, the joyful days of her childhood. This memory gave her the strength to survive.

The tragedy of Flora's lost years in the Soviet Union can never be forgotten, or forgiven; and none of us hearing her story can possibly imagine her ecstasy as the train pulled into Liverpool Street Station on 29 September 1984. She was clutching two suitcases and was almost penniless . . . but she was *home*.

The days that followed were overwhelming, beginning with the warm welcome given to her by Mr Philip Goldman (Chairman), Mrs Clare Solomon and Mrs Nita Blau at the Temporary Jewish Centre in London where she lived for some months.

It was not long before she was off to Lancaster for a reunion with Dr and Mrs John Edge, whose friendship had run through her life over twenty-six years.

'Naturally I wondered how much Flora would have changed,' Mrs Edge wrote to me, 'and I also wondered if I would recognize her. As she stepped off the train I recognized her indomitable walk, and was delighted to see her looking better than I could have imagined. I felt that her ability to find something amusing in the most terrible situations, and her very likeable personality, were what had brought her through a very shocking set of totally unjust persecutions. She also has a strong self-respect and I am sure that this has helped her, too.'

When it looked as though Flora was getting nowhere with the Soviet officials in her attempt to return to Britain, it was Mrs Edge who had the somewhat naïve idea that if Flora had a British passport she might just manage to book a flight back to England from a tourist resort on the Black Sea, or smuggle herself on to a boat going to Turkey.

'I put the idea to the Foreign Office, who at first turned down my idea of giving her a passport, but later worked out that if they did give her one it would in Russian eyes be confirming our Government's acceptance of her citizenship.'

Among the first letters Flora Leipman wrote on her return to Britain were to the Prime Minister, Mrs Margaret Thatcher, and to the Foreign Minister, Sir Geoffrey Howe, who had personally brought her case to the attention of the Soviet Minister of Foreign Affairs, Andrei Gromyko.

Sir Geoffrey Howe's reply was written on 31 October 1984: 'I share your happiness in your return to this country, and I am glad I was able to play a part in the outcome. I am full of admiration for your endurance of many difficult years and your persistence in keeping alive your claim to the right to return here.'

The following day Mrs Thatcher wrote from Downing Street: 'I join in hoping that your years in this country will indeed be passed here amidst kindness and consideration.'

Lord Bethell, European Member of Parliament and crusader for exiles from the Soviet Union, wrote about Flora's ordeal in *The Mail on Sunday*. His article brought a flood of letters from readers all over the country expressing sympathy for her tragic situation.

When the BBC was preparing a documentary about Flora's return to Glasgow they contacted Jenny Barrie and arranged a meeting in her flat. When the two women came face to face they looked at each other and embraced. There was no need for words.

For fifty years, since the Leipman family had left Glasgow, Leonard (Lenny) Okrim, one of their upstairs neighbours at 435 Sauchiehall Street, had tried to trace them but he had no idea that they had been engulfed into the whirlpool of the Soviet Union until he saw the television programme.

'Flora was an unforgettable girl, beautiful and very bright. I remember her and her brother Sammy – my friend from the Jewish Scouts – as if it was yesterday,' he recalls.

The reunion at the Garnetbank School was charged with emotion. Another classmate, Mrs Margaret Houston (née Devlin) remembers: 'Flora need have no fear that we survivors don't remember her. She was the girl most likely to succeed – so beautiful and bubbly that I used to envy her.'

Flora did walk down Sauchiehall Street, just as she had imagined in her dream in Russia, from one end to the other including Kelvingrove Park, each step bringing back memories of her childhood and of her family who lie in Russian soil. It was a bitter-sweet pilgrimage. None of the passers-by could have possibly known the thoughts of the lone woman stopping every now and then to savour her memories.

Today Flora Leipman lives in London in her own flat. Her first impression was that London had not changed. Selfridges, the Tower of London, the National Gallery, Westminster Abbey and even Big Ben were all standing as she remembered them fifty years ago – only they were cleaner.

Among her most enjoyable experiences of the past year were giving talks to the boys at Westminster School and at Gordonstoun about her lifetime and experiences in the Soviet Union. She has also been invited to speak at the Marble Arch Synagogue and several others.

When Miss Leipman met Lady Sutherland, wife of Sir Iain Sutherland, at a reception in London given by the Anglo-USSR Association, she asked her: 'Have you found it hard to adjust, Flora? Many people returning from the Soviet Union do have difficulties.'

Flora's heartfelt smile was answer enough. She had never felt the need to adjust. All through those fifty long years her thoughts had never left Britain.

GWEN ROBYNS

THE END

THE PAST IS MYSELF
by Christabel Bielenberg

'It would be difficult to overpraise this book. Mrs Bielenberg's experience was unique and her honesty, intelligence and compassion makes her account of it moving beyond words'
The Economist

Christabel Bielenberg, a niece of Lord Northcliffe, married a Geman lawyer in 1934. She lived through the war in Germany, as a German citizen, under the horrors of Nazi rule and Allied bombings. *The Past is Myself* is her story of that experience, an unforgettable portrait of an evil time.

'This autobiography is of exceptional distinction and importance. It deserves recognition as a magnificent contribution to international understanding and as a document of how the human spirit can triumph in the midst of evil and persecution'
The Economist

'Marvellously written'
The Observer

'Nothing but superlatives will do for this book. It tells its story magnificently and every page of its story is worth telling'
Irish Press

'Intensely moving'
Yorkshire Evening News

0552 99065 5

THE HOUSE BY THE DVINA
A RUSSIAN CHILDHOOD
by Eugenie Fraser

'Eugenie Fraser has a wonderous tale to tell and she tells it very well. There is no other autobiography quite like it'
Molly Tibbs, The Contemporary Review

A unique and moving account of life in Russia before, during and immediately after the Revolution, *The House by the Dvina* is the fascinating story of two families, separated in culture and geography, but bound together by a Russian-Scottish marriage. It includes episodes as romantic and dramatic as any in fiction: the purchase by the author's great grandfather of a peasant girl with whom he had fallen in love; the desperate journey by sledge in the depths of winter made by her grandmother to intercede with Tsar Aleksandr II for her husband; the extraordinary courtship of her parents; and her Scottish granny being caught up in the abortive revolution of 1905.

Eugenie Fraser herself was brought up in Russia but was taken on visits to Scotland. She marvellously evokes the reactions of a child to two totally different environments, sets of customs and family backgrounds. The characters on both sides are beautifully drawn and splendidly memorable.

With the events of 1914 to 1920 – the war with Germany, the Revolution, the murder of the Tsar, the withdrawal of the Allied Intervention in the north – came the disintegration of the country and of family life. The stark realities of hunger, deprivation and fear are sharply contrasted with the day-to-day experiences, joys, frustrations and adventures of childhood. The reader shares the family's suspense and concern about the fates of its members and relives with Eugenie her final escape to Scotland.

'A wholly delightful account'
Elizabeth Sutherland, The Scots Magazine

0552 12833 3

A SELECTED LIST OF AUTOBIOGRAPHIES
AND BIOGRAPHIES
AVAILABLE FROM CORGI BOOKS

12851 1		Childrens Hospital	**PEGGY ANDERSON**	£3.95
09332 7		Go Ask Alice	**ANONYMOUS**	£1.95
99054 X		Borstal Boy	**BRENDAN BEHAN**	£3.95
99065 5		The Past is Myself	**CHRISTABEL BIELENBERG**	£3.50
09373 4		Our Kate (Illus.)	**CATHERINE COOKSON**	£2.95
11772 2		'H' The Autobiograhy of a Child Prostitute and Heroin Addict	**CHRISTIANE F.**	£2.50
99271 2		My Happy Days in Hell	**GEORGE FALUDY**	£4.95
12727 2		Men	**ANNA FORD**	£2.95
12501 6		Beyond the Highland Line	**RICHARD FRERE**	£1.95
13070 2		Born Lucky: An Autobiography	**JOHN FRANCOME**	£2.95
12833 3		The House by the Dvina	**EUGENIE FRASER**	£3.95
99098 1		Autumn of Fury	**MOHAMED HEIKAL**	£3.95
99294 1		To Hell and Back	**NIKI LAUDA**	£2.95
99158 9		Brendan Behan	**ULICK O'CONNOR**	£2.95
99143 0		Celtic Dawn		£4.95
99247 X		The Ford of Heaven	**BRIAN POWER**	£3.50
99293 3		The Puppet Emperor		£3.95
12577 6		Place of Stones	**RUTH JANETTE RUCK**	£2.50
13058 3		The Marilyn Conspiracy	**MILO SPERIGLIO**	£2.50
12589		And I Don't Want to Live This Life	**DEBORAH SPUNGEN**	£3.50

ORDER FORM

All Corgi/Bantam Books are available at your bookshop or newsagent, or can be ordered direct from the following address:
Corgi/Bantam Books,
Cash Sales Department,
P.O. Box 11, Falmouth, Cornwall TR10 9EN.

Please send a cheque or postal order (no currency) and allow 60p for postage and packing for the first book plus 25p for the second book and 15p for each additional book ordered up to a maximum charge of £1.90 in UK.

B.F.P.O. customers please allow 60p for the first book, 25p for the second book plus 15p per copy for the next 7 books, thereafter 9p per book.

Overseas customers, including Eire, please allow £1.25 for postage and packing for the first book, 75p for the second book, and 28p for each subsequent title ordered.

NAME (Block Letters) ....

ADDRESS..

....